GETTING DEVELOPMENT RIGHT

Also by Eva Paus

Global Giant: Is China Changing the Rules of the Game? coedited with Penelope
 Prime and Jon Western, 2009.
Global Capitalism Unbound: Winners and Losers from Offshore Outsourcing, 2007.
*Inversión extranjera, desarrollo y globalización: ¿Puede Costa Rica emular a
 Irlanda?* 2007.
*Foreign Investment, Development and Globalization: Can Costa Rica Become
 Ireland?* 2005.
Rates of Change: Modelling Population and Resources, coauthored with Harriet
 Pollatsek, 1992.
*Struggle Against Dependence: Nontraditional Export Growth in Central America
 and the Caribbean*, 1988.

GETTING DEVELOPMENT RIGHT

Structural Transformation, Inclusion, and Sustainability in the Post-Crisis Era

Edited by

Eva Paus

GETTING DEVELOPMENT RIGHT
Copyright © Eva Paus, 2013.

First published in 2013 by
PALGRAVE MACMILLAN®
in the United States—a division of St. Martin's Press LLC,
175 Fifth Avenue, New York, NY 10010.

Where this book is distributed in the UK, Europe and the rest of the world,
this is by Palgrave Macmillan, a division of Macmillan Publishers Limited,
registered in England, company number 785998, of Houndmills,
Basingstoke, Hampshire RG21 6XS.

Palgrave Macmillan is the global academic imprint of the above companies
and has companies and representatives throughout the world.

Palgrave® and Macmillan® are registered trademarks in the United States,
the United Kingdom, Europe and other countries.

ISBN: 978–1–137–36090–8 (paperback)
ISBN: 978–1–137–34075–7 (hardcover)

Library of Congress Cataloging-in-Publication Data

Getting development right : structural transformation, inclusion, and
sustainability in the post-crisis era / edited by Eva Paus.
    pages cm
    Includes index.
    ISBN 978–1–137–34075–7 (hardback)—ISBN 978–1–137–36090–8 (pbk.)
    1. Economic development—Developing countries. 2. Developing
countries—Economic conditions—21st century. 3. Developing countries—
Economic policy—21st century. 4. Sustainability—Developing countries.
5. Sustainable development—Developing countries. I. Paus, Eva.

HC59.7.G44 2013
338.9009172′4—dc23   2013020428

A catalogue record of the book is available from the British Library.

Design by Newgen Knowledge Works (P) Ltd., Chennai, India.

First edition: September 2013

10 9 8 7 6 5 4 3 2 1

In memory of my father

CONTENTS

ILLUSTRATIONS

FIGURES

Tables

Acknowledgments

In editing this book I have incurred many debts, foremost to the contributors for their cooperation and willingness to revise their manuscripts. Many of the contributions were presented in an earlier version at the conference 'The Triple Crisis of Development' that took place at Mount Holyoke College in March 2012. The conference was hosted by the Dorothy R. and Norman E. McCulloch Center for Global Initiatives. I am most grateful for the financial support of Dottie and Sandy McCulloch and of the Mary E. Tuttle Fund. I thank my friends and colleagues for all the spirited discussions we had when we team-taught the course that led up to the conference: Catherine Corson, Tim Farnham, Vinnie Ferraro, Holly Hanson, Matt McKeever, Shahrukh Khan, and Jon Western.

Special thanks go to Jean Costello for her superb assistance in copyediting the book, to Jennifer Medina for her valuable assistance throughout the whole process, and to Joan Davis for her capable work indexing the book.

Contributors

Edward Barbier is the John S. Bugas Professor of Economics, University of Wyoming.

Eva Bellin is the Myra and Robert Kraft Professor of Arab Politics, Department of Politics and the Crown Center for Middle East Studies, Brandeis University.

Paolo Brunori is Professor of Economics, University of Bari, Italy.

Elisa Calza is a research assistant in the Division of Production, Productivity and Management at ECLAC (Economic Commission for Latin America and the Caribbean), Santiago, Chile.

Mario Cimoli is the director of the Division of Production, Productivity and Management at ECLAC, and Professor of Economics, Universitá Cá Foscari, Venice, Italy.

Francisco H. G. Ferreira is Lead Economist, Development Research Group, World Bank.

Thandika Mkandawire is Professor of African Development, London School of Economics.

JoséAntonio Ocampo is Professor of Professional Practice in International and Public Affairs, Columbia University.

Eva Paus is Professor of Economics and Carol Hoffmann Collins Director of the McCulloch Center for Global Initiatives, Mount Holyoke College.

Vito Peragine is Professor of Economics, University of Bari, Italy.

Gabriel Porcile is an economic officer in the Division of Production, Productivity and Management at ECLAC (Economic Commission for Latin America and the Caribbean) and Professor of Economics, Federal University of Parana and Researcher, CNPQ, Brazil.

Dani Rodrik is the Albert O. Hirschman Professor of Social Science at the Institute of Advanced Study in Princeton.

Diego Sánchez-Ancochea is University Lecturer in the Political Economy of Latin America, University of Oxford.

Deborah Seligsohn is a researcher at the University of California, San Diego.

CHAPTER 1

Introduction: Getting Development Right

*Eva Paus**

The celebratory tone about the emergence of the BRICs (Brazil, Russia, India, China) and the improved growth in Sub-Saharan Africa and Latin America during the 2000s obscures the reality that, for large parts of the developing world, the challenges of development are more acute than ever. After three decades of Washington Consensus policies, deepening globalization, and China's and India's rapid growth and increasing international competitiveness in ever more goods and services, many latecomers face three critical challenges: structural transformation, inclusion, and environmental sustainability.

This book brings together prominent scholars and practitioners from around the world who look beyond the current global crisis and short-term growth opportunities and take a long-term perspective in the analysis of inclusion, environmental sustainability, and structural transformation. The book deliberately includes an analysis of all three challenges to explore the relations among them in the articulation of a new development strategy. When we approach each challenge separately, we obfuscate possible trade-offs with the other challenges and miss the opportunity to devise policies that can minimize the tensions between the goals and maximize win-win outcomes. Our intention is to initiate an exploration of a more integrative policy response, cognizant of the complexity and contingency of the inter-relations among these challenges. The chapters in this book, taken together, suggest several important policy areas where we might achieve a double or even triple dividend. But they also show that the adoption and implementation of such policies depends critically on the political will to change current rules and behavior and to translate loft rhetoric into hard-nosed action.

After nearly 200 years of divergence, "Divergence Big Time" (Pritchett 1997), many developing countries have seen some income convergence with the countries of the Organisation for Economic Cooperation and Development (OECD) during the 2000s. But it is unlikely that this trend can be sustained. What the basis for growth is matters. Informed by structuralist thinking (Ocampo et al. 2009), we argue that growth can only be sustained if it is based on a change in the structure of production toward higher-productivity activities. Starting in the 1980s, most countries in Latin America and Africa embraced the free market policies of the Washington Consensus which focused on efficiency and static comparative advantages and paid little attention to the importance of structural change for sustained growth. The result has been productivity-reducing structural change (Rodrik, this volume), where labor has moved to activities with lower, not higher, productivity. Productivity-enhancing structural change generates more decent jobs, while productivity-reducing structural change fosters the expansion of low-paid jobs and informality.

Furthermore, China (and a few other developing countries in Asia) did not follow Washington Consensus policies and fared rather differently. A very successful process of structural transformation has undergirded three decades of high economic growth in China. China's impressive performance has meant that both low- and middle-income countries have seen a dramatic increase in income divergence with China (see figure 1.1). China's ability to compete in low- as well as high-tech products has increased the urgency for other middle-income countries to focus their strategy on promoting structural change toward higher value-added activities.

Inclusion is a broad concept with economic, political, and social dimensions. Here we focus primarily on reductions in poverty and inequality. The general trend over the past 20–30 years has been a decline in extreme poverty rates and an increase in inequality. One of the great achievements of the last decades has been a significant decrease in the rate of extreme poverty. The percentage of people living on less than $1.25 a day (2005 PPP)

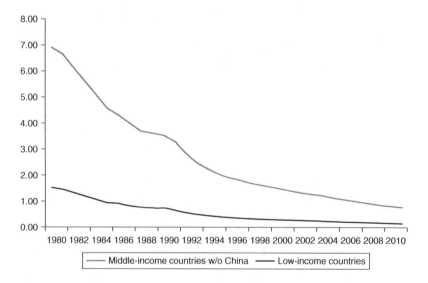

Figure 1.1   GDP p.c. in country groupings relative to GDP p.c. in China (based on constant 2005 PPP).

Table 1.1 Number (in millions) and percentage of people living below $1.25 a day (2005 PPP)

	1981	1984	1987	1990	1993	1996	1999	2002	2005
World									
Absolute number	1,896	1,808	1,720	1,813	1,795	1,656	1,696	1,603	1,377
Headcount ratio	51.8	46.6	41.8	41.6	39.1	34.4	33.7	30.6	25.2
East Asia and Pacific									
Absolute number	1,072	947	822	873	845	622	635	507	316
Headcount ratio	77.7	65.5	54.2	54.7	50.8	36	35.5	27.6	16.8
Of which China									
Absolute number	835	720	586	683	633	443	447	363	208
Headcount ratio	84	69.4	54	60.2	53.7	36.4	35.6	28.4	15.9
Eastern Europe and Central Asia									
Absolute number	7	6	5	9	20	22	24	22	17
Headcount ratio	1.7	1.3	1.1	2	4.3	4.6	5.1	4.6	3.7
Latin America and Caribbean									
Absolute number	42	52	52	43	42	52	55	58	46
Headcount ratio	11.5	13.4	12.6	9.8	9.1	10.8	10.8	11	8.2
Middle East and North Africa									
Absolute number	14	12	12	10	10	11	12	10	11
Headcount ration	7.9	6.1	5.7	4.3	4.1	4.1	4.2	3.6	3.6
South Asia									
Absolute number	548	548	569	579	559	594	589	616	596
Headcount ratio	69.4	55.6	54.2	51.7	46.9	47.1	44.1	43.8	40.3
Of which India									
Absolute number	421	416	428	436	444	442	447	461	456
Headcount ratio	59.8	55.5	54.2	51.7	46.9	47.1	44.1	43.9	41.6
Sub-Saharan Africa									
Absolute number	214	244	260	299	319	355	382	390	391
Headcount ratio	53.7	56.2	54.8	57.9	57.1	58.7	58.2	55.1	50.9

Source: Chen and Ravallion (2008).

fell from 51.8 percent in 1981 to 25.2 percent in 2005. The global average conceals important regional differences. While the extreme poverty rate in China decreased from 84 to 16 percent, Sub-Saharan Africa and South Asia saw a much smaller decline, and the two regions now account for the vast majority of the extreme poor (see table 1.1). The United Nations (2012:7) predicts that, in 2015, 1 billion people will still be living in extreme poverty, with 80 percent in South Asia and Sub-Saharan Africa.

Inequality offers a rather different picture from the trends in extreme poverty. We already noted what happened to intercountry inequality, which is captured by income divergence and convergence. The two most important exceptions to the continued increase in inequality among rich and poor countries are China and India. A telling indicator of global intercountry inequality is the ratio of the average income of the richest country to that of the poorest country. In 1820, that ratio was 3:1. Today it is 100:1 (Milanovic 2011:100)! Intracountry inequality has been on the rise over the last two decades, in developing and developed countries alike (Milanovic 2011).[1] A notable exception is Latin America. Historically, this region has been one of the most unequal in the world, but in the 2000s inequality in Latin America declined (Cornia 2012, López-Calva and Lustig 2010).

The growing threats to environmental sustainability have many different dimensions, from deteriorating water and air quality to the increasing conversion of forests and wetlands to cultivated land, to rising global temperatures. The focus on environmental sustainability adds another critical dimension to inequality: intergenerational inequality. It was the Brundtland Report in 1987 that first urged us to aim for "development that meets the needs of the present without compromising the ability of future generations to meet their own needs."

Emissions of carbon dioxide (CO_2), the major driver of global warming, have been growing unabatedly since 1960, with growth accelerating during the 2000s (see figure 1.2). Until the beginning of the industrialization process in the early 1800s, the atmosphere contained about 275 ppm (parts per million) of CO_2. Today, the number is 392![2] A global grassroots movement to solve the climate crisis, 350.org, argues that 350 ppm is the safe level of CO_2 in the atmosphere, if we want to avoid disastrous and irreversible climate impacts. The 4th Report of the Intergovernmental Panel on Climate Change (IPCC 2007) set the limit at 450 ppm to keep the global temperature rise to 2–2.4 percent, widely seen as the point beyond which major irreversible damage will occur.

Whatever the exact number for the tipping point, it is clear that there is urgency to slow the increase in CO_2 levels and then reduce them.[3] While today's industrialized countries bear the main responsibility for the increase in CO_2 in the atmosphere for most of the last two centuries, the rise in CO_2 emissions over the last 30 years has increasingly been driven by developing countries. In 2009, high-income OECD countries accounted for about 36 percent of CO_2 emissions, down from 60 percent in 1960. Over this period, China's share in global emissions increased from 8.3 percent to

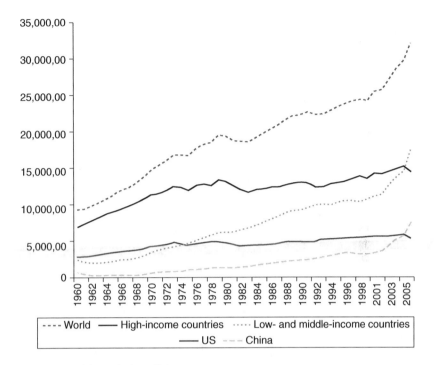

Figure 1.2 CO$_2$ emissions (kt).

Source: Based on World Development Indicators.

24 percent. China's share for the latter year is roughly the same as that for all low- and middle-income countries combined, excluding China and India.

The principle of "common but differentiated responsibilities," established in the UN Framework Convention on Climate Change (UNFCCC) in 1992, captures the need and capacity of industrialized countries to take the lead against climate change.[4] Martin Khor (2010:65) translates the principle of "common but differentiated responsibilities" for the reduction of greenhouse gas (GHG) emissions into a three-pronged approach:

> (1) the developed countries have to take the lead in changing their production and consumption patterns (the economic model); (2) Developing countries would maintain their development goals and take on sustainable methods and paths; (3) Developed countries commit to enable and support the developing countries' sustainable development through finance, technology transfer and appropriate reforms to the global economic and financial structures.

Developing countries cannot afford to ignore the triple challenge of environmental sustainability, inclusion, and structural transformation. If they do not pay sufficient attention to the consequences of growth for the environment, the inevitable increase in CO$_2$ emissions will affect people everywhere, but particularly and most immediately those who are most vulnerable. Increasing ecological scarcity and climate change have a disproportionate impact on the world's poor, most of whom live in agricultural and remote areas in developing countries. So it is highly questionable that growth without regard to environmental consequences will benefit the poor in the future (Barbier and Markandya 2013).

If developing countries continue to follow Washington Consensus policies, it will probably mean a continuation of the centuries-old trend of divergence between rich and poor countries, as productivity-reducing structural change is likely to continue. In addition, the growing divergence between most developing countries and China (and increasingly India), due to the underlying divergence in production patterns, will make it ever more probable that declining wages, rather than increasing productivity, will become the basis for international competitiveness in the countries lagging behind (Paus 2012).

The contributors to this book offer many general and specific policy suggestions to address the challenges of structural transformation, inclusion, and environmental sustainability. Several recommendations are likely to render double and even triple dividends: A shift in policy focus to promoting structural change can engender productivity-based growth and convergence. That, in turn, would pave the way for the creation of more decent jobs and greater intracountry equality.[5] The adoption, and eventual domestic development, of technology for a green economy can be the driver of structural change while also increasing environmental sustainability and thus intergenerational equality. The right management of natural resources can generate rents for structural transformation as well as contribute to environmental sustainability and poverty reduction. And social policies can support structural change as well as reduce intracountry inequality.

Each of the three sections in this book focuses primarily on one of the three challenges: structural transformation, inclusion, and environmental sustainability. In the remainder of this introduction, I summarize the main arguments and policy recommendations of the three sections highlighting the prospects for multiple dividends where possible. I conclude with a brief exploration of the challenges for policy implementation.

STRUCTURAL TRANSFORMATION

There are many reasons why developing countries might grow for a certain period, for example, a commodity price boom, a construction boom, or an influx of remittances. But growth can only be sustained if it is based on broad-based upgrading where production is shifted increasingly toward activities with greater technological spillovers, increasing returns, and higher demand elasticities, within and across sectors. The underlying assumption of this structuralist view is that different activities have different potential to generate dynamic benefits (Ocampo et al. 2009). Empirical evidence shows that developing countries with a larger share of their activities in higher-value activities experience higher growth (Hausmann et al. 2007, Ocampo and Vos 2008:33–57).

Structural change was the rationale behind import substituting industrialization (ISI). Though policy implementation was often beset with problems, it is important to separate the legitimacy of the rationale from the deficiencies in implementation (Paus 2011). With the rise of the Washington Consensus in the 1980s, the focus of the dominant paradigm shifted from the creation of dynamic comparative advantages to static comparative advantages, short-term efficiencies, and macro stabilization. Trade liberalization, an open-arms approach to foreign direct investment and a retrenchment of the government's role in production and sectoral development has led to deindustrialization and large informal sectors in Latin America and Sub-Saharan Africa.

The contributors in part I of this book (Rodrik, Cimoli et al., and Mkandawire) concur that the right kind of structural change is key for sustained growth and for lowering the intercountry inequality between latecomers and industrialized countries. In the current age of globalization, not only manufacturing but also internationally traded services and higher value-added activities in the primary sector can contribute to pro-growth structural change. Coming from different entry points, the authors argue for a more activist government to promote and enable such a shift in the structure of production and employment to higher value-added activities. They stress the importance of synergistic coordination of macro policies and industrial policies.

Two possibilities for double dividend strategies emerge from the chapters. Cimoli et al. highlight the potential of green technology to reconcile growth and environmental sustainability. This argument is central in Ocampo's chapter later in the book and discussed there in great detail. Mkandawire stresses that social policies can, and must, contribute to both structural change and greater inclusion.

Not All Structural Change Is Created Equal

After nearly 200 years of income divergence between most developing countries and today's industrialized countries, convergence has been the name of the game in the first decade of the twenty-first century, for all areas of the developing world. Dani Rodrik explores whether this convergence trend is likely to continue. Comparing the orthodox and structuralist views of the driving forces behind convergence, Rodrik argues that the structuralist perspective is more helpful for understanding what is going on. Different economic sectors have different productivities and different potential to generate dynamic benefits, and the challenge for developing countries is to move labor from lower- to higher-productivity sectors. When this process of transformation works as it should, we see productivity convergence between poorer and richer countries as well as among sectors within the developing countries.

But the process does not necessarily work as it should. Rodrik argues that the nature of structural change differentiates the development performance in Asia from that in Latin America and Africa over the last two decades. It was growth-enhancing in the former, but growth-reducing in the latter. While the Washington Consensus policies that dominated in Latin America and Africa were successful in stimulating productivity growth in manufacturing, that sector shrank and a lot of labor ended up in the informal sector and low-productivity services.

To engender growth-enhancing structural change, Rodrik advocates productivist policies: a combination of some sound fundamentals (market-friendliness and macro stability) and unorthodox policies to support new industries, including undervalued exchange rates. He argues against one-size-fits-all policies and recommends pragmatic and experimental policies.

An Environment Conducive to the Accumulation of Technological Capabilities

Mario Cimoli, Gabriel Porcile, and Elisa Calza focus on the development of technological capabilities and the diffusion of technological progress as the engine behind structural change toward higher valued-added activities. Informed by evolutionary economics, they emphasize that technological learning takes time and is subject to path dependency. In the catch-up phase, developing countries build endogenous technological capabilities by adapting technology imported from the industrialized countries; producers learn by doing. Industrial, macro, and institution-building policies need to create an environment that is conducive to learning. That includes deliberate temporary price distortions to give producers time and incentives to learn.

Cimoli et al. underscore the need for macro policies consistent with ongoing learning. Recurring macro shocks, volatility in exchange rates, and periods of overvalued exchange rates discourage the production of tradables, especially those with higher technology content where endogenous capabilities are still developing. They can generate a process of gradual weakening of technological capabilities (as expenditures on R&D decline, human capital is lost, producer-client interactions are disrupted, etc.), which reduces the growth potential of the economy.

The authors warn that the current austerity policies in the North with the resulting slowdown in growth violates an implicit principle of reciprocity where developing countries buy capital goods from the North and need to sell their exports to the North to earn the foreign exchange that finances the technology imports. They emphasize the need for a new global contract for international cooperation among countries at different levels of technological capabilities.

Toward a Transformative Social Policy

Thandika Mkandawire analyzes the shifting priorities and understandings of social policies under ISI and neoliberalism and argues for social policies that protect, redistribute, and contribute to structural transformation. He contends that developing country governments were cognizant of the productivist aspects of social policies under ISI, with spending on education, training regimes, and the use of social security funds to increase savings and investment rates (e.g., Singapore's Central Providence Fund). Though social policy was couched in universalist terms during this period, the incipient welfare regimes that transpired were highly segmented.

Under neoliberalism, social policy focused on the protective function, with the redistributive and productivist functions relegated to low levels of importance. With the emphasis on fiscal discipline, social investment was cut back and many social programs were privatized. The protective function of social policy was no longer based on notions of solidarity and systemic instability. Policies to reduce poverty were targeted in nature and emphasized conditional cash transfers and investment in human capital by the poor.

Mkandawire offers three recommendations for social policies that should accompany and legitimize a new development model. First, he suggests anticyclical social policies by building in automatic stabilizers. Second, cognizant of the great need for labor flexibility in the current globalization process, he advocates that governments take the high road to labor market flexibilization by combining adequate unemployment compensation with aggressive retraining programs (as exemplified by the Nordic countries) and not the low road of growing labor insecurity through short-term contracts and little training. And third, he calls for new social pacts that bind capital as well as labor.

China and the Middle-Income Trap

China plays a critical role in understanding the current development landscape. That is particularly true for the possibilities for structural transformation. Since the onset of reforms in the late 1970s, China has been highly successful in transforming the structure of its economy and exports, with high increases in productivity and rapidly growing international competitiveness in high- and low-tech products (Gallagher and Porzecanski 2010). Between 1978 and 2007, total factor productivity growth accounted for nearly 80 percent of GDP per capita growth (Zhu 2012:108).

China did not follow Washington Consensus policies. Successive governments pursued a gradual and selective opening to the international economy and adopted deliberate policies to advance domestic capabilities and maximize the absorptive capacity for technological spillovers from FDI and trade. While China is an example for other latecomers with respect to structural transformation, its unprecedented growth has been accompanied by a dramatic increase in inequality and ecological damage.

The point I want to stress here is that the combination of growth-reducing structural change in much of Latin America and Africa, growth-enhancing structural change in Asia, and China's competitiveness in international markets in both low- and high-tech goods (see figure 1.3) has raised the specter

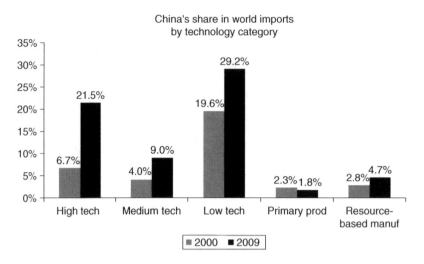

Figure 1.3 China's importance in world imports by technology category.

Source: Author's calculations based on UN-Comtrade database and the classification by Lall (2000).

of a middle-income trap for others. Producers in many middle-income countries find themselves increasingly unable to compete with producers in low-wage countries in the export of standardized products, but they have not developed the capabilities to compete, on a broad basis, in the exports of skill and knowledge-intensive goods and services. These countries now run the risk of being pushed onto the low road of change, where declining wages, not rising productivity, form the basis for competitiveness and growth. To avoid the middle-income trap, developing countries need to shift the policy focus to active support for upgrading within and across economic sectors, with a strong emphasis on building endogenous capabilities for innovation (Cimoli et al. 2009, Lee 2013, Paus 2012).

INCLUSION

Growth-enhancing structural change leads to sustained productivity growth that is the basis for a reduction in intercountry inequality between rich and poor countries. For a long time, the "inverted U" of the Kuznets curve captured economists' thinking about the evolution of intracountry inequality in the course of the development process. Inequality first increased as people were moving from agriculture to manufacturing where income and productivity were higher and more differentiated skill sets led to greater disparities within the manufacturing sector. Once a country reached a certain income level, political demands for greater income equality and more widespread access to education became the drivers behind declining inequality.

Today most economists agree that not much can be said at a general level about the link and causality between inequality and growth (e.g., Banerjee and Duflo 2003), and that the nature of the relationship between growth and inequality is contingent upon context and policies. Institutional arrangements and policies at the national level are important determinants of intra-country inequality. Over the last 30 years, income inequality in China has increased dramatically, with the Gini index going from 29.1 in 1981 to 42.5 in 2005 (World Bank 2005). Inequality was driven primarily by the disparities in growth among the different provinces (Milanovic 2011:80). In Latin America, on the other hand, growth in the 2000s was accompanied by a reduction in inequality, with the Gini index declining by 3.25 points on average. The decline was greater in left of center regimes where inclusion was a deliberate goal: 9 points in Argentina, 6.3 points in Venezuela, and 5.6 points in Ecuador (Cornia 2012:7). The reduction was the result of deliberate public policies, especially conditional cash transfers and education, as well as a reduction in the skill premium.

The contributors in part II of the book approach inclusion from different angles. Brunori et al. concentrate on the concept of inequality of opportunity that shifts the focus from inequality outcomes to underlying reasons. Sánchez-Ancochea and Bellin explore the interactions between political and economic factors in analyzing the possibilities for inclusion. Where Sánchez-Ancochea investigates whether globalization creates possibilities for a new politics that promotes both structural change and social inclusion, Bellin probes the connection between political and economic inclusion. Both authors point to hopeful signs for change, through transnational alliances among consumer and worker groups to affect labor standards in global production networks and the political momentum that led to the Arab Spring. But they argue that change at the macro level requires overcoming structural power imbalances and the challenges of political organization, and that the creation of decent jobs is critical for the achievement of economic inclusion.

Not All Inequality Is Unjust

The concept of "inequality of opportunity" aims to distinguish between "just" and "unjust" inequality. It is based on the belief that unequal outcomes may be just to the extent that they reflect different efforts by different individuals, and that such inequality is needed to create incentives for hard work and innovation. But inequality that is due to differences in circumstances over which individuals have no control, for example, parental background, race, gender, may be considered unfair, neither good for the individuals involved nor for the economy as a whole, as human potential is wasted.

Paolo Brunori, Francisco Ferreira, and Vito Peragine present a meta study of eight empirical works on inequality of opportunity. While acknowledging the limitations for cross-country comparisons due to the different types of circumstances included in the studies, different outcome indicators (income, consumption, labor earnings), different years covered in the empirical studies, and different estimations (parametric and nonparametric), they bring together estimates on inequality of opportunity for 41 countries, levels as well as ratios. The inequality of opportunity ratio (IEO-R) is the share of overall inequality accounted for by unequal opportunities; it is a lower bound estimate since it does not capture all the circumstances, but only the ones accounted for in the study.

Brunori et al. show that the IEO-R varies considerably across countries, from a low of 0.02 in Norway to a high of 0.32 in Brazil and 0.34 in Guatemala. They find that the IEO-R is closely correlated with overall inequality, and also with lack of intergenerational mobility. The policy implications are that governments should remove the obstacles that cause inequality in outcomes beyond people's control. Interventions can be compensatory (for certain groups of individuals, certain areas of the country) or oriented toward addressing unequal opportunities ex ante, for example, public education, access to childcare, and stronger support for families with children. Access to education is particularly important, given the role of parental years of schooling in social mobility.

Globalization and the Possibility for New Politics

Does globalization provide opportunities or constraints for a new politics that promotes a strategy of structural transformation and social inclusion? In exploring this question, Diego Sánchez-Ancochea focuses on the implications of local producer and worker participation in global production networks (GPNs) in Central America and the Dominican Republic. He investigates whether participation in GPNs generates political dynamics that are favorable for sustainable growth in real wages, redistributive social policies, and production upgrading.

During the 1990s and the 2000s, the export structures of these countries shifted toward labor-intensive manufactured goods, due to the incorporation into GPNs. The combination of low wages, proximity to the US market, special duty-free access provisions to the US market, and generous host-country tax incentives to attract transnational corporations (TNCs) into export processing zones were the driving forces behind this change. Sánchez-Ancochea argues that the countries' new dependence on GPNs offers three political opportunities. First, the diffusion of corporate social responsibility and consumer pressures in value chains forced suppliers in some instances to be more respectful of labor rights at the micro level (e.g., in El Salvador). Second, the emergence of international labor alliances in the context of preferential trade agreements created new pressures for labor-friendly legislation (e.g., in the Dominican Republic). And finally, as domestic producers within GPNs are forced to constantly upgrade their operations and find new sources of competitive advantage, they may be more inclined to demand social spending aimed at enhancing productivity.

Sánchez-Ancochea argues that the possibilities for consolidating micro achievements at the macro level are severely limited by structural constraints that emanate from the unequal power relations in GPNs. On the one hand, domestic producers in small countries have little power vis-à-vis TNCs and the intense competition among producers across countries means that rents in the GPNs are appropriated primarily by TNCs, not local producers. On the other hand, the existence of a large reserve army of labor, both domestically and internationally, makes it very difficult for workers to negotiate better wages and working conditions. In face of such structural constraints, Sánchez-Ancochea recommends policies that promote wage growth in conjunction with incentives for producers to pursue technological learning and innovation in new sectors.

Political and Economic Inclusion/Exclusion

Eva Bellin investigates the relationships between political and economic inclusion and exclusion. Focusing on countries in the Middle East and North Africa (MENA), she demonstrates the complexities of the interactions between inclusion in the economic and political spheres. Democratic regimes are neither necessary nor sufficient to deliver economic inclusion.

After independence, authoritarian regimes in MENA countries had pursued a strategy of "Arab Socialism," where social policies and government employment generated substantial economic inclusion. As a result, with the exception of Egypt and Yemen, poverty rates in MENA countries are the lowest in the developing world. And social indicators like education, infant mortality rates, and life expectancy have improved considerably. In the 1990s and the 2000s, however, a demographic bulge together with very low growth under Washington Consensus policies resulted in high unemployment rates, with youth unemployment running at 30 to 40 percent. Anger over economic grievances, Bellin argues, was a major factor in the buildup of the popular steam that led to the Arab Spring.

Bellin suggests that while one might expect increased political participation to lead to greater demands for and action on economic inclusion, that has not happened so far. She offers several explanations. First, given the relatively high levels of inclusion reflected in low poverty, relatively low inequality and high social indicators, it is harder for governments to pursue easy options for greater economic inclusion. Second, the new governments do not have a clear strategy of how to achieve growth and increase decent jobs. And third, groups are not very well organized, there is no history of democracy, and voters are more prone to fall for false promises. Bellin sees a ray of hope in the fact that the leaders of some of the new governments are looking to learn economic lessons from Turkey, Indonesia, and Malaysia, all countries with a Muslim majority.

Environmental Sustainability

Future growth in developing countries must not be as fossil fuel-intensive as the industrialization process of today's developed countries. The consequences of growth that is unresponsive to its environmental impact will be felt most immediately and forcefully by the rural poor in developing countries. In its 2013 Human Development Report, the UNDP (2013:10) issued dire warnings:

> While environmental threats such as climate change, deforestation, air and water pollution, and natural disasters affect everyone, they hurt poor countries and poor communities most. Climate change is already exacerbating chronic environmental threats, and ecosystem losses are constraining livelihood opportunities, especially for poor people. Although low HDI [Human Development Index] countries contribute the least to global climate change, they are likely to experience the greatest loss in annual rainfall and the sharpest increases in its variability, with dire implications for agricultural production and livelihoods. The magnitude of such losses highlights the urgency of adopting coping measures to increase people's resilience to climate change.

Moving to a green economy is seen as essential for the possibility to reduce the nexus between economic growth and CO_2 emissions. The Green Economy Report (UNEP 2011:16) suggests that growth and employment in a green economy "should be driven by public and private investments that reduce carbon emissions and pollution, enhance energy and resource efficiency, and prevent the loss of biodiversity and ecosystem services." Governments play the key role in initiating and supporting these investments through expenditures, regulation, and policy reform.

The concept of the green economy dates back at least to the late 1980s (Markandya et al. 1989). But it only gained traction in the context of the global crisis of 2008 when green technology became a focal point for jump-starting growth while also addressing ecological threats. The European Commission (2010) devised the *EU 2020 Strategy* that was to reduce resource use, increase resource efficiency, and develop new areas of competitiveness. The OECD (2011) published a green growth strategy as well, as did the Association of Academies of Sciences in Asia (AASA 2011). The green economy became the organizing principle for a new structure of global governance at the Rio 20+ Conference in June 2012 (Corson et al. 2013).

The contributors in part III of this book that focuses on environmental sustainability analyze the complexities of the green economy (José Antonio Ocampo), the importance of natural resource management for sustainable development (Edward Barbier), and the rising consciousness of the importance of environmental sustainability in China (Deborah Seligsohn).

Ocampo and Barbier point to the possibilities of double and triple dividend strategies. Ocampo suggests that the adoption and development of green technology can promote structural change and address ecological deterioration. Barbier argues that a better strategy of natural resource management can support structural transformation, reduce poverty, and lower environmental stress.

A low-carbon growth strategy in the South is highly dependent on developed countries taking the lead by changing their own consumption and production patterns and supporting the South in the transition to a green economy. The Green Economy Report (UNEP 2011) estimates that the funding needs to support a transition to a green economy are $1.3 trillion, 2 percent of global GDP in 2011 (in current dollars). Ocampo stresses that developing countries need to have access to clean technologies at low or no cost and suggests possible mechanisms for such technology transfer. Barbier shows that the amount of funding needed to support a transition to a green economy in developing countries is dramatically higher than the amounts provided to date.

The Green Economy

Ocampo discusses the macro and meso dimensions of the green economy. On the macro side, he stresses the importance of the social discount rate which is used to calculate the cost of actions to mitigate climate change and the benefits of doing so. The lower the discount rate, the higher the value we attach to the welfare of future generations. Existing studies suggest that the adoption of policies to mitigate climate change will lead to a reduction in output in the short run (as energy costs will rise), but an increase of output in the long run (e.g., UNEP 2011). The extent of the decline in growth depends on assumptions about how extensively low-carbon technologies will be used and how much production and consumption will shift in developed countries. But the cost of inaction (reflected in a reduction in productivity) is estimated to be even higher.

Ocampo argues that governments play a critical role in bringing about greener growth. It is generally agreed that governments need to use tax policies to reign in negative externalities and spending policies to promote activities with positive externalities. In addition, however, there is a greater need for stricter regulations and for public investment. Government investment, for example, in infrastructure, should "lock in" private investment conducive to environmental sustainability. Public and private investments have to become the drivers of structural change in developing countries. Governments should treat green economy industries like infant industries with the necessary support in the learning process. Government policies also need to give better access to basic services to the poor in energy, water, and sanitation. An additional reason why government action is critical is the speed of change required to address global warming, both in developed and developing countries.

Developing countries have to develop the absorptive capacity for green technology. And since most technology aimed at mitigating climate change is developed in OECD countries, developing countries need access to technology on an open basis, with knowledge-sharing platforms, freely available technologies, et cetera. Bilateral investment treaties and protection of intellectual property rights protection under the TRIPS agreements (Trade-related Intellectual Property Rights under the WTO) would need to be reformed to make such transfers possible.

Natural Resource Management and Poverty Reduction

Barbier highlights that most developing countries depend directly on natural resources, that natural resource use and land degradation has been rising in developing countries, and that a high percentage of the poor is concentrated in remote and ecologically fragile areas in countries with high export dependency on natural resources. He argues for a new development strategy with natural resource management at the core. Such a strategy would be more environmentally and economically sustainable and significantly reduce rural poverty in remote areas. It is a strategy with the potential for a triple dividend.

Whether natural resources are a curse or a blessing depends on institutions and policies. Barbier points to Malaysia, Thailand, and Botswana as examples of countries that have successfully used resource rents for investment in social capabilities and upgrading. In addition to strategic rent management, Barbier argues that governments need to target the poor directly in less favored and more remote areas. His policy recommendations include direct financing for eco-services schemes, which need to maximize direct participation of the poor; improved access for the poor to markets for affordable credit and insurance; a reduction in transportation costs to make nonagricultural activities feasible; more effective governance structures in support of poor communities' use of common pool resources; and stronger legal rights for local communities so that they can better control the goods and services from the ecosystems on which their livelihood depends.

Developed countries need to provide considerable financial support for the move to more sustainable resource-based development and poverty eradication in developing countries. Barbier identifies three sources of funding: environment and development funds, international payments for eco-services systems, and taxes on international trade or financial transactions. His survey of actual and potential funding mechanisms highlights the enormous gap between the funds needed and the funds currently supplied. Moreover, the funding sources that could raise the largest amounts of revenue (a global carbon tax or a currency transaction tax) are also the ones that face the greatest political resistance.

Growth and Environmental Sustainability in China

Deborah Seligsohn analyzes how environmental concerns have changed significantly in China in the course of the last decade. A confluence of political, economic, and institutional developments has changed the government's willingness and capacity to act on energy and environmental concerns. Energy security issues in the first half of the 2000s, greater institutional capacity and confidence (not least due to the process that led to China's accession to the WTO in 2001), the SARS crisis in 2003 and its aftermath, and a growing middle class with a desire for a safer quality of life have all contributed to a broadening of the government's understanding of development.

Seligsohn sees the Songhua River spill in November 2005 as a catalyst in raising environmental awareness and demands for action. Ultimately, the response to the environmental disaster led to the inclusion of specific environmental targets in the next five-year plans and the elevation of the State Environmental Protection Administration (SEPA) to the level of ministry. Similarly, Seligsohn argues that the clean air that was achieved during the 2008 Olympics in Beijing (due to severe production regulations and driving restrictions) resulted in greater demands for continued action on air quality improvement afterwards.

Growing concern about the impact of climate change has led the Chinese government to undertake ambitious green initiatives. These include large investments in renewable energy, promotion of fuel-efficient cars, expansion of rail transport, pollution control, and improvements in the electricity grid. The government has raised taxes on diesel and gasoline and reduced taxes on fuel-efficient cars. And China is the largest recipient in the world of carbon emission reduction credits, receiving currently $2 billion under the Clean Development Mechanism (CDM) (Barbier and Markandya 2013:159).

But even though China now accounts for 50 percent of global GHG emissions, it is still a middle-income country. In 2011, China had a GDP p.c. of $7,418 (constant 2005 PPP); that was 26.5 percent of the average GDP p.c. in the European Union and 17.5 percent of that of the United States. It is not surprising that in such a context, the meaning of "common but differentiated responsibility" is contested in international climate negotiations.

Toward an Integrative Strategy

To get development right, developing countries have to address the triple challenge of structural transformation, inclusion, and environmental sustainability. The chapters in this book, taken together, suggest four important policy areas for a more integrative response to these challenges.

1. A shift in the focus of the development strategy to structural transformation can lead to sustained productivity growth and the creation of more decent jobs. That can bring about a decline in intercountry inequality as well as intracountry inequality.
2. Social policies can be structured to increase inclusion as well as enable structural transformation.
3. In developing countries that are rich in natural resources (and that includes a large number of countries), a good strategy for managing natural resources can generate rents to support structural transfor-

mation. Targeted policies for the poor in these countries can reduce environmental degradation as well as poverty.

4. The move to a green economy can lower carbon intensity of production, advance structural change, and reduce inter- and intracountry inequality. In the short run, developing countries would import and adapt clean technology, and as domestic capabilities evolve, the domestic development of green technology can become a driving force of structural change in the medium and long term.

In addition to complementarities, there are also trade-offs, especially between the short run and the long run. The case of China shows very clearly that three decades of high growth came at the expense of the environment and equality. If a developing country wants to move to a green economy, it is quite possible that that will result in slower growth in the short run. The decline in growth will depend on the extent of technology and funding transfer from the North and the degree to which the country is willing to go ahead without much outside support. In the long run, however, growth can be higher and certainly more sustained.

The authors in this book make clear that the implementation of any of these policy responses requires an active and interventionist government: the use of industrial policies to support broad-based upgrading and growth-enhancing structural change, with particular emphasis on the development of technological capabilities; the adoption of macro policies consistent with continued learning in production; public investment to broaden social capabilities and to provide the basis for crowding in private investment in clean technology; spending and tax policies to deal with positive and negative externalities; targeted policies to address the sources of inequality of opportunity and the structural causes of rural poverty; and regulations and incentives that are needed to entice behavioral changes in consumption and production.

Policies in each country have to be specific, of course, to the needs, possibilities, and most pressing constraints of that country. Many developing countries have a dual production structure, with a small number of highly productive companies on the one hand and many low-productivity small firms on the other. Government policies have to respond to this reality with a dual set of policies that support upgrading advances for firms at both ends of the productivity spectrum.

Although the four areas and policies can be separated into individual pursuits, sustained achievements in one area are often contingent on complementary developments in another area. For example, when industrial and social policies do not cohere, we will not get a double dividend outcome, and the single dividend outcome can be much diminished. Santiago Levy (2012), a former undersecretary of finance in Mexico, captures this possibility aptly when he muses that "thanks to CCT [conditional cash transfer] programs, poor youngsters will enter the job market with more human capital, but they may not find more productive jobs."

Productivity-enhancing structural change is needed not only to create more decent jobs, but also to generate resources to fund social policies on an ongoing basis. Especially in countries without access to natural resource rents, governments may find it difficult to sustain social policies in the absence of productivity-enhancing structural change that generates the resources to support them (Martínez Franzoni and Sánchez-Ancochea 2012).

In *The Globalization Paradox*, Rodrik (2011:xviii) argues that the political trilemma of the world economy is that "we cannot simultaneously pursue democracy, national determination, and economic globalization." The implementation of a more integrative strategy requires that we modify the rules that currently govern economic globalization. More specifically, external boundaries on policy space have to be redrawn to increase national determination. Then governments can adopt the necessary pro-development policies without fear of retaliation by other governments (under provisions of the WTO) or foreign companies (under the provisions of bilateral investment treaties). The areas where new boundaries and understandings are needed the most include renegotiations of bilateral investment agreements to protect the right of sovereigns to adopt the required development-friendly policies (Abugattas and Paus 2008); a broader understanding of intellectual property rights to enable low-cost transfer of green technology (Ocampo, this volume); and the possibilities for capital controls to maintain development-friendly macro stability and prevent or mitigate crises (Gallagher 2011).

Headwinds

There are strong headwinds against the changes needed for the adoption and implementation of an integrative strategy. They are particularly powerful against a move to a green economy, since such a transition implies a dramatic change in consumption and production patterns in the North, and significant North-South transfers, in funds and access to technology. When asked about the role of the private sector in reducing the carbon footprint, Peter Lacy, Asia-Pacific managing director of sustainability services at Accenture, replied: "You are talking about everything being produced with 10 to 15 per cent of the energy and carbon intensity that it is now—and it needs to operate at that level, too. There's no way of describing that as anything other than an industrial revolution" (Murray 2012).

One of the difficulties in motivating action on the environmental sustainability front is the uncertainty about the exact extent and nature of the impact of continued global warming. Furthermore, the fact that such effects will only materialize in the medium to long run makes it easy for concerns about environmental threats to be trumped by concerns that are deemed more pressing in the short run. Barbier (2012) sketches out how the political difficulty of implementing different green economy actions varies with the

Table 1.2 Challenges for implementing a green economy

		Local and immediate benefits versus global and long-term benefits		
		Fewer trade-offs	*Some trade-offs*	*More trade-offs*
Political difficulty of implementation	Easy	Energy conservation Land-use planning	Improved drinking water and sanitation Development of fuel-efficient vehicles	Carbon sequestration projects
	Moderate	Public urban transportation	Low-cost clean energy supply Removal of fossil fuel subsidies Subsidies for clean energy R&D	Ocean conservation and fisheries management International payment for ecosystem services Large-scale water management projects
	Hard	Pollution regulation and pricing	Natural resource management Sustainable intensification of agriculture Water pricing Removal of water subsidies Carbon pricing	Global carbon tax High-cost clean energy removal Removal of agricultural subsidies

Source: Barbier (2012).

trade-offs between local and immediate benefits versus global and long-term benefits (see table 1.2).

The ongoing economic worries in the Eurozone countries and the pervasive focus on austerity, balanced budgets and tax decreases in the United States and much of Europe do not provide a propitious context for governments in which to prioritize big outlays for a green economy. Indeed, after the initial embrace of the green economy as a way out of the economic crisis that began in 2008, enthusiasm seems to have waned in industrialized countries, as evidenced by the lack of new international commitments at Rio 20+ in June 2012 and the concurrent G20 meetings in Mexico (Barbier 2012).

Tailwinds

There are also tailwinds that support changes. The power of successful examples and demonstrated failures can provide a strong impetus, especially at the micro and national level. The failure of the Washington Consensus to engender sustained growth and create more decent jobs together with successful structural transformation in countries that pursued more interventionist policies (especially China) has opened space for a shift in the dominant paradigm in development policy. If Justin Lin's work (2012) is any indication, structural change is making its way back into the corridors of development policy-making power at the World Bank.

The primary drivers of change can be the top down or bottom up. Political will and leadership can bring about important changes at the national level. We saw, for example, that in South American countries where inclusion was a deliberate policy goal, the decline in intracountry inequality was particularly strong during the last decade. The Kingdom of Bhutan is a powerful example of how strong government leadership can bring about decisive steps in the move to a green economy. In this small country, with a GDP p.c. of $5,162 (constant international 2005 PPP) in 2011 and a population of around 750,000, environmental considerations have been enshrined in the Constitution and economic policies. The Constitution requires Bhutan to preserve 60 percent of its territory as forest. The goal of the government's 11th development plan (2013–2018) is carbon-neutral and organic growth, and industrial policy promotes only green and clean sectors for growth.[6]

It is not coincidental that such impressive steps have been taken by a country whose leader had rejected GNP as the end-all goal toward improving people's welfare back in the 1970s. Instead, he had argued, we should focus on gross national happiness with its four pillars of equitable socioeconomic development, preservation of culture, conservation of the environment, and good governance. In such a social context, it is clearly easier to accept a slowdown in growth in the short run for the sake of environmental sustainability.

Social movements can be another important driver of change. They can raise awareness and increase public pressure for change. Under the right conditions, such pressure can translate into powerful change. In the aftermath of the Fukushima nuclear accident in March 2011, public pressure to move away from nuclear power in Germany combined with extensive media coverage and a vulnerable Merkel government led the German government to announce in May 2011 that the country would phase out all reliance on nuclear energy by 2022.

Mary Robinson, the former head of Ireland and now CEO of the Mary Robinson Foundation: Climate Justice, argues for the critical importance of grassroots efforts to bring about the change we need. She suggests (2013:304) that "we will succeed only if we adopt a participatory, bottom-up, climate justice approach that brings out the human rights and gender equality aspects, with particular focus on the empowerment of women."

The Need for New Social Pacts

Whether and how any of these four elements will be implemented and which elements can be implemented more easily than others depends on political processes and the constellation of power alliances at the local, regional, national, and international levels. Several contributors in this book stress that the implementation of an integrative strategy requires a new social pact, at the national level and the international level.

A global pact for an integrative strategy is probably the hardest to achieve. Historically, major changes in the global structure of governance came about after major upheavals in the world: the League of Nations after WWI and the Bretton Woods Institutions at the end of WWII. But the existence of these, and other, institutions today and the deep economic interrelations among most countries in the world provide reason for hope that we can find peaceful ways to bring about a new global compact. At the Durbin Climate Change Conference in late 2011, governments committed themselves to adopt a universal legal agreement on climate change no later than 2015. That is also the year when the agenda of the Millennium Development Goals expires. Thus, key elements of a more integrative strategy are on the agenda of all governments in the short run.

The greatest challenge to bringing about the needed changes is the disjuncture in speed of the different processes of change. In the absence of a change in policies, divergence and the growth of CO_2 emissions will continue. The implications of these trends heighten the urgency for action. But political processes work slowly and take time to bring about change.

Notes

* I am grateful to Luis Abugattas, Ed Barbier, Catherine Corson, Nicole Doerr, Shahrukh Khan, Diego Sánchez-Ancochea, and Jon Western for helpful conversations and feedback on different parts of the introduction. The usual disclaimer applies.

1. The income share of the top decile in the United States has reached heights last seen in the 1920s (The World Top Incomes Database. http://topincomes.g-mond.parisschoolofeconomics.eu/#Database).
2. http://350.org/about/science.
3. At the current rate of increase, CO2 increases by 2 ppm each year (http://350.org/about/science).
4. Article 3 of the agreement states that "parties should protect the climate system for the benefit of future and present generations of human kind on the basis of equity and in accordance with their common but differentiated responsibility and respective capabilities. Accordingly, developed countries should take the lead in combating climate change and the adverse effects thereof."
5. Martínez Franzoni and Sánchez-Ancochea (2012) argue that in addition to growth-inducing structural change, we need institutional changes in labor-capital relations and a sustained increase in minimum wages.

6. www.undp.org/content/undp/en/home/presscenter/articles/2012/09/12/bhutan-s-gross-national-happiness/.

References

Abugattas, Luis and Eva Paus. 2008. "Policy Space for a Capability-Centered Development Strategy for Latin America." In *The Political Economy of Hemispheric Integration: Responding to the Globalization in the Americas*. Diego Sánchez-Ancochea and Ken Shadlen (eds.). New York: Palgrave Macmillan.

Association of Academy of Sciences (AASA). 2011. *Green Transition and Innovation: Towards a Sustainable Asia*. Heidelberg, Dordrecht, London, New York: Science Press Beijing and Springer Verlag.

Banerjee, Abhijit V. and Esther Duflo. 2003. *Inequality and Growth: What Can the Data Say?* http://economics.mit.edu/files/753.

Barbier, Edward B. 2012. "The Green Economy Post Rio+20." *Science* 338(6109):887–888.

Barbier, Edward B. and Anil Markandya. 2013. *A New Blueprint for a Green Economy*. London and New York: Routledge.

Chen, Shaohua and Martin Ravallion. 2008. The Developing World Is Poorer Than We Thought, But No Less Successful in the Fight against Poverty. Policy Research Paper 4703. World Bank.

Cimoli, Mario, Giovanni Dosi, and Joseph E. Stiglitz (eds.). 2009. *Industrial Policy and Development: The Political Economy of Capabilities Accumulation*. Oxford: Oxford University Press.

Cornia, Giovanni Andra. 2012. Inequality Trends and Their Determinants. Latin America over 1990–2010. Working Paper No. 2012/09. World Institute for Development Economics Research.

Corson, Catherine, Ken Macdonald, and Ben Neimark. 2013. "Introduction to Special Issue: Grabbing 'Green:' Markets, Environmental Governance and the Materialization of Natural Capital." *Human Geography* 15(1), 1–15.

European Commission. 2010. *Europe 2020: A Strategy for Smart, Sustainable and Inclusive Growth*. Brussels: European Commission.

Gallagher, Kevin. 2011. "Losing Control: Policy Space to Prevent and Mitigate Financial Crises in Trade and Investment Agreements." *Development Policy Review* 29(4):387–413.

Gallagher, Kevin and Roberto Porzecanski. 2010. *The Dragon in the Room: China and the Future of Latin American Industrialization*. Stanford: Stanford University Press.

Hausmann, Ricardo, Jason Hwang, and Dani Rodrik. 2007. "What You Export Matters." *Journal of Economic Growth* 12(1):1–25.

Intergovernmental Panel on Climate Change (IPCC). 2007. *Climate Change 2007: Synthesis Report*. Geneva: IPCC.

Khor, Martin. 2010. "Challenges of the Green Economy Concept and Policies in the Context of Sustainable Development." In *The Transition to a Green Economy: Benefits, Challenges and Risks from a Sustainable Development Perspective*. Jose Antonio Ocampo, Aaron Cosbey, and Martin Khor (eds.). New York: UNDESA DSD, UNEP, & UNCTAD.

Lall, Sanjaya. 2000. "The Technological Structure and Performance of Developing Country Manufactured Exports, 1985–98." *Oxford Development Studies* 28(3):337–369.

Lee, Keun. 2013. *Schumpeterian Analysis of Economic Catch-Up: Knowledge, Path Creation, and the Middle-Income Trap.* Cambridge: Cambridge University Press,

Levy, Santiago. 2012. "The Creator of CCTs Looks to a New Challenge to Social Inclusion." *Americas Quarterly* 6(2):54.

Lin, Justin Yifu. 2012. *The Quest for Prosperity: How Developing Economies Can Take Off.* Princeton and Oxford: Princeton University Press.

López-Calva, Luis and Nora Lustig. 2010. *Declining Inequality in Latin America: A Decade of Progress?* Washington, DC: Brookings Institution and UNDP.

Markandya, Anil, Edward Barbier, and David Pearce. 1989. *Blueprint for a Green Economy.* London: Earthscan.

Martínez Franzoni, Juliana and Diego Sánchez-Ancochea. 2012. The Double Challenge of Market and Social Incorporation Progress and Bottlenecks in Latin America. Working Paper No. 27, 2012. desiguALdadas.net Research Network on Interdependent Inequalities in Latin America.

Milanovic, Branko. 2011. *The Haves and the Have-Nots: A Brief and Idiosynchratic History of Global Inequality.* New York: Basic Books.

Murray, Sarah. 2012. "Carbon Emissions: Business Fails to Reduce Footprint." *Financial Times*, November 26. www.ft.com/intl/cms/s/0/3d35a44e-3239–11e2-916a-00144feabdc0.html#axzz2P1qH8ANM.

Ocampo, Jose Antonio, Codrina Rada, and Lance Taylor. 2009. *Growth and Policy in Developing Countries: A Structuralist Approach.* New York: Columbia University Press.

Ocampo, Jose Antonio and Rob Vos. 2008. *Uneven Economic Development.* London and New York: Zed Books and United Nations.

Organisation for Economic Cooperation and Development (OECD). 2011. *Towards Green Growth.* Paris: OECD.

Paus, Eva. 2011. "Latin America's Middle Income Trap." *Americas Quarterly* Winter 5(1):71–76.

———. 2012. "Confronting the Middle Income Trap: Insights from Small Latecomers." *Studies in Comparative International Development* 47(2):115–138.

Pritchett, Lant. 1997. "Divergence, Big Time." *Journal of Economic Perspectives* 11(3):3–17.

Robinson, Mary. 2013. *Everybody Matters: My Life Giving Voice.* New York: Walker Publishing Company.

Rodrik, Dani. 2011. *The Globalization Paradox: Democracy and the Future of the World Economy.* New York and London: W.W. Norton and Company.

United Nations. 2012. *The Millennium Development Goals Report 2012.* New York: United Nations.

United Nations Development Program (UNDP). 2013. *Human Development Report. The Rise of the South: Human Progress in a Diverse World.* New York: UNDP.

United Nations Environment Program (UNEP). 2011. *Towards a Green Economy: Pathways to Sustainable Development and Poverty Eradication.* New York: United Nations.

World Bank. 2005. *World Development Indicators 2005.* Washington, DC: World Bank.

Zhu, Xiaodong. 2012. "Understanding China's Growth: Past, Present, and Future." *Journal of Economic Perspectives* 26(4):103–124.

PART I

Transforming the Structure of Production

CHAPTER 2

Structural Change, Industrialization, and Convergence

*Dani Rodrik**

What I hope to do in my presentation is to give a perspective that draws on my research about the recent experience of economic growth in the developing world and emerging markets and what that suggests for the future of economic convergence. Convergence refers to the closing of the gap in living standards between the poor majority in the world and the rich minority. For hundreds of millions of people the last few decades have actually not been all that bad. These recent decades have been better than any they or their parents or previous generations had, not only in absolute terms but also in terms of relative performance compared to what was happening in the advanced parts of the world.

Figure 2.1 suggests very interesting trends in economic growth since the end of WWII. What I have done here is basically smooth out year to year fluctuations and the growth rates of different parts of the world economy so I can just show what the overall trend is. I have broken the world up into two groups—the developed world and the developing world. The developed world is basically North America, Europe, and Japan. The developing world is essentially all the rest—Latin America, Africa, the Middle East, and all of Asia except Japan.

* This is a lightly edited transcript of Dani Rodrik's keynote presentation at the conference. The talk is largely based on the following two papers: "Globalization, Structural Change, and Economic Growth" (with Margaret McMillan). In *Making Globalization Socially Sustainable*, Marc Bacchetta and Marion Jansen (eds.). Geneva: International Labor Organization and World Trade Organization, 2011; and "Unconditional Convergence," NBER Discussion Paper No. 17546, October 2011. The reader is referred to these papers for full references and data sources.

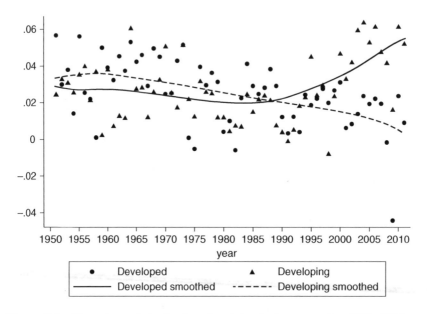

Figure 2.1   Growth trends in developed and developing countries, 1950–2011.

What you see is that for much of the period since WWII, the growth rate of the developed countries exceeded that of the developing countries. What that means is that advanced countries were growing faster and therefore the gap in terms of the living standards of the poor versus the rich was getting wider.

But something happened toward the middle part of the 1990s and particularly over the past 10–15 years or so. The growth rate in the developing world picked up in a very significant way, and the growth rate in the advanced parts of the world continued to decline. So now we have this striking divergence in economic performance between these two groups of countries to the point that just before the global financial crisis the difference between the annual average per capita growth rates of the rich versus the poorer countries of the world had opened up to 5 percentage points or more. This is a huge difference.

The good news here is that this experience of the last 10–15 years suggests that, on average, the developing world has been converging in terms of overall living standards with the advanced parts of the world. Not only that, they have been converging at a rather rapid rate as well.

The developing world is a very heterogeneous group that includes Asia; it includes not only highest performers China and East and Southeast Asian countries, but it also includes countries in Latin America and Sub-Saharan Africa. One of the striking features of the experience of the last 15 years or so is that in fact the pickup in growth has been rather uniform. In figure 2.2, I have broken up the overall trends in the developing parts of the world into

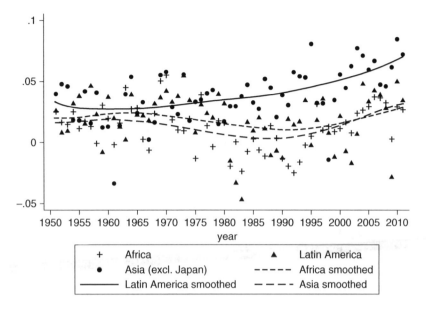

Figure 2.2 Developing country growth trend by region, 1950–2008.

three different regions—Asia, Latin America, and Africa. The picture with respect to Asia is, of course, something that points to the very significant success in achieving rapid economic growth in East and Southeast Asia, first starting with Taiwan and South Korea in the early 1960s and spreading onto Southeast Asia, Malaysia, Thailand, Indonesia. And, then, since the late 1970s, there is the Chinese growth boom. The line is trending up in part because China is becoming a bigger and bigger part of the Asian aggregate and therefore is pulling up the average as a result.

The other parts, Africa and Latin America, have not been doing nearly as well, and one can see in fact that through the 1980s and some of the 1990s the gap had been opening up. But the good news again is that recently even Latin America and Africa have been growing at a much higher rate than before. In fact, they have caught up and to some extent surpassed the growth rates they had experienced in the 1950s and the early 1960s, which by historical standards were quite high. Of course, Asia is growing much more rapidly than the rest. But the good news is that even Latin America and Africa are now growing more rapidly than they were in the 1980s and much of the 1990s.

This is a remarkable reversal in fortunes since the 1990s. It is in some ways exactly what should happen, a normal part of convergence. After all what developing countries need—the technology that they need to increase their productivity, the markets that they need to sell their products, the financing that they need in order to finance their investments—are already out there in a world economy that is globalized. They do not need to reinvent the technologies that the rich countries have already invented. Economic convergence should be the normal state of affairs, not the exception.

Historically, however, the kind of convergence that we have been experiencing recently is very much the exception rather than the rule. At some basic level, this is obvious. Otherwise we would not still have the world divided into the rich countries and the poor countries. But what is striking is that regardless of the time horizon, focusing on any relatively long period of time, there has not been a tendency for poor countries to grow more rapidly than rich countries. The predominant pattern is divergence, not convergence.

Figure 2.3 shows the relationship between initial per capita incomes in different countries and the subsequent growth rate they experienced over four different time horizons. We look all the way from the earliest period for which we can carry out this kind of systematic comparison—the period between 1820 and 2008. The most recent period is that between 1950 and 2008—the entire post-WWII period. The slope of the scatter plot tells us in each case that there has not been any tendency for poorer countries to grow more rapidly. Convergence would imply a downward slope, which we do not see. So what we have been experiencing in the last decade or so is unusual.

This recent trend forces us to ask two important questions. First, how do we interpret this period of recent convergence? Second, what does it tell us about the likelihood that it will continue, that we are going to be experiencing continued convergence? There are reasons to be both optimistic and pessimistic about the continuation of this trend of convergence. On the positive side, the kinds of policies that many developing countries have

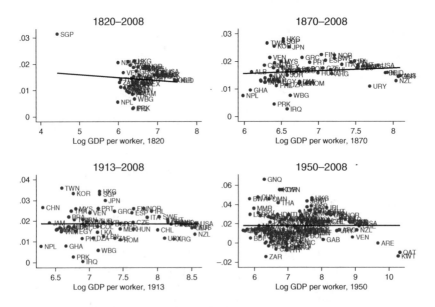

Figure 2.3   Lack of convergence over the long term.

been following are policies that are much more market friendly. They are also much more conducive to the integration of their economies into the world economies, and I will indicate in somewhat greater detail below that these policies are, in a conventional standard sense, much better policies. Therefore on those accounts, one might say we have the basis for continued convergence.

On the other hand, the period since about 2000 has been a rather special period that perhaps has artificially spurred the growth of a lot of the emerging developing parts of the world. This was a period of relatively high commodity prices, and since many developing countries are commodity exporters that tended to boost their economic growth. A number of developing countries grew very rapidly by borrowing a lot of money from international financial markets, as this was a period of financial globalization. It is not clear, given the state of the advanced countries, that we will continue with very high commodity prices or, given what has happened with the global financial crisis, that we are going to be experiencing continued flows of cheap short-term or long-term finance.

My basic point is that in order to be able to answer these questions, we need to have a perspective on economic growth. We need to have an understanding of what are the fundamental drivers of economic growth and how they are likely to change. So let me present two such perspectives, two interpretations you can use to analyze this growth performance and to make some judgments about the likelihood that these trends will continue.

First, the orthodox view. What I call the orthodox view is that convergence or sustained economic growth requires a set of well-known fundamentals. These fundamentals refer to a series of policies which, for lack of any other shorthand term, we might call Washington Consensus policies. What are those Washington Consensus policies? They are policies of opening up to the world economy, deregulating markets, privatizing state-owned enterprises or parastatals, providing adequate protection of property rights and enforcing contracts, and ensuring that the macroeconomic environment is conducive to low inflation and debt sustainability. The standard orthodox view is that doing all these good things produces high growth.

Now it turns out that this view has run into a lot of problems in recent decades. Just look at two examples, Brazil and Mexico. Mexico pretty much adopted the Washington Consensus wholesale and had certain additional advantages such as NAFTA and duty-free access to the North American market. Brazil did a fairly good job of adopting the Washington Consensus, but is probably not the most slavish adherent to it. What is striking when you look at the experience of Brazil and Mexico (and these are not exceptions in Latin America) is that their recent performance has paled in comparison with the performance that they had in the immediate postwar period. Mexico and Brazil may have done somewhat better since 2000, but their recent growth rates are a fraction of the rates they experienced before 1980. This is striking because the policies that Mexico and Brazil had in the 1950s, 1960s, and 1970s were policies that were utterly horrible from the perspective of the Washington Consensus. They had very high rates of trade protection, industrial policies were running rampant, subsidies and state-owned enterprises were pervasive, and inflation rates tended to be high. So the surprising thing from the orthodox perspective is that the improvement of policy "fundamentals" has led them not only to continue their under-performance relative to Asian countries, but also to grow substantially less rapidly than before.

The orthodox approach has reacted to these results by essentially enlarg-ing the set of policies that countries need to undertake. Rather than admit-ting defeat saying that maybe we have not gotten quite the right fix in terms of what you need to do to sustain growth, the approach has been to say well maybe it was not enough to liberalize trade and privatize state enterprises and deregulate the economy and run stable macroeconomic policies. Maybe countries needed deeper structural reforms. Maybe they needed to reform the labor markets at the same time. Maybe they needed to reform gover-nance. This ends up being an open-ended list that allows proponents of this view to always react to failure by saying there are even more things on the list that a government has not done.

The second perspective, which I find much more helpful in trying to understand what is going on, goes back to an earlier tradition in development economics, a structuralist tradition that emphasizes that poor countries are not just shrunk versions of advanced countries. The challenge of development is a challenge of changing structure. What it requires is to move resources from traditional low-productivity industries such as subsistence agriculture or low-productivity services to modern industries such as manufacturing or tradable services. The key policies are those that stimulate the expansion of the new industries, the entrepreneurship, and investment needed to absorb growing shares of employment. They will typically include a rather eclectic mix of policies, such as industrial policies or undervalued currencies that act to subsidize these modern industries.

To some extent the kind of policies that are required under the two perspectives may overlap. It is clear that if you are in an economy where the government stands ready to pounce on any entrepreneur who is actu-ally successful through taxes or bribery or other methods, then you will fail from both the orthodox and structuralist perspectives. Nobody will have sufficient incentive to invest in new industries. So there is a certain amount of overlap between the policy implications of the two perspectives. Similarly, hyperinflation is not very conducive to structural transformation either.

Still, even though there may not be a huge contradiction between these two ways of looking at things, they do imply different agendas and dif-ferent priorities. Sometimes the policies that the orthodox perspective prescribes, such as deregulation or the privatization of the financial sec-tor or opening up, may in fact undermine some structural transformation incentives by pushing some manufacturing industries into open competi-tion on world markets before they have had the time necessary to compete.

At the same time, policies that the structuralist perspective requires, such as industrial policies, direct policies of assistance to manufacturing industries, are going to conflict with the policy agenda of the Washington Consensus because governments are not supposed to be doing those kind of inventionist policies. So there is overlap, but there are also tensions and differing priorities.

Let me give you a sense of why the structuralist perspective is important and revealing. Structure is important because in developing countries there is huge heterogeneity in the productivity with which activities are carried out. This is true of all countries, but especially in developing countries. Even in some of the poorest African countries, one can find economic activities that are produced at levels of productivity that are close to the global benchmark. The problem is that too little of those economies' capital and, most importantly labor, are in those high-productivity activities. Most of them are locked in low-productivity activities.

Figure 2.4 shows productivity gaps for a set of nine African countries. Roughly 60 percent of the population is in agriculture which operates at about 50 percent of the productivity of the average for these economies. The manufacturing sector employs a very limited number of workers at much higher levels of productivity. To some extent, this cascade chart is a bit misleading because some sectors are highly capital-intensive (minerals) or require very high levels of skill. There is no way one can take farmers in traditional agriculture and put them all into the mineral sector. But it is certainly the case that one can put them to work in a lot of labor-intensive manufacturing activities, doubling or tripling their earnings, as well as increasing

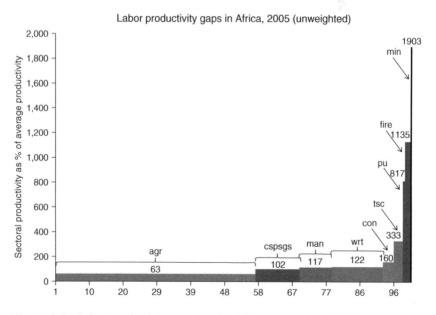

Figure 2.4 Labor productivity gaps in nine African countries, 2005 (unweighted).

economy-wide productivity. This is in fact how development takes place in practice. It takes place by taking people from low-productivity activities and putting them into high-productivity activities.

Similar gaps in labor productivity exist within these broad sectors as well. You can take each one of these sectors and break them up into subsectors. Even agriculture is a mix of traditional agriculture, subsistence agriculture, and maybe some horticulture or some floraculture where labor productivity is actually higher. So one sees huge heterogeneity there as well. Even within agriculture, by simply reshuffling production, reshuffling workers, one can get huge boosts in productivity and earnings without necessarily undertaking a lot of investment in that economy.

These structural gaps in productivity are a key feature of developing countries because we know that they tend to diminish over the course of development, as figure 2.5 shows. There is productivity convergence within economies as they grow. When the development process works as it should, we get not only convergence between rich and poor countries, but also convergence within previously poor economies. Structure matters less and less, if you are successful.

An important reason for these structural gaps is that not all productive activities are the same in terms of their capacity to generate dynamic productivity benefits over time. Let me focus here on the manufacturing sector, since that is where we have the most data. The manufacturing sector seems to be critical in the course of development, because it is a sector that seems

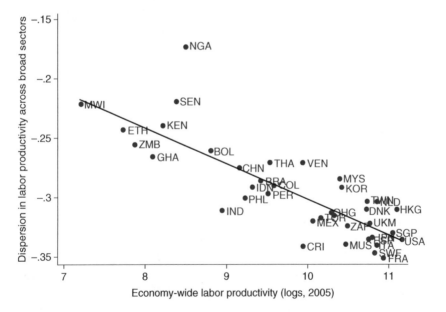

Figure 2.5 Relationship between inter-sectoral productivity gaps and income levels.

to exhibit automatic, unconditional convergence. It serves as an escalator for the economy. Once you are able to get your people, your workers into formal manufacturing—whether it is producing footwear or simple garments or into more complicated products like steel or automotive assembly—it turns out that those workers will be on the automatic escalator up in terms of sustained rapid convergence to the productivity frontier, regardless of what actually happens in the broader economic context. This is very striking because remember what I said about lack of convergence before. Earlier, I showed the absence of convergence of this sort going all the way back to 1820. But it turns out that there is a part of these economies where unconditional convergence does take place, and that part is manufacturing.

Figure 2.6 shows the evidence. Each one of the dots represent a four-digit manufacturing industry in the world. One can see that the lower the initial labor productivity in the industry, the faster the rate of productivity growth subsequently. The further you are from the productivity frontier, the more rapidly you will converge in that manufacturing activity. This is extremely good news. But it again highlights the structuralist message: growth and development are about getting your workers into the right sectors, and manufacturing may be key among them.

Now let us look at how structural factors map onto the actual performance of different parts of the world as well as few individual countries. I said earlier that Brazil and Mexico had been doing much more poorly in recent times compared to earlier periods. A large part of the explanation has to do with disadvantageous patterns of structural change.

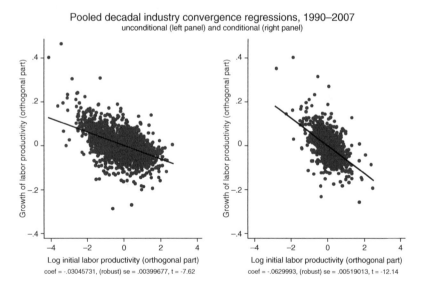

Figure 2.6 Why manufacturing is special: unconditional convergence.

Note: Each observation corresponds to a four-digit manufacturing industry in a specific country. Right panel includes country dummies.

Figure 2.7 shows a decomposition of growth in Latin America into two components: a "within" component, which measures productivity growth within individual sectors, and a "structural-change" component, which captures the effect of labor reallocations across sectors with different productivities. Before 1975, about half the region's growth was due to what was happening within sectors, and the other half was due to labor moving in the right direction from agriculture and other low-productivity activities to manufacturing and other high-productivity services. After 1990, we have had a remarkable change. The "within" component has remained the same, but the structural-change component has not only shrunk, but it has also turned negative! Now structural change actually serves to reduce overall growth. That means labor is going from activities where its productivity was higher to activities where its productivity is lower. This is growth-reducing structural change.

This perverse process is explained in part by the rapid shrinking of manufacturing in Latin America in terms of its labor share. In theory, the displaced labor should have ended up in higher-productivity services, but this has not happened. It has gone to informality and low-productivity services instead. This phenomenon goes far in explaining the difference between Latin America and Asia in the period since 1990. Figure 2.8 compares Latin America to Asia (as well as Africa and the high-income countries). It turns out that roughly two-thirds of the difference in the overall growth rate of Asia compared to Latin America and Africa is accounted for by these differential patterns of structural change. Asia for the most part has managed to get the right pattern of structural change going, while Latin America and

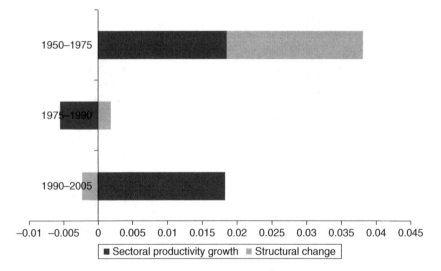

Figure 2.7 Productivity decomposition in Latin America across different periods (annual growth rates).

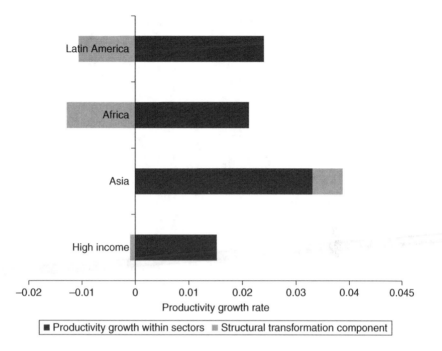

Figure 2.8 Decomposition of productivity growth by country group, 1990–2005.

Africa in recent years have not. And "within" productivity growth has not sufficiently compensated for the adverse structural change in the lagging regions.

It is also interesting to look at the individual countries that are behind those pictures. Let me just show you one bad case of structural change and one good case. The bad case has to come from Latin America and is Argentina (figure 2.9). The horizontal axis is the change in the employment share of these different sectors, and the vertical axis is their relative productivity. What is striking in the picture is the dramatic loss of employment between 1990 and 2005 in manufacturing—a relatively high-productivity sector—and the expansion of service activities that are not nearly as productive. This is in some ways development in reverse. The typical Asian case, with labor coming out of agriculture and into urban activities, is shown in Thailand (figure 2.10). It is striking how this "normal" case has been confined to a relatively small number of countries over recent decades.

What can we say about the kind of policies that account for these differential patterns? I call the set of policies that produce the desirable kind of structural change, productivist policies. Productivist policies rely in part on sound fundamentals. I do not want to throw away the chief insights of the Washington Consensus, which is that a country needs market friendliness and macro stability. But it also needs much more, and one does not,

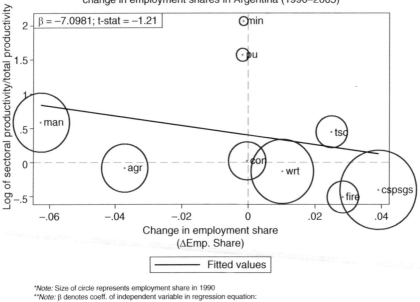

Figure 2.9 Growth-reducing structural change: Argentina.

Source: Authors' calculations with data from Timmer and de Vries (2009).

in fact, need to be a purist with respect to those fundamentals (as Asian countries have shown). You need in particular a layer of policies that are going to be supportive of new economic activities. In the past, such policies have taken diverse forms: a certain degree of repression of finance to enable a larger role for development banking, subsidized credit and other forms of industrial policies, and, very importantly, competitive currencies. One of the most effective ways in which you can subsidize modern tradable industries that spearhead structural change is to have an undervalued currency. In practice, currency policy has proved much more effective than direct industrial policies that are quite difficult to implement (see figure 2.10).

Let me conclude with a broad interpretation and a prognosis. It is true that today's policies around the world in the emerging markets and developing countries are much, much better in a conventional sense. It is also true, in general, that we have much better governance around the world. Many civil wars have ended in Sub-Saharan Africa. There are many more democracies in the developing world today than there used to be. But I think the empirical record is that these kind of fundamentals tend to increase the resilience of developing countries without necessarily igniting or sustaining economic growth. That is to say, these are the kinds of factors that ensure

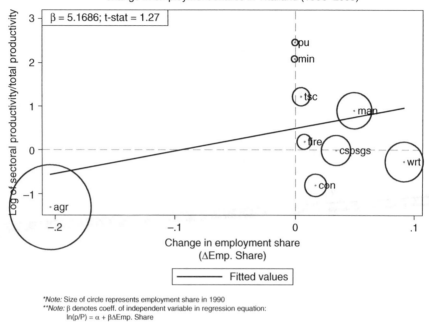

Figure 2.10 Growth-increasing structural change: Thailand.
Source: Authors' calculations with data from Timmer and de Vries (2009).

fewer negative outliers in terms of growth performance. But they do not ensure high economic growth and rapid convergence.

My argument is that growth requires something else. It requires an ability to diversify your economy and to accomplish structural change, and this is not something that is automatic. It is not something that happens just after you have established the fundamentals. It requires pragmatic, experimental, and often unorthodox policies in support of new industries. These unconventional policies are also often difficult to employ effectively. But so are conventional policies such as fiscal policies or education policies. The difficulty of industrial policy simply means that we ought to try and improve them.

Going forward we shall be facing a world economy that is going to be much more hostile to the conduct of unconventional, unorthodox policies that have supported growth in the past. There was a time when developing countries were pretty much left alone to pursue whatever currency policies, industrial policies, trade policies, financial policies they wanted to pursue. That external environment has changed significantly—most clearly in the context of the trade rules and with the changes in the WTO. But, in addition, I think we are moving into a world environment where the crisis in Europe and the likely slow growth in the United States in years ahead will make policy makers in the advanced parts of the world much less likely to condone unorthodox policies on the part of large developing countries. That will make it very difficult for China to continue with the type of policies it has. And it will make it very difficult for other medium- or large-sized economies in the developing world to replicate those policies. The challenge for them will be to develop adequate substitutes for fostering structural change.

CHAPTER 3

Still Blowin' in the Wind: Industrial Policy, Distorted Prices, and Implicit Reciprocity

Mario Cimoli, Gabriel Porcile, and Elisa Calza

INTRODUCTION

Structuralist and evolutionary theories agree on the fact that one of the main challenges of development is diffusing technological progress, so as to change the pattern of specialization by incorporating new sectors and reducing inter-sectoral disparities, raising productivity levels and improving income distribution; then, once external constraints are overcome, faster growth will allow for a decline in unemployment and underemployment in the subsistence sector.

Since its beginning in the 1950s, the Structuralist School has focused on the relationship between structural change and economic development. The focus is on how the diversification of the economy may generate spillover effects, backward and forward linkages, and positive technological externalities, which in turn accelerate capital accumulation. Development is based on qualitative change, the upgrading of industries and moving toward more dynamic sectors, with higher rates of demand growth and higher opportunities for technical change.

This chapter argues that undertaking a process of structural change based on the diffusion of technological progress, the upgrading of the production structure and the movement of labor toward high-technology activities and with increasing returns still presents a major and unavoidable challenge for economic development. Furthermore, structural transformation can help ease two other main developmental challenges: distribution and environmental sustainability. This chapter sheds some light on the transformation of the production structure and analyzes the underlying process that affects the pace of structural change, either accelerating it or slowing it down.

Technological capabilities are the engine for these transformations: they are the basis for the expansion of production and employment at the firm, sector, and industrial levels. Building and accumulating technological capabilities requires a continuous process of learning, time, and resources. The nature of learning processes tends to change according to the sector, the production environment, and the type of activities performed. When the Structuralist School developed its pioneering works in the 1950s and the 1960s, some sectors (such as manufacturing) were recognized to be able to boost learning activities more than others. Nowadays, learning has probably become more transversal across sectors and more related to specific highly technological-intensive activities in different sectors, which makes it an even more difficult process to analyze.

One of the main contributions of the Evolutionary School is having looked into the "black box" of these learning dynamics at the micro level. At least since the beginning of the 1970s, it has been recognized that in developing economies productivity growth relies on borrowing, imitating, mastering, and improving on the advanced technology used by countries that have reached the technological frontier. Significant factors favoring this process include the literacy and skill level of the workforce, the skills and technical competence of engineers and designers, and (increasingly) the existence of managers capable of running complex organizations efficiently (Dosi et al., 1990).

Given its peculiarities and its importance for long-term economic growth, the generation of technological capabilities and the transformation of the production structure in developing economies should not be left at the mercy of market forces and at the volatility of market signals (Cimoli et al. 2009). The idea that successful catching up requires active industrial policies[1] has only gradually reached mainstream economics. On the other hand, this is a well-established point in the tradition of economic history and heterodox growth theory,[2] where industrial policies represent the fundamental tools for reducing the technology gap and increasing international competitiveness.

However, active industrial policies are a necessary condition for reducing technological asymmetries and boosting structural change. In addition, a certain degree of coordination across economic policies has to be pursued too, and macroeconomic priorities should be set consistent with innovation and industrial targets. Obsessively pursuing what are believed to be the "right" macroeconomic prices can nullify the efforts of even the strongest industrial policy. For example, a decrease (appreciation) of the real exchange rate (RER) may induce a destruction of existing technological capabilities, when this appreciation is so strong or its volatility so high to affect negatively the development of strategic technological sectors by limiting their export performance and their expansion.

Even this "structuralist recipe" of active policies may turn out to be just a naive theoretical exercise for structural change, in practice unable to attain its goals in developing countries affected by a widening technology gap. In order to carry on with the process of structural change, the industrializing and catching-up countries have to expand their effective demand and to import from abroad the technological and capital goods that they need to upgrade the technological content of their production. The Structuralist School defined this mechanism as "the principle of implicit (or automatic) reciprocity": it states that the industrializing countries are "reciprocal," in the sense that they will buy capital goods from abroad, converting into technological import every dollar of foreign exchange they obtained from export revenues.

Under the "principle of implicit reciprocity," industrializing countries are implicitly sustaining the expansion of effective demand and growth in advanced countries. The shortcoming of this mechanism is its sustainability in the long run: the sustained import of technological goods will lead the catching-up countries to face serious disequilibria in the balance of trade in the long run, constraining their growth potential. A parallel expansion of exports can ward off this situation by guaranteeing the inflow of foreign exchange and helping to ease the external constraint on growth. This leads to another problem: feasibility. In fact, sustaining the export increase needed by industrializing countries is not possible without a mechanism of global political cooperation.

A corollary of the principle of implicit reciprocity argues that when industrializing countries are basing their structural upgrading on technological imports from technologically advanced countries, the latter should open their markets and implement expansionary policies to expand their autonomous expenditure. Besides helping sustain the rise of industrializing countries' exports and facilitating the process of structural change, this will represent a win-win solution of mutual growth for both groups of countries, allowing both to reach a higher growth rate than in the case of uncoordinated policies. In fact, if advanced countries will not offer space to sustain this expansion, protectionism and trade closure represent the only viable solution for industrializing countries to transform the production and employment structure and to generate the technological capabilities without incurring unsustainable trade imbalances (Cimoli and Porcile 2011a).

The time has come to rethink rules in a global world and to suggest solutions in which concerns with long-term growth, distribution, and environmental sustainability at the global level are paramount. Structural change proposes an answer to the developmental puzzle, and it still seems to be the only effective way to reach these aims. Moreover, the principle of implicit (or automatic) reciprocity and its corollary propose a win-win scenario of growth based on coordinated expansionary policies, and it proposes a new pillar for renewed global governance based on international coordination.

The chapter starts with discussing the importance and the characteristics of technological capabilities (first section), which are at the core of the process of structural change and long-term growth, and whose accumulation depend on a continuous process of learning. Then it considers the role that technological capabilities and learning play in the transformation of the production structure and diversification (second section) and how their characteristics shape the reaction of the production structure to macroeconomic shocks (third section). In particular, special attention has been given to understanding the process of the destruction of technological capabilities and of the loss of diversification that can follow a macroeconomic shock such as an appreciation (decrease) of the RER. We also highlight the importance of active industrial policies to foster technological learning, thus allowing for the development of endogenous technological capabilities and the reduction of the technology gap between advanced and industrializing countries. Finally (fourth section), we argue for international cooperation for structural change in catching-up countries as a renewed pillar for global economic governance. Given the threat of unsustainable external unbalances for industrializing countries due to the import of technological inputs, the corollary of the structuralist "principle of implicit reciprocity" represents a win-win solution of mutual growth for both industrializing and advanced countries.

TECHNOLOGICAL CAPABILITIES

Technological capabilities and learning are still among the main issues in the debate on the production structure and the process of diversification for development. This section aims at advancing our understanding of the characteristics of technological capabilities and of the underlying process of technological learning.

Both economic history and economic theory generally acknowledge a deep relationship between technical change and economic development. The building of technological capabilities is at the root of this relationship, where continuous processes of learning are responsible for the accumulation of capabilities. Since the mid-eighties, the Schumpeterian evolutionary literature has steadily developed new microeconomic tools for analyzing learning processes in catching-up economies.[3] The opening of the technological "black box" by the Schumpeterian literature has produced new insights into how learning and technological capabilities coevolve and why technology gaps rise or fall across nations and time (Cimoli and Dosi 1995).

Technological learning presents a set of interrelated features, which in turn characterize and shape the nature of technological capabilities. Technological learning requires real time and is subject to path-dependency, since the evolution of capabilities depends on previous experiences and directions of past learning. In this sense, the existence of cumulative processes that lead to vicious or virtuous cycles contributes to explain why some countries traverse to a path where learning, production capabilities, and institutions interact virtuously, while others remain in a state of hysteresis within a low-growth (divergence) trap. A consequence of these features is that countries and firms that are closer to the technological frontier tend to maintain an advantage in innovation and to increase their distance with respect to the laggards.

Furthermore, the building of certain physical and technological assets is generally irreversible, since these assets cannot just be abandoned or easily reconverted or replaced. This characteristic also has to do with the existence of a critical tacit component in technological learning, which cannot be obtained from importing capital goods or from reading manuals and other forms of codified information. It is embedded in processes and in the "way of doing things." Finally, there exists complementarity between sectors and capabilities, in such a way that externalities and increasing returns are crucial at both the industrial and economy levels.

These properties suggest that there is no reason for naïve optimism about convergence, since phenomena such as path-dependency and cumulative processes lead to strong inertia in the patterns of learning and specialization. Moreover, the generation of technological and production capabilities requires time and is based on progressive learning in organizations that implies the sequential deployment of various forms of tacit and incremental learning. However, as we will discuss in the following sections, catching up is possible when industrial and institution-building policies create a favorable environment for learning.[4]

Effective technological learning necessarily relies on active policies whose instruments and objectives change over time (Cimoli et al. 2009). Market signals alone are often not enough for fostering the accumulation of technological capabilities, and, in some cases, they actually compromise such accumulation. This occurs because learning takes place around existing technological capabilities, and investment concentrates in low-tech sectors that have already achieved comparative advantages and higher profitability. Learning-related reasons explain the historical evidence that shows that just prior to industrial catching-up, average industrial import tariffs are relatively low, but they rise rapidly in the catching-up phase and eventually fall when mature industrialization has been attained. Indeed, it is during the catching-up phase that the requirement of distorting (international) market signals is more acute, because learning-intensive industries are at this stage relatively fragile infants (Amsden 1989, Chang 1994, 2001).[5] In this process, the management of rents plays a key role to generate incentives and credible compulsions for learning (Khan and Blankenburg 2009).

PRODUCTION STRUCTURE AND DIVERSIFICATION

This section briefly presents the relationship between endogenous capabilities and structural change, highlighting their crucial role in engendering and boosting development processes. In order to foster the expansion of productivity, employment, and output, the accumulation of technological capabilities needs to come along with a transformation of the production structure.[6] Sectors are different in their potential for generating and accumulating technological capabilities; some of them can boost externalities, complementarities, innovation, and technological innovation and diffusion more than others. Thus, the diversification of production leads to the creation of higher-productivity activities and various forms of increasing returns, stemming from new skills, capabilities, and knowledge spillovers that a more complex economic structure makes possible.

This complex relationship between structural change and economic development was first explored by the pioneers of development theory.[7] A number of empirical studies describe how technological capabilities matured in a group of developing countries from the 1950s to the early 1980s, which enabled the reallocation of production factors from low-productivity to high-productivity sectors, and allowed them to gradually export medium- and high-tech goods and even become technology exporters (Fransman and King 1984). For these countries, industrialization became a way out of their "backward" condition: the increasing participation of industry in total value added would generate spillover effects, and this process would be reinforced by the continual development of new industries and new knowledge if demand and investment in new products were sustained.

The historical experience analyzed in these studies revealed how the manufacturing sector has held a special role in the process of structural change during the past decades. In fact, the increasing returns provided by the manufacturing sector made it a privileged locus for the development of technological learning, accumulation of technological capabilities, and diffusion of technology to the whole economic system. In addition, manufacturing started to account for a significant share of total employment, along with construction and services, and what happened to employment in manufacturing had significant repercussions for employment and productivity in the rest of the economy.

Industrialization based on the expansion of manufacturing allowed for moving toward higher-productivity sectors. A rising share of technology-intensive activities in manufacturing has been considered for a long time a good proxy for the process of learning in the whole economy, despite the fact that other sectors play an important role in the development of positive externalities. Nowadays manufacturing still is a good indicator of the intensity of learning in a developing economy, but its role is less relevant than in the past. Manufacturing no longer guarantees the same dynamic expansion of productivity and employment as it did in past industrialization waves. This especially holds in the actual economic context that has shown a continuous decline of the weight of manufacturing in terms of value added.

In effect, today, the generation of positive externalities, complementarities, and innovation has increasingly become less related to specific sectors than in the past: they are taking place in highly technological activities that are scattered across productive sectors, in activities where increasing returns prevail. In this sense, technological capabilities and learning still remain the main issues of the debate on the production structure and diversification, no matter where they are taking place. Thus, nowadays a strict "sectoral" approach is too limiting when analyzing the future sources of productivity and employment.

Today, as in the past, technology gaps and asymmetries between groups of countries still persist because the generation of technological capabilities is concentrated in the most dynamic activities (on the continuum of heterogeneous activities) and in sectors whose demand grows faster, while lower-end activities and slow-growing demand sectors prevail in catching-up and industrializing countries. This is why heterogeneity is the inevitable result of Schumpeterian competition, and why we can still define the catching-up countries as "dual" economies in the Lewis sense, despite of all the transformation that has occurred in the global economy during the past decades.

In fact, in most developing economies, technical change tends to be highly localized in a few low-end activities for export (both in the agricultural and industrial sector) with feeble effects on total demand and structural change. As a result, productivity tends to grow at higher rates than demand, which means that economies have a large surplus of labor in the subsistence sector or in sectors with extremely low levels of productivity (employment strata whose productivity is close to subsistence), generating persistent unemployment and subemployment.[8] On the other hand, in developed economies, the expansion of employment and productivity is grounded in the diversification of the economy, the expansion of high-tech activities, and the dynamism of domestic and international demand.

The process of development relies also on this movement of labor from low-productivity strata to high-productivity strata. Hence, catching-up and industrializing countries need to accumulate technological capabilities and grow at very high rates to be able to transfer the labor force which is underemployed in low-productivity sectors toward higher-productivity sectors; this is the only form of overcoming the heterogeneity in labor productivity. This implies that the only engine that could drain labor out of the subsistence sector and toward higher-productivity activities is the transformation of the production structure: it will not be possible to move workers to better jobs if there is no creation of new sectors, new activities within existing sectors, and technological upgrading. In less technologically advanced countries, job creation and the reduction of underemployment critically depends on the diversification of the production and export structures.

In the tradition of the Structuralist School and its followers, we are arguing that structural change is at the root of long-term economic growth. However, in the current global scenario and different from past decades, the impact of structural change on environmental sustainability cannot be ignored. This is a topic whose importance has increased in the global policy agenda. High rates of global growth may turn out to be unsustainable if the current patterns of production and technological change do not change, due to an excessive rise in the emissions of CO_2 and other contaminating substances. To make the acceleration of growth in catching-up countries compatible with the long-term goal of protecting the environment, policies for structural change and diversification should actively support activities and technologies that are more environmentally friendly. This would imply a built-in bias in favor of green growth and green technologies (ECLAC 2012).

This new environmental constraint may possibly lead to a delay in the process of structural change. Policies that protect nature and nonrenewable resources are strongly supported by public opinion in both developed and developing countries, and transforming the production structure toward sectors, activities, and technologies that are "greener"' may benefit from significant international cooperation. Thus, the combination of structural change and environmental sustainability represents a unique opportunity to boost the incorporation, adaptation, and diffusion of technologies that are on the international technological frontier (ECLAC 2012).

MACRO SHOCKS AND HYSTERESIS

This section presents what happens to the microeconomics of learning when an unexpected macroeconomic shock hits the economy, and the consequences it may have on long-term growth. The mandatory starting point of this analysis are the characteristics of technological capabilities, which play a fundamental role also in affecting economic growth during and after macro shocks (such as speculative shocks, price volatility in commodities and in the RER).

Due to the stickiness in capabilities, the technological and production systems cannot respond in a flexible way to fluctuations and changes in market signals. Furthermore, if macro shocks are recurrent, they may produce a process of a gradual but continuous weakening of capabilities and, finally, of productivity and growth potentials. The consequences may seem less dramatic than those from a financial crisis, but they may not be less costly in the long run, given their lasting effects in terms of loss of productivity and of potential growth: the more the shocks affect the microeconomics of learning and the process of accumulation of technological capabilities, the deeper and more persistent will be the impact on the whole economic structure (Cimoli and Porcile 2008, 2011a).

Figure 3.1 summarizes the interrelations between the loss of capabilities, productivity, and systemic effects during a period of recurrent shocks. An abrupt shock obliges the firm to readapt and reorganize the production process and, consequently, to redefine the required capabilities. These changes require time and resources and, despite the fact that the velocity with which the firm responds is crucial for remaining competitive in the market, the effects of re-adaptation on productivity will not be immediate: it takes time, and during this time there will necessarily be a slowdown in productivity growth. According to the Smith-Young-Kaldor perspective, output growth triggers increases in the division of labor and improves learning in each of the complementary activities as well as in the skills required in the use of equipment. Conversely, productivity growth falls when the expansion of production falls, and increasing returns are lost. In figure 3.1, this is represented by the negative slope of the first segment of the productivity curve.

After this initial aftershock slowdown (or even transitory fall) in productivity, this variable could grow again at the same rate or at a higher rate than at the moment of the shock. But if shocks are recurrent and/or uncertainty persists, the firm would have to constantly readapt its processes and the product mix, or it will have to adjust at a slower pace, at least until the emerging structure of relative prices becomes more transparent. In the end, the evolution of firm productivity with successive shocks and uncertainty will

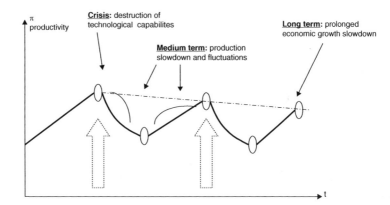

Figure 3.1 Productivity slowdown and destruction of technological capabilities.
Source: Cimoli and Porcile (2008).

look as if productivity was stagnant (or even constantly declining—the dotted negatively sloped line in figure 3.1), when it actually fluctuates. Adding up the productivity slowdown across firms gives a lower rate of productivity growth in the aggregate.

The short-term fluctuations in productivity may represent more than a temporary loss in the quantities produced: if fluctuations are recurrent, they also represent a loss of capabilities and therefore a loss of future potential growth. If technological capabilities and complementary assets are weak and/or have been destroyed, then, after the shock, productivity growth will slow down for a period of time that may eventually be longer than the adjustment process. In this way, when the shock ends, the economy will be less able to respond to new challenges, or to increase productivity at the same rate as before. When the destruction of knowledge has occurred, each shock may depress the rate of productivity growth even after the adjustment, for an indefinite time span. The country will be running at a slower pace than the rest of the world, being unable to advance and thus stay in the same place—a phenomenon that has been defined as "the Red Queen effect" (Cimoli and Porcile 2008).

This progressive destruction of technological capabilities represents one of the main threats to the process of structural change of industrializing and catching-up countries, since they are creating and consolidating their (still frail) endogenous capabilities. This point may hold for commodity-rich countries and in the case of recurring RER shocks.

In effect, specializing in primary commodities does not seem to represent the best option in the attempt to upgrade technological capabilities: when rising commodity prices favor the development of sectors that are less technology intensive and whose stimulus to human capital formation is weak, this may inhibit the surge of knowledge-intensive sectors, and the economic structure that emerges will have less technological capabilities and less diversification (fewer sectors), implying a reduction of systemic learn-ing and economic returns. Both effects come together and reinforce each other, giving rise to vicious circles that will hamper economic growth in the long run. Thus, commodities may provide early industrialization oppor-tunities, but they limit the possibilities for maintaining rapid development through deepening and diversification in the primary sector. Countries rich in natural resources can delay industrialization, but in general they cannot reach sustained growth without a strong industrial base that permits them to minimize the risks of price fluctuations (ECLAC 2008, 2010).

Another variable that has a significant influence on the direction and intensity of the diversification process in catching-up countries is the RER,[9] as stressed by the literature in recent years.[10] Since the RER is a signifi-cant policy variable affecting trade, its movements affect the pattern of spe-cialization, inducing a reallocation of resources across sectors and long-run growth. This reallocation does not just represent a quantitative change; it frequently implies beginning new activities and/or closing those that cease to be competitive.

Take for example a shock given by an appreciation (decrease) of the RER, as could be the case when the RER is used as anti-inflationary macroeco-nomic tool.[11] This shock may reduce diversification due to the disappearance of some activities and even sectors that cannot survive external competition. Furthermore, the negative shock of the RER is not neutral across sectors: the more technology-intensive tradable activities, where endogenous capa-bilities are weaker and external competition is tougher, will suffer the most. In other words, a real appreciation discourages the production of tradeable goods, particularly those of medium- and high-technology content. This will, in turn, lead to a decrease in the overall technological intensity of the production structure.

Hence, the first main lesson is that managing the RER has significant implications for the subsequent trajectory of technological learning. This is relevant in light of the experience of several economies in Latin America, which in the past decades went through periods of currency appreciation followed by severe external crises. Appreciation emerged either as result of cyclical improvements in the terms of trade (e.g., the case of a rise in the demand for commodities) or cycles of high liquidity in international finan-cial markets. In both cases, appreciation had structural impacts. The second main lesson is that industrial and technological policies are required in order to at least partially compensate for a real appreciation. By changing relative prices, these policies may prevent an appreciated RER from compromising the diversification process and the technological upgrading of production.

Most of the effects of shocks on the production structure and productiv-ity discussed here can be found in the historical experience of many Latin American economies. By comparing the productivity level in the region with that of the United States (considered here as the technological frontier), fig-ure 3.2 shows how relative productivity (of labor) has moved very slowly over time in Latin America. Since the 1980s, the index of relative productivity

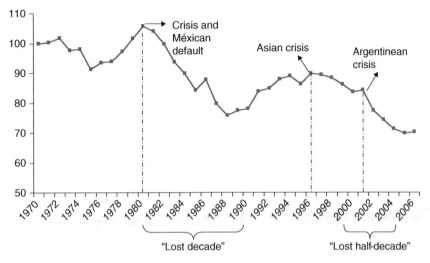

Figure 3.2 Productivity gap between Latin America and the United States.

Note: The relative productivity index of Latin America was calculated as the simple average of relative productivity index for four countries (Argentina, Brazil, Chile, and Mexico).

Source: Cimoli and Porcile (2011b).

between Latin America and the United States decreased (meaning that the productivity gap increased), and this fall was especially intense in the last part of the decade. Despite sustained economic growth between 2003 and 2008, the performance of the region in terms of relative productivity was the worst of the last 36 years—with the only exception of the eighties (the lost decade).

The effects of the shocks on Latin America are clearly visible in figure 3.2 (and they recall the shape of the productivity line in figure 3.1). The three main breaks in the curve represent a dramatic fall during the Latin American debt crisis of the eighties, followed by a moderate improvement in the early nineties; a new fall after the Asian crisis in the second half of the nineties; and another in early 2000s in the aftermath of the Argentinean crisis. These breaks are preceded by periods of slow increases of relative productivity, interrupted by negative shocks that reduce productivity, employment, and output and that destroy the existing technological capabilities in sectors with medium- or high-technological intensity, without the construction of new ones. Thus, the region seems still unable to break out of this vicious circle and unable to "close the gap" with the developed world (Cimoli and Porcile 2011b).

Summarizing, in general, every shock (in prices and/or GDP) will induce a productivity slowdown during the adjustment process. When the shock has an impact on the economic structure, and some sectors and capabilities are destroyed (R&D departments are closed, producer-user interactions ended, public research agencies underfinanced, human capital lost, and so on), productivity growth may fall after the adjustment. Given the destruction of technological capabilities, the efforts of the firms to adjust to new shocks will become increasingly less effective, and the ability to learn and restore productivity growth will be undermined. This will be particularly the case if shocks are frequent.

IMPLICIT RECIPROCITY AND ITS COROLLARY

Which global rules should be implemented to foster sustained and long-term global growth in the aftermath of the international financial crisis? So far, the focus has mainly been placed on the need for new rules for the international financial system, which is still probably the most urgent challenge that needs to be addressed in the next future. However, other dimensions of global growth have not yet been adequately considered, despite their important implications in the long run—among them, structural change and environmental sustainability. This section proposes a structuralist perspective on international trade and development as the starting point for discussing a new set of policies in which concerns with structural change, distribution, environment, and global growth are paramount. International cooperation is one of the main pillars of this approach.

As discussed before, industrializing countries need to accumulate technological capabilities and grow at very high rates in order to overcome heterogeneity in labor productivity and transfer the labor force underemployed in low-productivity activities toward higher-productivity ones. In other words, they need to undertake a process of structural change, which requires importing from more technologically advanced countries the technological and capital goods needed to upgrade the content of their production.

This need of industrializing countries to speed up growth and absorb the underemployed by upgrading the production structure is expressed in a key tenet of the Structuralist School: the principle of implicit (or automatic) reciprocity (Prebisch 1950, 1976). Based on structuralist ideas on trade and growth (Prebisch 1959), the principle states that the industrializing countries offer implicit (or automatic) reciprocity to industrialized countries because they will not accumulate reserves, but convert every additional unit of foreign exchange they obtain from exports into imports of capital and high-tech goods from the advanced countries and thus reduce the size of the subsistence sector.

The industrializing countries are "reciprocal" in the sense that, using their export revenues to buy capital goods from abroad, they will be sustaining the expansion of effective demand and growth also in advanced countries—thus helping to accelerate and maintain a higher rate of growth at global level. If the automatic reciprocity holds, industrializing and catching-up countries will not adopt mercantilist policies, but will use all their foreign exchange to buy imports from the advanced countries.

However, external disequilibria impose a limit on implicit reciprocity: the process of structural change and growth may be constrained by the availability of foreign exchange. The implicit reciprocity ensures that fiscal policy in industrializing countries is managed with a view toward filling in any gap between actual growth and the balance-of-payment-constrained growth. There are two rather different scenarios. An alleviation of the external constraint will motivate the government to pursue a more active fiscal policy aimed at reducing unemployment and underemployment. But if fiscal policy is used as the only instrument to sustain demand without diversifying and expanding exports and improving international competitiveness, then growth will be hampered by external disequilibrium. Thus, the external unbalances can only be avoided with a sustained expansion of exports, which will help to ease the external constraint on structural change and growth.[12]

The feasibility of an export increase does not depend solely on industrializing countries. Here lies the second and most interesting part of the story: the mechanism of international cooperation. A corollary of the principle of implicit reciprocity argues that the participation of industrializing countries in international trade is to a large extent a function of their own capacity to export. Thus, technologically advanced countries should open their markets and implement expansionary policies to sustain the rise of industrializing countries' exports, calling for international cooperation to reduce the lack of structural change at the global level.

Otherwise, the only possible alternative to this mechanism of international coordination is protectionism. If advanced countries will not offer space to sustain an expansion, protectionism and trade closure represent the only viable solution for industrializing countries to transform the production and employment structure and to generate the technological capabilities required to foster long-term economic growth without incurring unsustainable trade unbalances. Thus, in an interdependent international economy with significant technological and productive asymmetries, a purely market-led approach to international relations will fail to explore all the potential of trade for global growth.

The lesson of the implicit reciprocity and its corollary also holds when applied to macroeconomic policies. When both groups of countries coordinate expansive policies, industrializing countries can sustain the process of expansion of effective demand and diversification of production structures, combining consistently macro and industrial policies. But if the implementation of Keynesian expansive policies adopted by industrializing countries is not accompanied by similar policies in technologically advanced countries, because they pursue austerity and fiscal consolidation policies, then the efforts toward structural change in catching-up regions will be nullified and global growth will slow down.

Thus, the corollary of implicit reciprocity suggests that a "Keynes plus Schumpeter" policy-mix contains the ingredients required for catching up and a positive-sum game in the international system (Cimoli and Porcile 2011a). In fact, for industrializing countries, a purely pro-competitiveness policy and a purely activist fiscal policy will be self-defeating: a "pure" structural change approach may produce a mercantilist drive in trade policy, while a "pure" fiscal policy approach will meet the barrier of the external constraint. Furthermore, to achieve sustainable global growth, not just industrializing countries, but also advanced countries should support a combination of policies that stimulate structural change along with traditional Keynesian macroeconomic policies.

In sum, the principle of implicit (or automatic) reciprocity and its corollary propose a win-win solution of mutual growth for both industrializing and advanced countries. Advanced countries should stimulate the export of industrializing countries, as this would not compromise their own growth objectives; in turn, industrializing countries should combine fiscal and industrial policies in order to keep the rule of automatic reciprocity working. This approach combines supply-side and demand-side variables. Focusing solely on demand would lead to a stop-and-go dynamics, in which a fiscal stimulus by the government, or a rise in autonomous expenditure by the private sector, leads to an external crisis and the need to adopt austerity policies. In the long run, sustained growth requires structural change and technological catching-up. On the other hand, an exclusive focus on rationalization and accelerated productivity growth may give rise to unemployment at home and disequilibria in other parts of the world. A balanced view of the two sides of the growth equations is required.

There is a real threat that the technological asymmetries which characterize countries at different stages of structural change will turn into irreconcilable political asymmetries. This picture resembles the juxtaposition that is taking shape in the actual international scenario between the fiscal austerity policies adopted by advanced countries and the expansionary and diversification-led policies undertaken by some industrializing and catching-up countries. The corollary of the principle of implicit (or automatic) reciprocity offers a rationale for supporting the consolidation of international coordination across blocks or groups of countries that are at different developmental and technological stages. For this reason, implicit reciprocity could represent a new pillar for renewed global governance based on international coordination.

Concluding Thoughts

In the experience of many newly developed and emerging countries, structural change played a primary role as the engine of the development process. Their catching up has been based on the diffusion of technological progress and the gradual incorporation of new sectors, leading to changes in the pattern of specialization, increased productivity levels, a reduction of intersectoral disparities, and improved distribution.

However, the international scenario that the globalization process has been shaping during the past decades still presents many open challenges for development and growth. Various issues concerning economic development have remained unresolved—such as the stubborn persistence of unsustainable environmental deterioration, social exclusion with rising inequality, and the lack of structural change. And they have started to represent a heavy burden for global growth, in developed and developing countries alike. Technological asymmetries and gaps still exist between more advanced countries and those that are still lagging behind in terms of diversification of production; investigating the reasons for their persistence and proposing new policies and rules to deal with them is still one of the main challenges for pursuing global growth.

This chapter tried to shed some light on the transformation of the production structure, analyzing what underlies this process, and which forces are affecting the pace of structural change, either accelerating it or slowing it down. The analysis started with focusing on the role played by learning and technological capabilities, which are at the core of the process of structural change and long-term growth. Their characteristics shape the reaction of the production structure to shocks and volatility in prices and macroeconomic variables. In particular, we paid special attention to understanding the process of destruction of technological capabilities and of the loss of diversification that can follow a macroeconomic shock such as an appreciation (decrease) of the RER.

This chapter also proposed policy solutions to address the lack of structural change through new global governance rules. In fact, the shortcomings of the current international economic regulations have become evident after the outbreak of the financial crisis. The increasing asymmetries and the uncertainty that characterizes the post-crisis scenario have generated an urgency to rethink forms of governance and change the rules for a renewed development model.

Structural change requires the adoption of adequate industrial and technological policies. In newly industrializing countries, the role of industrial policy is to reduce the technology gap, increase international competitiveness, and allow for an expansion of exports in global markets, thereby alleviating the external constraint on growth. Moreover, for industrial and technological policies to be effective, a strong consistency between macroeconomic priorities and industrial and technological policy targets has to be pursued. Focusing on the "right" macroeconomic fundamentals without taking into account their impact on the production structure could nullify the effects of even the strongest industrial policy. In this sense, the experience of countries that succeeded in catching up—like Korea and more recently China—shows a macro policy committed to competitiveness and comprehensive industrial and technological policies.

A central problem in devising a new industrial policy for development is that industrial policies have often not been implemented correctly in the past. For instance, industrial policies were a significant force in many large Latin American economies until the late seventies, and they played an important role in promoting structural change. However, such a role was clearly insufficient. In particular, there was a tendency to concede subsidies, protection, and financial support to domestic and foreign firms in order to encourage industrial diversification. On the other hand, the use of this support by the firms was not regularly assessed or withdrawn when firms failed to attain the objectives of exporting and of technological learning. The governments gave the carrots but with no stick to oblige these firms to move along a learning path—protection granted rents without demanding a response by the firms in terms of learning. Thus, in Latin America, firms became extremely dependent on public support and did not move along the technological ladder with the required speed. In the late 1990s, industrial policies were altogether abandoned, and it is only in recent years, particularly after 2002, that these policies regained visibility on the political agenda, even if they were still adopted a defensive, reactive pattern as in the past. There have been defensive moves toward protection, not related to a well-defined development strategy, with specific goals and a time horizon for removing the protectionist barriers.

Reducing the lack of structural change and technological asymmetries at a global level needs more than the adoption of adequate policies in industrializing countries; it requires a consensus about new international rules for political cooperation. In the actual interdependent global economy, the time has come to propose solutions in which concerns with global growth and distribution are paramount. The principle of implicit (or automatic) reciprocity and its corollary do comply with structuralist views as regards the possibility of a positive-sum game in the international economy. They represent a good starting point for discussing a new set of coordinated global policies, since they propose a win-win scenario of global growth based on a mechanism of coordinated expansionary policies, with higher rates of growth and lower technology and income gaps, while at the same time focusing on a technological path compatible with environmental sustainability.

NOTES

1. Industrial policy is defined in this chapter in a very broad sense, including all measures that create incentives in favor of and/or directly allocate resources to industrial growth and technological change.
2. Amsden (1989), Bell (2006), Cimoli and Porcile (2009, 2011b).
3. See among others Bell (2006), Bell and Pavitt (1993), Fransman and King (1984), Katz (1984), Lall (1982), Teitel (1984, 1987), and Teubal (1984).
4. In the process of catching up, there is no clear-cut distinction between innovation and diffusion. The speed of diffusion is related to the capacity to acquire technology (in the form of capital goods, know-how, training, and so forth), adapt it to specific local conditions, and—gradually—develop specific competitive advantages in the international economy by means of incremental innovations. Initial efforts are concentrated on product design activities (most likely as a result of past incentives provided by import substitution policies) and, increasingly, on quality improvements and product differentiation. Attention has to be directed toward engineering, the organization of production, and the mechanized production processes. The organization can thus move toward the development of managerial capacities, such as the scientific design of production processes, the search for a higher division of labor (deskilling jobs and separating mental and manual labor), the organization of fixed product lines, and the implementation of vertical integration to improve learning.

5. Safeguarding the possibility of learning was indeed the first basic pillar of the infant industry logic. In order to maintain an inefficient industry (or plant) in the market, some sort of "learning protection" must be by force introduced for a limited period of time (Fransman and King 1984, Lall 1982).

6. Chang (2001), Cimoli et al. (2010), Dosi et al. (1990), ECLAC (2007, 2012), Rodrik (2008).

7. Hirschman, Prebisch, Rosenstein-Rodan, Gerschenkron, Chenery, and Sirkin are some of the classical authors in development theory.

8. This is the starting point of ECLAC's structuralist theory (Pinto 1970, 1976, Prebisch 1950, Sunkel 1978).

9. About this topic, see also Bértola and Porcile (2006), Cimoli (1992).

10. The literature is extensive; see for instance Bresser-Pereira (2008), Eichengreen (2007), Frenkel (2004), Freund and Pinerola (2008), Pacheco-Lopez and Thirlwall (2006), Rapetti (2011), Razmi et al. (2009), and Rodrik (2008). Early contributions are Baldwin (1988) and Baldwin and Krugman (1989).

11. For a better explanation of the theoretical model behind the way a shock in the RER may affect the production structure and diversification, see Cimoli et al. (2010).

12. For a discussion of the external constraint on growth from the perspective of the Latin American structuralism, see Rodríguez (2006). Recent revisions and extensions are Blecker (2009), Cimoli and Porcile (2011a), Setterfield (2009), and Thirlwall (2011).

References

Amsden, Alice H. 1989. *Asia's Next Giant: South Korea and Late Industrialization.* New York: Oxford University Press.

Baldwin, Richard. 1988. "Hysteresis in Import Prices: The Beachhead Effect." *The American Economic Review* 78(4):773–785.

Baldwin, Richard and Paul Krugman. 1989. "Persistent Trade Effects of Large Exchange Rate Shocks." *The Quarterly Journal of Economics* 104(4):635–654.

Bell, Martin. 2006. "Time and Technological Learning in Industrialising Countries: How Long Does It Take? How Fast Is It Moving (If at All)?" *International Journal of Technology Management* 36(1/2/3):25–38.

Bell, Martin and Keith Pavitt. 1993. "Technological Accumulation and Industrial Growth: Contrasts between Developed and Developing Countries." *Industrial and Corporate Change* 2(1):157–210.

Bértola, Luis and Gabriel Porcile. 2006. "Convergence, Trade and Industrial Policy: Argentina, Brazil and Uruguay in the International Economy, 1900–1980." *Revista de Historia Económica—Journal of Iberian and Latin American Economic History* 24(1):120–150.

Blecker, Robert A. 2009. Long-Run Growth in Open Economies: Export-Led Cumulative Causation or a Balance-of-Payments Constraint? Paper prepared for presentation at the 2nd Summer School on "*Keynesian Macroeconomics and European Economic Policies.*" Research Network Macroeconomics and Macroeconomic Policies, August 2–9. Berlin, Germany.

Bresser-Pereira, Luiz Carlos. 2008. "Dutch Disease and Its Neutralization: A Ricardian Approach." *Brazilian Journal of Political Economy* 28(1):47–71.

Chang, Ha-Joon. 1994. *The Political Economy of Industrial Policy.* London: Macmillan/St. Martin's Press.

———. 2001. "Infant Industry Promotion in Historical Perspective: a Rope to Hang Oneself or a Ladder to Climb with?" Document prepared for the conference "Development Theory at the Threshold of the Twenty-first Century," Economic Commission for Latin America and the Caribbean (ECLAC), August 2001.

Cimoli, Mario. 1992. "Exchange Rate and Productive Structure in a Technological Gap Model." *Economic Notes* 21(3):490–510.

Cimoli, Mario and Giovanni Dosi. 1995. "Technological Paradigms, Patterns of Learning and Development: An Introductory Roadmap." *Journal of Evolutionary Economics* 5(3):243–268.

Cimoli, Mario, Giovanni Dosi, and Joseph E. Stiglitz (eds.). 2009. *Industrial Policy and Development: The Political Economy of Capabilities Accumulation.* Oxford: Oxford University Press.

Cimoli, Mario and Gabriel Porcile. 2008. Volatility and Crisis in Catching-Up Economies: Industrial Path-Through Under the Stickiness of Technological Capabilities and "*The Red Queen Effect.*" Paper presented at the Mount Holyoke College Development Conference, November 14–16. Mount Holyoke College, South Hadley Massachusetts.

———. 2009. "Sources of Learning Paths and Technological Capabilities: An Introductory Roadmap of Development Processes." *Economics of Innovation and New Technology* 18(7/8):675–694.

———. 2011a. "Global Growth and Implicit Reciprocity: A Structuralist Perspective." *Cambridge Journal of Economics* 35(2):383–400.

———. 2011b. "Learning, Technological Capabilities and Structural Dynamics." In *The Oxford Handbook of Latin American Economies.* José Antonio Ocampo and Jaime Ros (eds.). New York and Oxford: Oxford University Press.

Cimoli, Mario, Gabriel Porcile, and Sebastián Rovira. 2010. "Structural Convergence and the Balance-of-Payments Constraint: Why Did Latin America Fail to Converge." *Cambridge Journal of Economics* 34(2):389–411.

Dosi, Giovanni, Keith Pavitt, and Luc L. Soete. 1990. *The Economics of Technical Change and International Trade.* Brighton: Harvester Wheatsheaf.

Economic Commission for Latin America and the Caribbean (ECLAC). 2007. "Progreso Técnico y Cambio Estructural en América Latina." División de Desarrollo Productivo, Santiago de Chile CEPAL.

———. 2008. *Structural Change and Productivity Growth, 20 Years Later Old Problems, New Opportunities.* LG/G.2367(SES.32/3). United Nations, Santiago de Chile.

———. 2010. *La hora de la igualdad. Brechas por cerrar, caminos por abrir.* LC/G.2432 (SES.33/3). United Nations, Santiago de Chile.

———. 2012. *Cambio estructural para la igualdad. Una vision integrada del desarrollo.* LC/G.2524(SES.34/3). United Nations, Santiago de Chile.

Eichengreen, Barry. 2007. The Real Exchange Rate and Growth. Working Paper N. 4, Commission on Growth and Development.

Fransman, Martin and Kenneth King. 1984. *Technological Capability in the Third World.* London: Macmillan.

Frenkel, Roberto. 2004. "From the Boom in Capital Inflows to Financial Traps." Initiative for Policy Dialogue Working Paper.

Freund, Caroline and Martha Denisse Pierola. 2008. "Export Surges: The Power of a Competitive Currency." The World Bank, Policy Research Working Paper 4750.

Katz, Jorge M. 1984. "Domestic Technological Innovations and Dynamic Comparative Advantage." *Journal of Development Economics* 16(1/2):13–38.

Khan, Mushtaq and Stephanie Blankenburg. 2009. "The Political Economy of Industrial Policy in Asia and Latin America." In *The Political Economy of Capabilities Accumulation: The Past and Future of Policies for Industrial Development*. Mario Cimoli, Giovanni Dosi, and Joseph E. Stiglitz (eds.). Oxford: Oxford University Press.

Lall, Sanjay. 1982. *Developing Countries as Exporters of Technology: A First Look at the Indian Experience*. London: Macmillan.

Pacheco-Lopez, Penélope and A. P. Thirlwall. 2006. "Trade Liberalization, the Income Elasticity of Demand for Imports and Economic Growth in Latin America." *Journal of Post-Keynesian Economics* 29(1):41–61.

Pinto, Aníbal. 1970. "Heterogeneidad estructural y modelo de desarrollo reciente de la América Latina." *En Inflación: raíces estructurales*. México, D. F.: Fondo de Cultura Económica.

———. 1976. "Naturaleza e implicaciones de la heterogeneidad estructural de la América Latina." *El Trimestre Económico* 37(145):83–100.

Prebisch, Raúl. 1950. *The Economic Development of Latin America and Its Principal Problems*. New York: United Nations.

———. 1959. "Commercial Policy in the Underdeveloped Countries." *American Economic Review* 49(2):251–273.

———. 1976. "a Critique of Peripheral Capitalism." *CEPAL Review* 1:9–76.

Rapetti, Martin. 2011. "Macroeconomic Policy Coordination in a Competitive Real Exchange Rate Strategy for Development." UMASS Amherst Economics Working Papers 2011–09. University of Massachusetts Amherst, Department of Economics.

Razmi, Arslan, Martin Rapetti, and Peter Skott. 2009."The Real Exchange Rate as an Instrument of Developing Policy." UMASS Amherst Economics Working Papers 2009–07. University of Massachusetts Amherst, Department of Economics.

Rodríguez, Octavio. 2006. *El Estructuralismo Latinoamericano*. México: Siglo XXI.

Rodrik, Dani. 2008. "The Real Exchange Rate and Economic Growth." *Brookings Papers on Economic Activity* 39(2):365–439.

Setterfield, Mark. 2009. "Neoclassical Growth Theory and Heterodox Growth Theory: Opportunities for and Obstacles to Greater Engagement." Working Papers 0901. Trinity College, Department of Economics.

Sunkel, Osvaldo. 1978. "La dependencia y la heterogeneidad estructural." *El Trimestre Económico* 45(1):3–20.

Teitel, Simon. 1984. "Technology Creation in Semi-Industrial Economies." *Journal of Development Economics* 16(1/2):39–61.

———. 1987. "Towards Conceptualisation of Technological Development as an Evolutionary Process." In *Structural Change, Economic Interdependence and World Development*. John H. Dunning and Mikoto Usui (eds.). London: Macmillan.

Teubal, Morris. 1984. "The Role of Technological Learning in the Exports of Manufactured Goods: The Case of Selected Capital Goods in Brazil." *World Development* 12(8):849–865.

Thirlwall, Anthony Philip. 2011. "Balance of Payments Constrained Growth Models: History and Overview." Studies in Economics 1111, Department of Economics, University of Kent.

CHAPTER 4

Social Policy and the Challenges of the Post-Adjustment Era

Thandika Mkandawire

Today, many developing countries are faced with the challenge of devising strategies that ensure both rapid growth and structural changes that are sustainable and socially inclusive. A key element of every development policy is social policy, meaning that any new model of development that emerges from the current state of disarray in policy thinking must be accompanied by social policies that complement this model and provide political legitimacy to it, protecting citizens from the risks that inevitably accompany any development model and enhancing the productive capability of the population.

This chapter begins with a discussion of development strategies and the associated social policies that prevailed before and during the era of structural adjustment. The neoliberal policy agenda, which has been dominant for close to three decades in many parts of the world, has not only reversed the policies of the previous models of industrialization, but brought in its wake a paradigm that reframed social policies, rendering them residual and confined to the provision of safety nets to the poor, thus undermining the incipient welfare regimes associated with previous models. These policies have left behind a legacy that must be addressed if developing countries are to overcome the many barriers to economic growth and structural change. The chapter then turns to an exploration of policy measures that can be developed in the post-Washington era.

THE "GOLDEN ERA OF INDUSTRIALIZATION"

The period between the end of WWII and 1973 has been described as the "Golden Age of Capitalism" (Marglin and Shor 1990) because of the quite high rates of growth in both developed and developing countries. It was also a period in which "embedded liberalism" reigned (Ruggie 1982), permitting individual countries to pursue a broad set of policies. As far as developed countries were concerned, this provided for the emergence of the "welfare state," while, in developing countries, it created space for the emergence of "developmental states." In the former, social policy was much more protectionist and redistributive in its immediate concerns; whereas in the latter, the leaning was toward more productivist aspects of social policies. However, it is important to underscore that these features—production, redistribution, and protection—were explicit or implicit aspects of all social policy, the difference being the weight attached to each.

The literature on development during the period insists on the dichotomy of "export-oriented" versus "import substitution," the former associated with the highly successful East Asian countries, the latter with most other developing countries. There were two great divergences in the models that eventually led to different social policy concerns. The first involved the relatively high levels of equality in the East Asian model, at least when compared to its African and Latin America counterparts. This equality was based on the "initial conditions" of massive land reform and high achievements in education. The second divergence involved the employment effects of the two strategies, which in some sense were a reflection of the source of earnings required for the acquisition of capital goods and technology. Resource-rich economies tended to rely on the export of raw materials, while labor-abundant economies relied on the export of labor-intensive exports. In a sense, both were obeying their "comparative advantages"; but the two approaches produced radically different results in terms of social policy. In addition, there were differences in the perception of the "population problem." Asian countries were confronted with high population density and growing populations with constant threats of famines, which immediately focused the attention of policy makers onto issues of food provision, population control, and labor utilization, in a way it did not in Latin America and Africa.

However, a number of common features in these models have received much less attention than the differences between them. First, both strategies sought to accelerate economic growth through interventionist policies; both aimed at structural transformation through industrialization supported by industrial policy. Many developing countries consciously embarked on processes of "arching up," understood as requiring economic growth and structural change. The latter was viewed not only as a consequence of economic development, but also as a means to achieve it: by moving labor to high-productivity activities and repositioning the economy through the diversification of exports. Policy was then aimed at directly inducing such structural change through high levels of accumulation, sectorial policies, and technology acquisition. Both strategies aimed to diversify the export structure through industrialization. Related to this was the belief that such structural shifts called for a "big push," requiring the mobilization of investment resources by the state. Market forces could not be left to achieve this, as private individuals would not provide for the kind of long-term funding required for rapid change, nor would the time preference of individuals allow for the sacrifices required for increasing savings. Coordination by the state was essential: hence the prevalence of "planning," industrial policies, and forced savings schemes. Underpinning all this was the deployment of skilled human labor.

With respect to social policies, the two models shared two features. The first was that they had strong Bismarckian characteristics, especially an insistence on professional belonging as the basis for access to collectively negotiated rights. How much welfare the model could provide depended significantly upon how many jobs it could create. In many African countries, paternalistic enterprises provided their employees with a wide range of social benefits, including health facilities, pensions, education, and housing allowances. Variants of this model were adopted by successful East Asian developmental states. It is perhaps the assumptions about full employment and high-savings orientation that distinguish this model from the welfare regimes in Latin America, which are based on targeted social provision and state-provided social protection, but feature low savings, low employment, and debt-prone, inflationary fiscal regimes.

In the context of the full employment that prevailed in East Asia, there was often a tendency to obviate the protection concerns of social policy. However, such models are not able to cope with high levels of unemployment, as occurred in Africa and Latin America, or with the slowing down and structural change of the economy, the demographic aging, and the financial liberalization that followed the East Asian crisis in 1997.

Highly segmented welfare regimes were another feature shared by the two models. Although social policy was couched in the language of universalism, the economic models associated with it and the structural changes they engendered inevitably led toward highly segmented welfare regimes. Those in the formal sector enjoyed high levels of welfare rights as compared with those in small or informal labor markets. The segmentation was the combined result of the Bismarckian principle of access to social welfare through wage employment, and the dualism of the process of industrialization in terms of scale of production units, technologies used, and degree of formality. This often created highly organized labor in large-scale, oligopolistic firms, able to bargain for a share of the profits and rents earned by the oligopolies, often generating a "wage-technique" spiral, in which the first sought higher productivity by adopting capital-intensive techniques that, in return, provoked demands from labor for a higher share of the earnings (Arrighi 1973, Frankema 2012). In the worst case, this led to what Peter Evans terms "an anti-Schumpeterian triangle" of state, labor, and capital "where protected workers, protected entrepreneurs and the state elites and employees engaged in rentier games, driven by a political logic rather than by the driving force of competition and innovating" (Filgueira 2007).

This segmentation of welfare was also a feature of the East Asian model, despite its more export-oriented and relatively labor-intensive industrialization. Governments actively participated in technological development and tended to walk on two technological legs, encouraging capital intensity in one sector, while promoting labor intensity in the other. Much of the export production came from large firms. The role of capital-intensive models in employment generation came not so much from direct employment, but from their linkages with smaller more labor-intensive industries. Such linkages were not simply spontaneous or market-driven technological choices, but constituted part of the national labor market policy and other social policies, that encouraged or insisted on local sourcing, as well as forward and backward linkages in the economy (Seguino 1997). Thus, while the technologies adopted were dualistic, the rapid growth of the labor-intensive industry provided a near-full employment regime that, until the financial crisis of 1997, did not entail any further social protective measures other than lifetime employment.[1]

In retrospect, due to a number of factors, the segmentation was generally less pronounced than what was to occur later. First, in a relatively closed labor market, "the absence of international market discipline enabled long-term wage regulation programs that sought to suppress wage gaps across industries and between blue- and white-collar workers" (Frankema 2012). In other words, skilled labor was not competing in open global markets where it would have garnered a premium above national earnings. Second, the pursuit of various measures of "labor compression," through "solidary wages" or social policies that provided a "social wage" underpinned various social pacts, at times through outright repression. All too frequently, this "wage compression" widened the gender gap through a gender-divided market in which women were predominantly low-paid and in labor-intensive industries, thus effectively subsidizing the export industries that relied on inputs from this sector, or benefited from the foreign exchange earned by these industries (Seguino 1997).

However, by the end of the 1960s, it was recognized that growth had been accompanied by poverty and inequity. The structural change that had taken up rapidly had generated different dualisms than those contemplated in the classical model of Arthur Lewis—not between modern and traditional models, but within the modern sector itself. The main concern then revolved around adding equity to the equation, and addressing the new dualism. It was clear that in the absence of deliberate policies to shape patterns of growth, there was no guarantee that it would occur in amounts sufficient to make a discernible dent into poverty, let alone equity issues. Consequently, a new generation of strategies aimed at meeting basic human needs or inducing "growth with equity" were proposed by the International Labor Office (ILO) and the World Bank respectively (Chenery et al. 1974, ILO 1972). These strategies were short-lived, however, their demise being linked to the economic crisis of the 1970s and the ideological ascendancy of neoliberalism in leading developed countries and international financial institutions (IFIs), the Bretton Woods institutions. Many developing countries had to turn to the IFIs for financial support, where they were confronted with pristine neoclassical stylization of economies. Yet even in its brief heyday, the basic needs strategy attracted considerable skepticism from important quarters in the development establishment.

Social Policy under Neoliberalism

Structural Adjustment without Structural Change

While much of the fairly high economic performance of the 1960s and the 1970s was associated with interventionist state development policies, by the 1980s, the fiscal crisis of the state (due to debt and the collapse of trade-based revenue sources) and the welfare state led to an assault on interventionism. Many of the new challenges arose from the way in which the "crises" of the 1970s and the 1980s were addressed under the influence of the International Financial Institutions (IFIs).

The preoccupation of development policy with structural change became overwhelmed in the 1980s by concerns with stability and debt management, and notions of "structural adjustment." These policies either reversed the structural changes induced by previous polices or led to a freezing of existing structures. Structural change requires not only general macroeconomic policies, but also sector-specific interventions through industrial policy, education, agricultural policy, etc. Such a position was anathema to an analysis insisting on a few macroeconomic indicators and relying on the market to determine micro- and sector-level developments.

"Structural adjustment" has generally worked against the movement of labor from low- to high-productivity activities. In a number of countries, the policies have led to deindustrialization, and in turn, to the reversal of structural changes. McMillan and Rodrik (2011) demonstrate that while structural change in East Asia has been of the growth-inducing type, the situation in African and Latin America has been the opposite: "In other words, rationalization of manufacturing industries may have come at the expense of inducing growth-reducing structural change." Indeed, in the case of Latin America and Africa, structural change has made a sizeable negative contribution to overall growth, while Asia is the only region where the contribution of structural change has been positive. This historically perverse "structural adjustment" has produced new social problems of informalization and pauperization of large sections of the urban population. However, social policies to address these new social problems have been dismissed as evidence of "urban bias" or pandering to organized urban interests.

From Growth without Equity to Stagnation

Earlier calls for "Growth with Equity" or "Meeting Basic Needs" arose at a time when it appeared that developing countries had mastered the growth part of the equation. The crisis of the 1970s brought economic growth to a dramatic halt and side-stepped the concerns over growing inequality and unemployment. The policy response ignored the structural nature of these new problems, and simply attributed them to "market distortions," meaning that for much of the 1980s and the 1990s, economic growth and structural change played a secondary role in policy circles occupied with stabilization and dismantling of interventionist policies. Growth was often derived from such stabilization and structural adjustment measures. High growth rates would contribute to the alleviation of poverty, especially if it was assumed that there would be no changes in income distribution. The simple assertion was that "growth is good for the poor" (Burnside and Dollar 2000), the implication being that governments need not devise deliberately pro-poor growth policies, but simply seek to maximize economic growth by sticking to the prescriptions of the IFIs.

Most governments in developing countries assumed that growth was central to development and criticized the World Bank for undermining growth prospects by their adhesion to deflationary policies. The issue then was not whether growth was good for the poor, but whether the adjustment policies applied during the 1980s and the 1990s were good for growth. The overwhelming evidence is that they were not (Easterly 2000, Przeworski and Vreeland 2000).

In addition, every growth process entails structural change and redistribution of income. Whether growth is actually good for the poor depends on the nature of the changes and the social policy regime that accompanies them. The period of Structural Adjustment Programs (SAPs) has also been one of regression in terms of income distribution and increasing absolute and relative poverty. Part of this was deliberately triggered. The incentives proposed under SAPs are premised on a shift in income toward nonwage earners (mostly owners of capital), in order to provide the requisite incentives for investment. The victims of this growing inequality were not the "usual suspects" who have all along pursued highly inegalitarian development strategies. Even South Korea failed to restore the high level of social equality upheld during previous decades, and thus demonstrated the problems of sustaining equity, despite a fairly impressive economic recovery from the crisis of 1997. Inequality in South Korea has reached levels "unprecedented" since the early 1980s. There has been a dramatic decompression of wages, leading to widening gaps in employment status and income levels across labor markets (Yun 2009).

In sum, the neoliberal model had no explicit model of growth. In formulaic policy pronouncements, the mantra was that "getting the fundamentals right" (as enshrined in the Washington Consensus) would be enough to trigger growth. In this highly axiomatic framework, there was no need to specify how stabilization policies actually lead to growth, or what policies and institutions would make such growth equitable. There is simply no automatic connection from growth to equality. Indeed, considerable evidence exists to suggest the contrary in the absence of deliberate redistributive measures.

From Segmentation by Regulation to Segmentation by the Market

Social policy relies on a strong fiscal base. By the mid-1980s, within the new ideological disposition toward stabilization and structural adjustment, social policy was associated with the fiscal crisis of the state, and thus treated as one more source of economic instability and inflation. Moreover, the association of social policy with state intervention opened it up to neoliberal attack as one of the sources of economic failure. Social expenditure was seen to detract from stabilization and would have to be curtailed, if fiscal deficits were to be checked. This policy shift led to cutbacks in social investment, privatization of social programs, and the abandonment of social planning as an integral part of policy making. It should be added here that pressure from NGOs for popular participation has also contributed to a growing sense of marginalization of social policy as a state preoccupation, let alone responsibility.

Neoliberal economists attributed high levels of inequality in the pre-adjustment era to the segmented welfare states that the patterns of industrialization and social policies had generated. The segmentation of social policy during the interventionist developmental era left room for an assault on social policy on neoliberal populist grounds, leading in some cases to an abandonment of the segmented welfare regime. The "neopopulist" language employed against such regimes spoke of rent-seeking groups that "captured" state polices and produced inefficient welfare states, which only benefited "insiders." The point, however, is not the segmentation of welfare, but the speed at which the welfare state is spread and unified. Historically, all welfare regimes have started off as segmented and, over time, have moved toward more unified systems through an extension into welfare states and more socially inclusive polices. Trends in many developing countries were toward such universalization, with the rate of de-segmentation and universalization depending on political factors and the structural changes in the economy.

Presumably, it was thought, liberalization of markets would pull the rug from under this interventionist order and "level the playing field." But neoliberal policies have achieved something entirely different. In many cases, the coverage of social protection programs has been reduced without thereby reducing segmentation (Lloyd-Sherlock 2009).[2] Instead there has been a sharp segmentation between formal transnationalized sectors of the economy on the one hand and informalized ones on the other hand. In addition, within each of these sectors there has been a sharp differentiation in wages as a result of wage decompression and deregulation. As a consequence, social policy has become segmented, and neoliberal reforms simply abolished the incipient welfare states, leading to commercialization of welfare services and retrenchment of the state. Skilled workers have managed to escape state-sustained welfare systems toward social provision by the market, leaving the poor to rely on family, informal markets, or poorly funded welfare programs.

Residual Role for Social Policy

The neoclassical understanding of the workings of the market has had implications for social policy in developing countries, especially during the reign of the structural adjustment and stabilization programs imposed by the Bretton Woods institutions during much of the last four decades. First, the deflationary bias of these policies meant that only the minimally protective aspects of social policy were protected, while the redistributive and productive aspects were set aside or downplayed. This resulted in the destruction of long-term productive capacity by lowering investment in "human capital," and produced an even more uneven distribution income.

Second, in the axiomatic framework of neoclassical economics, social policy appears merely as a corrective mechanism for addressing "market failure," not as a way to address transcendental values. Primacy and normalcy are given over to the market. However, in the more dogmatic neoliberal version, even these market failures provide no argument for state-managed social policies, as "government failures" are likely to be worse than market failures. Social policy was thus assigned a residual role, largely that of politically sugar-coating policies that entrenched insecurity through massive layoffs, engendered by deindustrialization and retrenchment of the state.

Transfers and Targeted Social Policies

Partly in response to criticisms of their deflationary bias, the growing political salience of poverty and inequality, and the growing literature on the dynamics of growth and development that point to the failure of adjustment to address problems of poverty and place economies on a long-term growth path, the IFIs embarked on policies that would include a "social dimension" and give them a "human face." However, this was to be achieved without fundamentally altering the theoretical underpinnings of the model. Thus, although, in 1990, the World Bank signaled a return to poverty concerns and a departure from the excessive focus on debt management and stabilization, it proposed a strategy for poverty alleviation that assumed its SAPs would provide the "enabling environment," if governments would only get their policies right. But having achieved the weakening of the fiscal position of the state, orthodox proponents now argued that such an anemic state had to abandon its developmental or redistributive ambitions and confine itself to the limited agenda of regulation of the market and providing some ameliorative social services for the poor and vulnerable.

The new initiatives of the IFIs were focused on conditional cash transfers (CCTs) and social risk management. Both were seen as ideologically compatible with market-driven policies. Moreover, cash transfers were regarded as market compatible, with the advantage of promoting investment in human capital by the poor. These programs also fit with the new " social risk management" paradigm being pushed by the IFIs (Holzmann and Jørgensen 2001), which has reduced poverty to something episodic, caused by transient shocks rather than structural determinants. This paradigm is thus a retreat from notions of social protection that built on solidarity and the mitigation of the negative impact of systemic instability and universalism (McKinnon 2004). The assumption was that markets generally functioned well, but that there may be small "market failures" that would necessitate short-term interventions.

Significantly, these policies were often detached from broader economic and social provision, compounding the segmentation of policies attributed to state interventionist policies of the past. Although this was designed to shift aid from development projects to social programs, such programs lacked the transformative features of social policy in its comprehensive sense. Within these approaches, if the transformative role of social policy is admitted at all, it is often confined to the micro level: this restriction is part of the ring-fencing of the core macroeconomic adjustment model from the incursions of the social agenda that might sabotage its stabilization purpose.

The new economic regime insisted upon what was described as "incentive-compatible" allocation of social expenditure. Closely associated with the severe budget constraints imposed on governments and a shift away from ideologies of solidarity and social citizenship, the new policies were focused on targeted forms of social protection for the poor and vulnerable. The programs were associated with overall bureaucratic reforms that often redefined the relationship between state and citizen. In light of the overall turn toward the market, there was an insistence that the same "market logic" be used in the management of public services. The arguments were the same: exposure of bureaucrats to the exigencies of the market would make them more efficient, and the commercialization of services would provide clients with a wide range of services. New public management reforms were introduced to bring markets inside state organizations. The appropriateness of these managerial reforms, their actual efficiency, and the impact on the integrity of the public institutions has been the subject of considerable debate (Bangura and Larbi 2006, Terry 2005). The most compelling case against such measures is that they treat citizens as clients. This implies a market-based model that may cut against democratic values of accountability, (as opposed to accounting), fairness, justice, and inclusiveness.

New policies included "smart targeting" or CCTs, which demanded reciprocal action on behalf of the recipients. Although programs such as Opportunidades in Mexico and Bolsa Familia in Brazil are said to overcome the traditional problems of targeting and to have disproportionately benefited the poor, "the progressive effect of these schemes is dwarfed by the inequality generated by the security system as a whole, in which half of the budget goes to the richest income quintile" (Lloyd-Sherlock 2009:359). In terms of budgetary allocations, these programs do not suggest the "political will" claimed by the champions of the programs. Opportunidades amounts to only 0.3 percent of Mexico's GDP, and only one-tenth of the country's two main social security systems (Lloyd-Sherlock 2009). And Bolsa Familia accounts for only 0.36 percent of the budget, which compares in stark terms with the average of 13 percent for social expenditure (Cornia and Martorano 2010).

FACING THE CHALLENGES: TOWARD A MORE TRANSFORMATIVE SOCIAL POLICY

Three challenges arise from the analysis above. The first involves devising a macroeconomic framework that enables economies to stabilize their real variables, especially output and employment. The second is to highlight the transformative role of social policy, especially in its contribution to output growth and structural change. And the third lies in ensuring that social policy plays its protective and redistributive roles.

Building in Automatic Stabilizers through Social Policy

The challenge today is to adopt socially responsible macroeconomic policies that facilitate economic growth and structural adjustment while addressing the problems of instability. In the last decade, many developing countries have enjoyed fairly high growth rates, largely due to improved terms of trade. These have occurred largely within a neoliberal framework, although both democratic policies and the increased foreign exchange due to improvements in the balance of payments provide these economies with more policy space. Indeed, the economic recovery has provided failed macroeconomics with a new lease on life, either by associating it with the recovery, or through benign neglect. However, the problems of that model persist and developing countries may once again make the earlier mistake of having growth without a set of macroeconomic tools that address the cyclical patterns of that growth.

If, in the post-WWII era, social policy in developing countries was the handmaiden of developmentalism, in their developed counterparts, it was interwoven with the ontology of Keynesian economics, which was fundamentally preoccupied with issues of stabilization and maintenance of full employment or putting back to work those who had lost employment due to the Depression. In this model, social policy provided both the objective of macroeconomic policy and an important instrument in achieving macroeconomic stability. The "Keynesian Welfare System" was, not surprisingly, focused on the protective and redistributive aspects of social policy. And if it paid any attention to growth at all, it was through the channel of better capacity utilization, and by augmenting aggregate demand through state expenditures on social programs, or in redistributing income in favor of those with a higher propensity to consume.

The general view was that Keynesianism and the social policies it spawned did not address the problems of supply that were the main issue in the developing countries.[3] In the eyes of developmentalists, the welfare state was guilty by its association with an economic analysis that was not deemed appropriate for developing country needs. Earlier structuralists who were concerned with under-consumption considered demand relevant for developing countries as well (Furtado 1965, Nurkse 1953). In general, however, development economics confined itself to the supply side (FitzGerald 2002). Concerns over the level and patterns of demand rarely took on the counter-cyclical issues they had in advanced "Keynesian welfare states," where social spending has served as an important countercyclical cushion.

In an age of demand compression, it may seem foolhardy to consider the growth effect of social policy through Keynesian aggregate demand effects in poor countries. In the age of liberalization, domestic demand has ceased to be of particular interest, with the focus now centered on being "open" and meeting international demand. However, one striking feature of social spending in developing countries is its pro-cyclicality (Ocampo 2008). There is, therefore, renewed interest in the demand management aspect of economic policy, partly in response to the pro-cyclical neoliberal policies. These ideas have reappeared in the context of the current crisis and the belief that developing countries could play a countercyclical role by stimulating their economies. China is being urged to invest more in housing and health services in order to stimulate its domestic economy (Ocampo 2008). What is needed is a social policy that can play the Keynesian role of providing automatic countercyclical stabilizers within a fundamentally growth-oriented framework.

Social Policy, Human Capital, and Investment

Earlier development economics recognized the importance of "manpower" as something that would have to be addressed by any planning. In more recent years, new growth theories have afforded human capital a central role through their recognition of technological change as "endogenous": meaning that it is underpinned by a number of deliberate and structured factors in society. There is always a discrepancy between social and private returns of growth-enhancing investment, such as health and education, due to the presence of positive externalities. This has been one major argument for public intervention in such social investments, which government must undertake if the economy is not to be stuck in a "low development trap." However, in the age of adjustment, the arithmetic of "rates of return" was narrowly deployed to push for "user charges" and a reduction of state expenditure on secondary and tertiary education. Furthermore, the retrenchment of labor in the 1980s and the 1990s in many developing countries led to an increase in informalization, which weakened the "training regimes" for which formalization of labor markets and training are an important ingredient. Informalization has also led to the "devaluation of skills acquired during the import substitution phase in Latin America" (Cimoli and Correa 2002).

By the mid-1990s, it was clear that this had been a mistake, and institutions such as the World Bank returned to funding higher education. In terms of skills in the labor force, many developing countries found that their public institutions were either privatized or simply starved of funds. However, the problem of access was still couched in the language of finance. Rather than pointing the way to comprehensive, transformative social policy, the analysis has instead pointed toward financial market reforms to make credit accessible to the poor (e.g., microcredit). Conventional economists have interpreted the problem of low education of the poor as a financial market failure.

Structural change and economic growth are both the consequences and causes of technological change. The process demands new skills, while discarding those made obsolete by the process of what Schumpeter referred to as "creative destruction." Effective policies are not those that fight, Ludditelike, against such changes, but those which both protect citizens from the "destructive" effects of such changes and enhance their adaptive capabilities. In both these tasks, social policy plays a central role. Social policy links education and training to economic performance by determining levels of school enrolment and accessibility to various institutions of training, and providing incentives to firms and individuals to acquire skills. It helps in the coordination of decisions by different actors about the acquisition of these skills. The literature on Varieties of Capitalism has identified the associated "training regimes" as one of the constituent elements of welfare regimes, defined as the "ensemble of institutions... and specialized actors... engaged in the organization and provision of education and training as well as the specific customs, rules, and regulations governing their internal functioning and mutual coordination within different national policy frameworks" (Buechtemann and Verdier 1998).

Partly because of a moral aversion to instrumentalizing social policy, research on the developmental state has not paid much attention to the role of social policy, except perhaps to dismiss its concern for production as "instrumental" as opposed to policy in the Western advanced countries, where it presumably is concerned with only matters of intrinsic value. In recognition that the developmental states had extensive social policy, academics have coined new labels for these states: "Confucian oekonomic welfare state" (Jones 1990), the "productivist welfare state" (Holliday 2000), or the "developmental welfare state" (Gough 2004). However, this is partly based on a misreading of the latter. The welfare state was always an attempt to reconcile production with other values such as equity and social inclusion, a point succinctly articulated by Esping-Andersen with respect to social democracy's reconciliation of efficiency and equity through what he calls "productive social policy."

To fully exploit the "destructive creativity" of capitalism, welfare states set up a system of protection and training of labor. The Schumpeterian side of the welfare state is therefore not evidence that the welfare state has turned into a "workfare" state. The "productivist" side of the welfare state has become more transparent in responses to pressures of globalization. Global competition has compelled the European welfare regimes to pay greater attention to the productive role of social policy, not simply in the "workfare" mode that displaces the welfare state (Angkinand 2009, Holden 2003, Jessop 1994, Torfing 1999), but in the "social investment" mode that extends the welfare state to manage what are perceived to be knowledge-based economies (Giddens 1998, Morel et al. 2012). This new concern with "social investment," captured by the notion of "training regimes," suggests that skill formation and training regimes are often embedded in much larger welfare policy concerns, with ramifications that go beyond the economic to include the impact on political and social relations (including gender). It further suggests that in advanced economies, at least, there is a strong correlation between key components of social protection (employment, unemployment, and wage protection) and the dominant skill profile of the workforce. Similar differences can be identified among "training regimes" in developing countries.

Structural change is an extremely disruptive process. Much of the social protection system of modern welfare states has been geared toward addressing the many problems that this poses to society. Such systems can determine the tempo and direction of the movement of labor and, more specifically, they "can change the balance among the five fundamental types of mobility events that contribute to the process of structural change, namely (a) entry into the labor force by young workers or recent immigrants, (b) job mobility of those already in the labor force, (c) exit and reentry of mid-career workers, (d) exit and entry into the labor force by women during their childbearing years, and (e) retirements and other long-term exits" (Diprete et al. 1997). Neoliberal policies have insisted on "labor market flexibility" premised on the principle of the right of the employer to hire and fire individuals to ensure efficiency and full employment.

However, there are other notions of "flexibility" compatible with both efficiency and social rights. These involve not the protection of the job, but protection of the workers through adequate unemployment compensation and massive and constant retraining and redeployment of labor. It is this approach that makes Nordic labor markets among the most flexible and receptive to technological change. The key argument here is that some of the rigidities created by social policies may, paradoxically, provide the Schumpeterian space for innovation and planning, because the much-vaunted "exit option" may actually militate against growth-inducing commitment (D'Antoni and Pagano 2002). In addition, reduced employment flexibility may have the opposite effect: longer tenure (which, in turn, is enhanced by less flexible labor markets) raises the time horizon of workers, who consequently might not try to maximize current wages and may limit their search for alternative jobs (Acemoglu 2002). Michie and Sheehan (2003:123) show "that the "low road" of labor flexibility practices encouraged by labor market deregulation—short-term and temporary contracts, a lack of employer commitment to job security, low levels of training, and so on—are negatively correlated with innovation."

For many developing countries, the main challenge lies in reversing the huge turnabout in education and training that occurred during the adjustment era. What is required, then, is a social policy that can enhance the human capacities of labor, and facilitate mobility between industry and geographical areas.

Social Protection, Financial Markets, and Investment

The way in which pension funds are collected and managed can shape the financial sector while the financial sector, in turn, can impact the returns and portfolio choices available to the pension system. The way in which labor income and welfare is regulated thus influences whether savings will flow into the banking system (Vitols 2001:175–176). The IFIs understood this financial nexus. The sheer magnitude of funds involved relative to national financial institutions has made such resources a focus of attention in the design of financial systems for economic growth.

The liberalization of financial markets and introduction of stock markets were closely related to the privatization of pension funds. The Pinochet regime dramatically illustrated the elective affinity between social security systems and financial institutions. Following this experience, many developing counties have been forced to privatize their pension funds, mainly to kick-start stock markets. The argument is that such stock markets will contribute to the "deepening" of financial markets, which will, in turn, contribute to higher growth. That is a contested position considering that none of the higher performing developmental states have relied on such stock markets (Singh 1996).

The link between social security funds and development finance has been a feature of "late industrializers," and other latecomers have emulated German "universal banking" and the Bismarckian state the most. The firm- or industry-level policies that ensured wage compression and lower levels of household inequality, and that placed great emphasis on solidaristic retirement provisions were important factors in supporting the bank-based system in Germany (Vitols 2001). "This elective affinity between solidaristic labor regimes and bank-based financial regimes is important in controlling the relative size of the market segment of the financial system" (Vitols 2001:176).

Although pension funds constituted large amounts of money in some developing countries, remarkably little was said about their developmental role in earlier literature. The most iconic providence fund is Singapore's Central Providence Fund, which has played a vital role in the generation of savings. Citizens were forced to contribute to the fund, which accounted for 25 percent of gross national savings in 1985. The fund's contributions enabled Singapore to raise gross national domestic savings to as much as 40 percent on average in the 1980s (Huff 1995). In a similar vein, in South Korea, the pension system was designed "as a source of capital rather than as a means of old-age income security" (Jung and Walker 2009:427). Huge funds were collected in the process, constituting 30 percent of GDP in 2006. In South Korea, as in Japan, a substantial portion of the pension funds were lent to the Ministry of Finance, which in turn used these funds to invest in various public projects (Iglesias and Palacios 2000). The pension system was used particularly to finance heavy and chemical industries (Jung and Walker 2009, Kim 2005, Kwon 2004a).

Many other countries had similar "forced savings" schemes, many of which were wholly or partially privatized during the era of neoliberalism (Huber and Stephens 2000, Mesa-Lago 2002, Singh 1996, World Bank 1994). While, admittedly, many of these countries may not have allocated these funds wisely, privatization, rather than a reexamination, of the investment portfolio has denied the state access to useful funds for investment in infrastructure.[4] Privatized pension funds now tend to find their way into real estate speculation in shopping malls, or buying treasury bonds to finance government deficits, or are simply transferred abroad as part of the portfolio diversification.

The new consensus on poverty was based on the view that risk and vulnerability are the main factors to be addressed. This view was in contradiction with the focus of the IFIs on contributory pensions. The funding of some of these schemes has not been reliable, dependent as they are on volatile and transient sources of income. There is ample evidence suggesting that noncontributory benefits improve citizens' well-being and sense of security. What is needed, then, is the inclusion of schemes that are universal, noncontributory, and financed from the regular budget, and a social policy that not merely accommodates financial markets, but tames them.

"Patient Capital," "Patient Labor"

A major challenge in relating labor and financial markets in the process of development lies in finding systems that ensure both "patient capital" and "patient labor," in order to underpin their accumulation and innovation systems. In the context of catching up, patient labor in the labor market should have, as a counterpart, patient capital in the financial market. A policy designed to shift more people into the modern sector would encourage high profitability and high investment in the high-productivity sector. This requires that the share of labor in value added is restrained, allowing for high profits, and that capitalist consumption is restrained, and the reinvestment of profit is high.

One important feature of the East Asian developmentalist state was the "high profit-high growth" nexus behind the high levels of growth (Akyüz and Gore 1996).[5] How was this achieved? A number of arguments have been advanced in the literature on the developmentist state, including the nationalism of the bourgeoisie, the coercive force of the state, and its ability to "stabilize" labor and, through carrots and sticks, make the business class buy into its project and retain the autonomy necessary to force capitalists to invest (Koo and Kim 1992). This appears to have obfuscated an important aspect of economic and social policy in these countries: measures to support high profits ensured lower wages and labor peace, accompanied by restrictions on the use or allocation of such profits.

There were a number of instruments that ensured the proper use of surplus. These included "severe restrictions on luxury consumption, both directly through restricting the import and domestic production of luxury consumption goods, and indirectly through high taxation and restrictions on consumer credits, although the mix of measures differed across countries" (Akyüz et al. 1998). Other measures involved restricting earnings from the financial sector. This was achieved through state control or ownership of the banks, elimination of speculative investment opportunities, and restrictions on the outflow of capital.

One implication of the organizational structure of industry is that wages in the sector will be set not by marginal productivity in the labor-intensity sector, but rather by the outcome of wage bargaining. The political challenge, then, is to develop both patient labor and patient capital. The achievement of such conditions is a matter of high political-economic order and defines the "welfare regime."

The state should act as a kind of broker that ensures that the "ex post distribution of resources is such that it corresponds to those incentives that were ex ante necessary to induce the necessary investments." It can also intervene in the economy to make high reinvestment of profits the preferred behavior of capital owners. Here, "social pacts" can play an important role: one of the functions of social policy has been to give credence to such arrangements, either through state regulation or state-guaranteed "wage bargains."

It is important to underscore the importance of mutually binding pacts. Many of the social pacts of the 1990s (especially in Southern Europe and Ireland) suffered from one-sidedness. They were generally about labor restraining and sharing the burden while capital, especially in its financial form, was left unbound.

Legitimation and "Social Embedding" of the Development Project

In the case of late industrializers, structural changes can be extremely disrupting, tearing asunder long-established social bonds, long-held norms, and worldviews. It is thus not surprising that many late industrializers adopted a number of social policies at much lower levels of economic development than those followed by the "pioneers." In the language of Karl Polanyi (1946), this constituted one way of "embedding" the market in the social sphere, which was broader than that of the bourgeoisie.

The problem of legitimacy takes on a more urgent task in new democracies, where many hitherto disempowered groups insist that democracy go beyond the formal and yield substantive returns. While, in the 1980s, new democracies tended to adopt orthodox policies (Mkandawire 2004), they are now under enormous pressure to move toward "developmental welfare states" (Adésínà 2007, Kwon 2004b, Riesco 2007). We should bear in mind that the idea of legitimacy is not only confined to democracies as is sometimes implied in the literature on developmental states. The quintessential developmental states of East Asia were authoritarian: their efficacy has been attributed to their "autonomy," which left them unencumbered by social claims. Given such a characterization, more attention has been paid to what Michael Mann (1987) refers to as the "despotic power" of the state ("the range of actions which the elite is empowered to undertake without routine, institutionalized negotiation with civil society") than to the "infrastructural power" (defined as the "capacity of the state to actually penetrate civil society and to implement logistically political decisions throughout the realm"). The extraction of resources (human or material) from society without recourse to force is a key element of such infrastructural power. The earlier view of "autonomy," which associated it with authoritarian rule, was modified with the notion of "embedded autonomy," which pointed to a special relationship between the state and business and the many mechanisms of consultation between them (Evans 1995).

However, this focus on the "embeddedness" of the state with respect to narrow sections of society tended to neglect the implicit or explicit social policies of authoritarian states aimed at other sections of society, except to the extent that it enhanced human capital. Indeed, this restricted view of "embeddedness" led to the characterization of East Asia as a "social policy free zone" (Chang 2004).

Even in its most authoritarian moments, the developmental state had to adopt policies that gained it legitimacy in the eyes of the population or, at least, those sections of the population central to its industrialization project, capital and labor. The literature certainly exhibits some ambiguities. While measures by the state to "embed" itself in bourgeois society are suggested as a source of its effectiveness, the instrumentalization of social policies, extending the embeddedness of the autonomous state to other social classes is viewed negatively—and regarded as being aimed simply at pacifying the workforce or as "pre-emptory means to address existing or expected distributional conflicts or to facilitate the industrialization process, rather than to reduce social inequalities" (Chung 1992:3, Deyo 1989, Holliday 2000, Midgley 1986). However, for all the repression and labor unrest witnessed under the Asian developmental strategy, there is also ample evidence to suggest widespread adhesion by the population to the otherwise top-down development project. The Gramscian hegemony of such a project has been attributed to all sorts of factors: docility, Asian values, Confucian deference to authority, acquiescence under the duress of brute force, patriotism, or self-sacrifice. But there is a persuasive literature on how politics and social policy played their part in "buying peace" in Korea (Ringen et al. 2011). The idea of "industrial citizen" in Korea and Japan represented a means of integrating labor into the developmental model. China's current discussion about a "harmonious society" speaks to the same problematique: brute force alone could have sustained the developmental projects of these countries for just as long.

Concluding Thoughts

The era of neoliberal dominance brought in its wake both an economic model and social policy regimes that followed the dictate of the market. In many cases, this not only failed to address the social problems that had arisen during the "Golden Era" developmentalist period, but generated new problems as well, while weakening state capacity to address the new challenges. More recently, renewed growth has taken root in many developing countries, but it remains highly vulnerable, and is generating new social problems of its own.

What are required, therefore, are strategies of development that deepen structural change, and include effective social policies with which to address the old and new problems of overcoming poverty and inequality. The issue at hand is not a return to the segmented developmental welfare state of yore, but, instead, to move toward a more inclusive and universal developmental welfare state, which can contribute directly to the process of growth and structural change, while ensuring that citizens' welfare and social rights are safeguarded and enhanced.

Notes

1. A more recent model referred to "export populism," which has been initiated in Argentina. This is based on exportable commodities, taxed to subsidize "wage food" (Richardson 2009).

2. Thus in Chile, coverage of the social security system, previously about 72 percent of the population, dropped to only 60 percent or less of the workforce by 2000 (Borzutzky 2005).

3. Dudley Seers considered the application to which Keynesianism was applied as a "special case" (Seers 1963). The Indian economist V. K. Rao argued that Keynesian economics was "simply not relevant for developing countries."

4. Mismanagement of these funds was often attributed to political interference. Privatization was advanced on the grounds that it would insulate pension scheme from political interference. However, the experience of Argentina, through the 2008 nationalization of its private individual accounts system, suggests that privatization is not irreversible (Kay 2009).

5. With respect to high share of profits in the East Asian economies, You argues:

   A high business saving rate may be due to a high share of business profits in the distribution of income and/or a high profit-retention ratio. Can we say then that the high rates of business savings in East Asia derive from the income distribution that is unusually favorable to profits? The answer is a qualified yes. All the East Asian countries have relatively high profit shares (equivalently, low wage shares), but almost a half the developing countries have profit shares similar to or higher than the East Asian level. (You 1998:49).

REFERENCES

Acemoglu, Daron. 2002. "Technical Change, Inequality, and the Labor Market." *Journal of Economic Literature* 40(1):7–72.

Adésínà, Jìmí (ed.). 2007. *Social Policy in Sub-Saharan African Context: In Search of Inclusive Development*. Basingstoke: Palgrave Macmillan.

Akyüz, Yilmaz, Ha-Joon Chang, and Richard Kozul-Wright. 1998. "New Perspectives on East Asian Development." *Journal of Development Studies* 34(6):4–36.

Akyüz, Yilmaz and Charles Gore. 1996. "The Investment-Profit Nexus in East Asian Industrialisation." *World Development* 24(3):461–470.

Angkinand, Apanard P. 2009. "Banking Regulation and the Output Cost of Banking Crises." *Journal of International Financial Markets, Institutions & Money* 19(2):240–257.

Arrighi, Giovanni. 1973. "International Corporations, Labour Aristocracies, and Economic Development In Tropical Africa." In *Essays on the Political Economy of Africa*. Giovanni Arrighi and John S. Saul (eds.). New York: Monthly Review Press.

Bangura, Yusaf and George A. Larbi (eds.). 2006. *Public Sector Reform in Developing Countries: Capacity Challenges to Improve Services*. Basingstoke: Palgrave Macmillan / United Nations Research Institute for Social Development (UNRISD).

Borzutzky, Silvia. 2005. "From Chicago to Santiago: Neoliberalism and Social Security Privatization in Chile." *Governance* 18(4):655–674.

Buechtemann, Christoph F. and Eric Verdier. 1998. "Education and Training Regimes: Macro-Institutional Evidence." *Revue d'Economie Politique* 108(3):291–320.

Burnside, Craig and David Dollar. 2000. "Aid, Policies, and Growth." *The American Economic Review* 90(4):847–868.

Chang, Ha-Joon. 2004. "The Role of Social Policy in Economic Development: Some Theoretical Reflections and Lessons from Asia." In *Social Policy in Development Context*. Thandika Mkandawire (ed.). London: Palgrave.

Chenery, Hollis B., Richard Jolly, Montek S. Ahluwalia, C. L. Bell, and John H. Duloy. 1974. *Redistribution with Growth*. London: Oxford University Press for the World Bank.

Chung, Moo-kwon. 1992. State Autonomy, State Capacity, and Public Policy: The Development of Social Security Policy in Korea. PhD diss. Indiana, University.

Cimoli, Mario and Nelson Correa. 2002. Trade Openness and Technological Gaps in Latin America: A "Low Growth Trap." LEM Working Paper 2002/14. Pisa: Laboratory of Economics and Management, Sant'Anna School of Advanced Studies.

Cornia, Giovanni Andrea and Bruno Martorano. 2010. Policies for Reducing Income Inequality: Latin America during the Last Decade. Working papers 1006. New York: UNICEF, Division of Policy and Strategy.

D'Antoni, Massimo and Ugo Pagano. 2002. "National Cultures and Social Protection as Alternative Insurance Devices." *Structural Change and Economic Dynamics* 13(4):367–386.

Deyo, Frederic C. 1989. *Beneath the Miracle: Labor Subordination in the New Asian Industrialism*. Berkeley: University of California Press.

Diprete, Thomas A., Paul M. De Graaf, Ruud Luijkx, Michael Tåhlin, and Hans-Peter Blossfeld. 1997. "Collectivist versus Individualist Mobility Regimes? Structural Change and Job Mobility in Four Countries." *American Journal of Sociology* 102(2):318–358.

Easterly, William. 2000. "The Lost Decades: Developing Countries Stagnation in Spite of Policy Reform, 1980–1998." *Journal of Economic Growth* 6(2):135–157.

Evans, Peter. 1995. *Embedded Autonomy: States and Industrial Transformation*. Princeton, NJ: Princeton University Press.

Filgueira, Fernando. 2007. "The Latin American Social States: Criticak Junctures and Critical Choices." In *Democracy and Social Policy*. Yusaf Bangura (ed.). Basingstoke: Palgrave Macmillan.

FitzGerald, Valpy. 2002. Globalisation and the Transmission of Economic Ideas. Paper presented at the UNRISD/ILO Meeting on "Globalisation, Culture and Social Change," Geneva.

Frankema, Ewout. 2012. "Industrial Wage Inequality in Latin America in Global Perspective, 1900–2000." *Studies in Comparative International Development (SCID)* 47(1):47–74.

Furtado, Celso. 1965. "Development and Stagnation in Latin America: A Structural Approach." *Studies in Comparative International Development (SCID)* 1(11), 159–175.

Giddens, Anthony. 1998. *The Third Way: The Renewal of Social Democracy*. Cambridge: Polity Press.

Gough, Ian. 2004. "East Asia: The Limits of Productivist Regimes." In *Insecurity and Welfare Regimes in Asia, Africa and Latin America: Social Policy in Development Contexts*. Ian Gough, Geof Wood, Armando Barrientos, Philippa Bevan, and Peter Davis (eds.). Cambridge: Cambridge University Press.

Holden, Chris. (2003). "Decommodification and the Workfare State." *Political Studies Review* 1(3):303–316.

Holliday, Ian. 2000. "Productivist Welfare Capitalism: Social Policy in East Asia." *Political Studies* 48(4):706–723.

Holzmann, Robert and Steen Jørgensen. 2001. "Social Risk Management: A New Conceptual Framework for Social Protection, and beyond." *International Tax and Public Finance* 8(4):529–556.

Huber, Evelyne and John D. Stephens. 2000. The Political Economy of Pension Reform: Latin America in Comparative Perspective. Occassional Paper No. 7. Geneva: UNRISD.

Huff, W. G. 1995. "The Developmental State, Government, and Singapore's Economic Development since 1960." *World Development* 23(8):1421–1438.

Iglesias, Augusto and Robert J. Palacios. 2000. "Managing Public Pension Reserves—Part I : Evidence from the International Experience." *World Bank Pension Reform Primer*.

International Labor Office (ILO). 1972. Employment, Incomes and Equality: A Strategy for Increasing Productive Employment in Kenya. Geneva: ILO.

Jessop, Bob. 1994. "The Transition to Post-Fordism and the Schumpeterian Workfare State." In *Towards a Post-Fordist Welfare State*. Roger Burrows and Brian D. Loader (eds.). New York: Routledge.

Jones, Catherine. 1990. "Hong Kong, Singapore, South Korea and Taiwan: Oikonomic Welfare States." *Government and Opposition* 25(4):446–462.

Jung, Chang Lyul and Alan Walker. 2009. "The Impact of Neo-Liberalism on South Korea's Public Pension: A Political Economy of Pension Reform." *Social Policy & Administration* 43(5):425–444.

Kay, Stephen J. 2009. "Political Risk and Pension Privatization: The Case of Argentina (1994–2008)." *International Social Security Review* 62(3):1–21.

Kim, Dae-Hwon. 2005. "State and Development in Korea after the Asian Crisis." In *Beyond Market-Driven Development: Drawing on the Experience of Asia and Latin America*. Makoto Noguchi and Costas Lapavitsas (eds.). New York: Routledge.

Koo, Hagen and Eun Mee Kim. 1992. "The Developmental State and Capital Accumulation in South Korea." In *State and Development in the Asian Pacific Rim*. Richard P. Henderson and Jeffrey Applebaum (eds.). Newbury Park, CA: Sage Publications.

Kwon, Huck-ju. 2004a. "The Economic Crisis and the Politics of Welfare Reform in Korea." In *Social Policy in Development Context*. Thandika Mkandawire (ed.). London: Palgrave.

———. 2004b. *Transforming the Developmental Welfare State in East Asia*. Basingstoke: Palgrave Macmillan.

Lloyd-Sherlock, Peter. 2009. "Social Policy and Inequality in Latin America: A Review of Recent Trends." *Social Policy & Administration* 43(4):347–363.

Mann, Michael. 1987. "Ruling Class Strategies and Citizenship." *Sociology* 21(3):339–354.

Marglin, Stephen A. and Juliet B. Shor. 1990. *The Golden Age of Capitalism*. Oxford: Clarendon Press.

McKinnon, Roddy. 2004. "Social Risk Management and the World Bank: Resetting the 'Standards' for Social Security?" *Journal of Risk Research* 7(3):297–314.

McMillan, Margaret S. and Dani Rodrik. 2011. Globalization, Structural Change and Productivity Growth. NBER Working Paper 17143. Cambridge, MA: National Bureau of Economic Research.

Mesa-Lago, Carmelo. 2002. "Myth and Reality of Pension Reform: The Latin American Evidence." *World Development* 30(8):1309–1321.

Michie, Jonathan and Maura Sheehan. 2003. "Labour Market Deregulation, 'Flexibility' and Innovation." *Cambridge Journal of Economics* 27(1):123–143.

Midgley, James. 1986. "Industrialization and Welfare: The Case of the Four Little Tigers." *Social Policy & Administration* 20(3):225–238.

Mkandawire, Thandika. 2004. "Disempowering New Democracies and the Persistence of Poverty." In *Globalisation, Poverty and Conflict*. Max Spoor (ed.). Dordrecht: Kluwer Academic Publishers.

Morel, Nathalie, Bruno Palier, and Joakim Palme. 2012. *Towards a Social Investment Welfare State? Ideas, Policies and Challenges*. Bristol: Policy Press.

Nurkse, Ragnar. 1953. *Problems of Capital Formation in Underdeveloped Countries*. Oxford: Basil Blackwell.

Ocampo, Jose Antonio. 2008. "The Links between Economic and Social Policies: A Conceptual Framework." In *Pursuing Decent Work Goals: Priorities for Research*. Gerry Rodgers and Christine Kuptsch (eds.). Geneva: ILO.

Polanyi, Karl. 1946. *The Great Transformation: The Political and Economic Origins of Our Time*. Boston: Beacon Press.

Przeworski, Adam and James Raymond Vreeland. 2000. "The Effects of IMF Programs on Economic Growth." *Journal of Development Economics* 62(2):385–421.

Richardson, Neal. 2009. "Export-Oriented Populism: Commodities and Coalitions in Argentina." *Studies in Comparative International Development (SCID)* 44(3):228–255.

Riesco, Manuel (ed.). 2007. *Latin America: A New Developmental Welfare State Model in the Making?* Basingstoke: Palgrave Macmillan.

Ringen, Stein, Huck-ju Kwon, Ilcheong Yi, Taekyoon Kim, and Jooha Lee. 2011. *The Korean State and Social Policy: How South Korea Lifted Itself from Poverty and Dictatorship to Affluence and Democracy*. London: Oxford University Press.

Ruggie, John Gerard. 1982. "International Regimes, Transactions, and Change: Embedded Liberalism in the Postwar Economic Order." *International Organization* 36(2):379–415.

Seers, Dudley. 1963. "The Limitations of the Special Case." *Bulletin of the Oxford Institute of Economics and Statistics* 25(2):77–98.

Seguino, Stephanie. 1997. "Gender Wage Inequality and Export Led Growth in South Korea." *The Journal of Development Studies* 34(2):102–132.

Singh, Ajit. 1996. "Pension Reform, the Stock Market, Capital Formation and Economic Growth: A Critical Commentary on the World Bank's Proposals." *International Social Security Review* 49(3):21–43.

Terry, Larry D. 2005. "The Thinning of Administrative Institutions in the Hollow State." *Administration & Society* 37(4):426–444.

Torfing, Jacob. 1999. "Workfare with Welfare: Recent Reforms of the Danish Welfare State." *Journal of European Social Policy* 9(1):5–28.

Vitols, Sigurt. 2001. "The Origins of Bank-Based and Market-Based Financial Systems: Germany, Japan, and the United States." In *The Origins of Nonliberal Capitalism: Germany and Japan in Comparison*. Wolfgang Streeck and Kozo Yamamura (eds.). New York: Cornell University Press.

World Bank. 1994. *Averting the Old Age Crisis: Policies to Protect the Old and Promote Growth, A World Bank*. New York: Oxford University Press.

You, Jong-Il. 1998. "Income Distribution and Growth in East Asia." *Journal of Development Studies* 34(6):37–65.

Yun, Ji-Whan. 2009. "Labor Market Polarization in South Korea: The Role of Policy Failures in Growing Inequality." *Asian Survey* 49(2):268–290.

PART II

Democratizing Development

Inequality of Opportunity, Income Inequality, and Economic Mobility: Some International Comparisons

Paolo Brunori, Francisco H. G. Ferreira, and Vito Peragine

INTRODUCTION

The relationship between inequality and the development process has long been of interest, and both directions of causality have been extensively investigated. The idea that the structural transformation that takes place as an economy develops may lead first to rising and then to falling inequality—known as the Kuznets (1955) hypothesis—was once hugely influential. The view that inequality may, in turn, affect the rate and nature of economic growth has an equally distinguished pedigree, dating back at least to Kaldor (1956). In the 1990s, a burgeoning theoretical literature suggested a number of mechanisms through which wealth inequality might be detrimental to economic growth, when combined with credit constraints and increasing returns, because of political channels, fertility effects, et cetera. See Voitchovsky (2009) for a recent survey of that literature.

But popular concern about inequality in developing (and developed) countries does not originate exclusively—or even primarily—from its possible instrumental effects on growth, on the growth elasticity of poverty, on health status, on crime, or on any number of other factors that are possibly influenced by the distribution of economic well-being. Many of those who worry about inequality do so because they consider it—or at least some of it—"unjust." Most development economists, however, share the broader profession's discomfort with normative concepts such as justice and, until recently and with some distinguished exceptions, have had little to say about it.

That is a pity. Behavioral economics has taught us that notions of fairness and justice affect individual behavior—in the precise and well-documented sense that they induce sizable deviations from the behaviors predicted by purely self-regarding models of rationality (e.g., Fehr and Fischbacher 2003, Fehr and Gachter 2000, Fehr and Schmidt 1999). Some recent experimental evidence suggests that, in assessing outcome distributions, people do distinguish between factors for which players can be held responsible, and those that are beyond their control (Cappelen et al. 2010). If fairness matters to economic agents and alters their behavior, then understanding fairness ought to matter even to the purest positive economist. If people assess distributional outcomes differently depending on how much of the inequality they observe is thought to be "fair" or "unfair", then it may be useful to measure the extent to which inequality is unfair.

Efforts in this direction have in fact begun. Drawing primarily on the welfare economics literature on "inequality of opportunity" (I.Op.), researchers have started to measure unfair inequality in both poor and rich countries. In that literature, there is now widespread agreement on the basic principle of what equality of opportunity refers to: inequalities due to circumstances beyond individual control are unfair, and should be compensated for, while inequalities due to factors for which people can be held responsible (sometimes called "efforts"), may be considered acceptable. But this broad concept can be interpreted in a number of different ways, some of which have been shown to be mutually inconsistent. And there is an even greater array of actual indices that have been proposed to implement these concepts, and used to measure inequality of opportunity in different countries or at different times. The relatively high ratio of different (and incomparable) approaches to actual empirical applications means that it has so far been difficult to make a reasonably broad comparison of inequality of opportunity levels across countries.

This chapter takes a first step toward making such a comparison, by drawing on two specific approaches that have been relatively widely used. The first is the measurement of ex-ante inequality of economic opportunity (IEO). The second is the measurement of (children's) access to basic services adjusted for differences associated with circumstances—commonly known as the Human Opportunity Index (HOI). The latter is not a measure of inequality of opportunity per se; it is better seen as a development index that is designed to be sensitive to inequality of opportunity. Our objective is a modest one: we collect and summarize the results of empirical applications of these two measures to as many countries as possible, and describe the correlations between these measures and a number of other indicators of interest, including GDP per capita, overall income inequality, and two measures of intergenerational mobility.

We hope that the collected evidence on the degree of inequality of opportunity in different countries, and its pattern of association with other variables, might help to shed light on the nature of the (often increasing) inequalities observed today in many areas of the world, and may help in the design of redistributive public policies. The chapter is organized as follows. The second section contains a brief overview of the concepts and approaches to the measurement of inequality of opportunity. This provides essential background not only for an understanding of where the inequality of opportunity measures come from and what they do, but also of what they do *not* do, and the concepts they do *not* capture. The third section contains our review of inequality of opportunity measures for 41 countries, and examines how they correlate with other indicators. The next section presents a comparison of HOI applications across 39 developing countries, and how it correlates with other relevant indices, including the United Nations' Human Development Index (HDI). The fifth section contains a discussion of the results, including some policy implications. The last section concludes.

CONCEPTS AND MEASUREMENT

The economics literature on inequality of opportunity builds explicitly on a few key contributions from philosophy, including Arneson (1989), Cohen (1989), and Dworkin (1981a, 1981b).[1] The basic idea, as noted above, is that outcomes that are valued by all or most members of society (such as income, wealth, health status, etc.), and that are often termed "advantages," are determined by two types of factors: those for which the individual can be held responsible, and those for which he/she cannot.[2] Inequalities due to the former—which we will call "efforts"—are normatively acceptable, whereas those due to the latter—which we call "circumstances"—are unfair, and should in principle be eliminated.

More specifically, the idea of equality of opportunity is composed of two basic principles: the *compensation* principle, stating that "inequalities due to circumstances should be eliminated" and the *reward* principle, which concern the relationship between effort and final advantage.[3] In its simplest form, the trajectory from these basic principles to the construction of indices designed to measure inequality of opportunity quantitatively begins with defining a single individual advantage (let's call it income, y) and assuming that all of its determinants can be classified into either a set of circumstances (C) or a scalar index of effort (e). Circumstances include a vast list of personal characteristics that are beyond the control of the individual, such as gender, age, ethnicity, place of birth, or parental background. Effort is difficult to observe or measure empirically, and so it is often obtained as a residual component, once the circumstances have been selected. The theory of inequality of opportunity is built upon the idea that these circumstances and efforts determine advantage.

If the set of circumstances is finite, and each circumstance variable is discrete, we can partition the population into groups of individuals that are fully homogeneous in terms of circumstances. Each of these subgroups is called a *type* and, by definition, individuals within each type differ *only* in their effort level. For example, if the only two circumstances were gender (male or female) and race (black or white), then there would be four types in the population: white men, black men, white women, and black women. Evidently, the greater and more finely characterized the set of circumstances, the larger the number of types, and the more homogeneous the people within each one.

The ex-ante approach to the measurement of inequality of opportunity seeks to evaluate—that is, attribute a numerical value to—the opportunity set faced by each individual. Inequality of opportunity would be *eliminated* when all types faced opportunity sets with the same value. If that did not hold, inequality of opportunity could be *measured* by computing an appropriate inequality measure over the counterfactual distribution where each person's advantage is replaced by the value of his or her opportunity set. In other words: the idea of the ex-ante approach is that inequality of opportunity is the inequality in the value of people's opportunity sets.

Then two questions must be answered before a precise measure can be proposed. First, how should opportunity sets be valued? And second, what inequality index should be applied to the counterfactual distribution? Most attempts to evaluate the opportunity set faced by individuals in a given type are based on information on the income distribution *within the type*. The advantage prospect of individuals in the same type is interpreted as the set of opportunities open to each individual in that type. A specific version of this model, extensively used in empirical analyses, further assumes that the value of the opportunity set can be summarized by a single statistic such as its mean.[4]

Hence, starting from a multivariate distribution of income and circumstances, a *smoothed distribution* is obtained, in which each individual income is replaced with the average income of the type the individual belongs to: this distribution is interpreted as the distribution of the values of the individual opportunity sets. In this model, measuring opportunity inequality simply amounts to measuring inequality in the smoothed distribution. Clearly, focusing on the mean imposes full neutrality with respect to the inequalities within types. On the other hand, there is no clash between the compensation and reward principles under this ex-ante approach: compensating differences due to circumstances (i.e., differences between types) lowers inequality of opportunity, while the measure is insensitive to the extent of the reward to effort within types.

For an alternative approach, called the "ex-post approach" that does not endorse such a strong neutrality within types (but where the compensation and reward principles may clash) and instead focuses on the income inequality among individuals at the same level of effort, see Aaberge et al. (2011) and Roemer (1998). For a discussion and a comparison of the two approaches, see Fleurbaey and Peragine (2012).

Most measures of inequality of opportunity computed in practice have followed the ex-ante approach. Notable exceptions include Checchi et al. (2010) and Checchi and Peragine's (2010) work on inequality of opportunity in Europe, which reports both ex-ante and ex-post measures. The particular version of the ex-ante approach that we have described above—where the value of opportunity set for all individuals in a given type is simply the mean income observed for that type—has been applied to at least some 40 countries, by a number of authors. The specific inequality measure used does vary across some of the papers but most use the mean logarithmic deviation, following Checchi and Peragine (2010) and Ferreira and Gignoux (2011). In a few cases, as detailed below, the Theil (T) index and even the variance are employed. Despite these differences, as well as a variety of caveats on data comparability across—or even within—studies, the eight papers reviewed in the third section comprise the most closely comparable sources on actual I.Op. measures across countries that we are aware of.

In closing this section, we turn to another approach that has been applied to a number of countries in recent years, namely the HOI of Barros et al. (2009, 2011). This index is defined over a different set of advantages (which, confusingly, are sometimes referred to as "basic opportunities"), namely access to certain basic services, such as piped water, electricity, or sanitation. The HOI (for service j), denoted by H^j, is given by the average access rate to the service in the population, penalized by the degree of dissimilarity in that coverage across types. It is clearly analogous to the Sen welfare function, where mean outcomes are adjusted by one minus a measure of inequality. The dissimilarity across types is given by the dissimilarity index commonly used in sociology. In this application, it simply computes an appropriately normalized (and population-weighted) average deviation in service coverage from the mean, across types.[5] Sometimes an aggregate index is calculated as an average of H^j across a number of different services.[6] Various versions of the HOI have now been computed for at least 39 countries, and basic results are compared in the fourth section.

Ex-Ante Inequality of Opportunity in 41 Countries

As noted above, the ex-ante approach to the measurement of inequality of opportunity essentially consists of computing an inequality measure over a counterfactual distribution, where individual advantages are replaced with some valuation of the opportunity set of the type to which the individual belongs. In this section, we review eight papers that have adopted this approach and applied it, in total, to 41 countries, ranging from Guinea and Madagascar (with annual per capita gross national incomes [GNIs] of $980 measured in purchasing power parity (PPP), to Luxembourg, with a per capita GNI of almost PPP$64,000). The eight papers are Belhaj-Hassine (2012), Checchi et al. (2010), Cogneau and Mesplé-Somps (2008), Ferreira and Gignoux (2011), Ferreira et al. (2011), Piraino (2012), Pistolesi (2009), and Singh (2011).

All of these papers use a measure of economic well-being as the advantage indicator: household per capita income, household per capita consumption, or individual labor earnings. All use the mean value of this indicator for each type as the value of the type's opportunity set. We refer to the measure generated by this specific version of the ex-ante approach as an index of IEO. There are, in fact, two closely related versions of the index: the absolute or *level* estimate of inequality of opportunity (IEO-L) is given simply by the inequality measure computed over the smoothed distribution, where each person is given the mean income of their types: $I(\hat{y})$. The ratio of IEO-L to overall inequality in the relevant advantage variable (e.g., household per capita income) yields the relative measure, IEO-R[7]:

$$IEOR = \frac{I(\hat{y})}{I(y)} \tag{1}$$

The partition of types varies across studies, ranging from six types to 7,680 (although in four of the eight studies, the range is a more comfortable 72–108 types). Due to data limitations, some authors compute IEO-L using a parametric shortcut. After estimating the reduced-form regression of income on circumstances:

$$y = C\beta + \in \tag{2}$$

and obtaining coefficient estimates $\hat{\beta}$, these authors used predicted incomes as a parametric approximation to the smoothed distribution:

$$I(\hat{y}), \text{where } \hat{y}_i = C_i \hat{\beta} \tag{3}$$

Parametric estimates are also presented either as levels (IEO-L) or ratios (IEO-R), analogously. This approach follows Bourguignon et al. (2007), and its advantages and disadvantages are discussed in some detail in Ferreira and Gignoux (2011). Empirically, parametric estimates of inequality of opportunity tend to be a little lower than their nonparametric counterparts but, at least in the case of Latin America, the differences are not great: proportional differences between the two average 6.6 percent in Ferreira and Gignoux (2011).

The fact that the parametric estimates are conservative—that is, generally lower than the nonparametric ones—is consistent with another important property of these estimates of IEO-R and IEO-L. They are, in each and every case, *lower-bound* estimates of inequality of opportunity. A formal proof of the lower-bound result is contained in Ferreira and Gignoux (2011), but the intuition is straightforward. The vector of circumstances that is observed empirically—and used for partitioning the population into types—is a strict subset of the theoretical vector of all circumstance variables. The existence of unobserved circumstances—virtually a certainty in all practical applications—guarantees that these estimates of I.Op.—whether parametric or nonparametric—could only be higher if more circumstance variables were observed.

As discussed in Ferreira and Gignoux (2011), the existence of effort variables, observed or unobserved, is entirely immaterial to this result, since (2) is written as a reduced-form equation, where any effect of circumstances on incomes *through* their effects on effort (such as years of schooling or hours worked) is captured by the regression coefficients, and hence influence the smoothed distribution. In a setting where some variables are treated as observed efforts (as in Bourguignon et al. 2007), equations (2) and (3) capture the *reduced-form* influence of circumstances on advantages, both directly and indirectly through efforts. By construction, therefore, the only omitted variables that matter for IEO-L and IEO-R are omitted circumstances.[8]

Table 5.1 presents the estimates of IEO-L and IEO-R for each of the 41 countries studied by the eight aforementioned papers. The table also lists their GNI per capita, overall inequality and, when available, a measure of intergenerational earnings elasticity (IGE) reported in the literature, a measure of the intergenerational correlation of education from Hertz et al. (2007), and the HOI. Whereas overall inequality, IEO-L and IEO-R, come from the eight studies mentioned above, the other variables come from other sources. GNI per capita comes from the World Bank's World Development Indicators database. Our measure of intergenerational correlation of education is simply the correlation coefficient between the parents' education and the child's education, where both are measured by years of completed schooling, as reported by Hertz et al. (2007). Parental education is the average of mother's and father's attainment "wherever possible" (Hertz et al. 2007:11). The correlation we report is what the authors call a measure of "standardized persistence."

The measures of IGE reported in table 5.1 come from 11 different studies published over the last ten years, namely Azevedo and Bouillon (2010), Cervini-Plá (2009), Christofides et al. (2009), Corak (2006), D'Addio (2007), Dunn (2007), Ferreira and Veloso (2006), Grawe (2004), Hnatkovska et al. (2012), Hugalde (2004), Núñez and Miranda (2007), and Piraino (2007). Denoting parental earnings (or income) by y_p and the adult child's earnings by y_c, these elasticity estimates generally come from an equation of the form:

$$\log y_c = \beta \log y_p + \varepsilon \qquad (4)$$

An elasticity (β) of 0.4, for example, would mean that income differences of 100 percent between two fathers (say), would lead to a 40 percent gap between their sons (on average). As in the case of our IEO-L and IEO-R measures, the datasets and econometric methods used for estimating this elasticity are not homogeneous across studies. This comparative exercise is very much in the same spirit as Corak (2012), and the same caveats he discusses are applicable here. The values for HOI reported in table 5.1 come from Molinas Vega et al. (2011) for Latin America, and World Bank (2012a, 2012b) for Africa.

Table 5.1 should be read in close conjunction with table 5.2, which provides some basic information on each of the eight studies used to construct the inequality of opportunity estimates in table 5.1. Table 5.2 describes which

Table 5.1 Inequality of opportunity, income inequality, and economic mobility in 41 countries

Country	GNI per capita PPP	Total inequality	IEO-L	IEO-R	Method	Intergenerational income elasticity	Intergenerational correlation of education	HOI
Austria (1)	39,410	0.1800	0.0390	0.2167	parametric			
Belgium (1)	37,840	0.1450	0.0250	0.1724	parametric		0.400	
Brazil (3)	10,920	0.6920	0.2230	0.3223	parametric	0.5733	0.590	75.90
Colombia (3)	9,000	0.5720	0.1330	0.2325	parametric		0.590	79.25
Cyprous (1)	30,160	0.1706	0.0510	0.3000	parametric	0.3430		
Czec Rep. (1)	23,620	0.1760	0.0190	0.1080	parametric		0.370	
Denmark (1)	40,140	0.0830	0.0120	0.1446	parametric	0.0710	0.300	
Ecuador (3)	9,270	0.5800	0.1500	0.2586	parametric		0.610	76.25
Egypt (5)	5,910	0.4230	0.0491	0.1160	nonparametric		0.500	
Estonia (1)	19,500	0.2430	0.0260	0.1070	parametric		0.400	
Finland (1)	37,180	0.1360	0.0130	0.0956	parametric	0.1353	0.330	
France (1)	34,440	0.1630	0.0210	0.1288	parametric	0.4100		
Germany (1)	38,170	0.1910	0.0350	0.1832	parametric	0.2130		
Ghana (2)	1,600	0.4000	0.0450	0.1125	nonparametric		0.390	39.30
Greece (1)	27,360	0.2000	0.0340	0.1700	parametric			
Guatemala (3)	4,610	0.5930	0.1990	0.3356	parametric			51.73
Guinea (2)	980	0.4200	0.0560	0.1333	nonparametric			
Hungary (1)	19,280	0.2080	0.0210	0.1010	parametric		0.490	
India (8)	3,560	0.4218	0.0822	0.1949	parametric	0.5500		
Ireland (1)	32,740	0.1880	0.0420	0.2234	parametric		0.460	
Italy (1)	31,090	0.1960	0.0280	0.1429	parametric	0.4095	0.540	
Ivory Coast (2)	1,650	0.3700	0.0500	0.1351	nonparametric			
Latvia (1)	16,360	0.2290	0.0280	0.1223	parametric			
Lithuania (1)	17,880	0.2280	0.0350	0.1535	parametric			
Luxemburg (1)	63,850	0.1480	0.0350	0.2365	parametric			
Madagascar (2)	980	0.4400	0.0920	0.2091	nonparametric			22.62

Netherlands (1)	42,580	0.1920	0.0360	0.1875	parametric	0.2200		0.360
Norway (1)	57,130	0.1300	0.0030	0.0231	parametric	0.2050		0.350
Panama (3)	12,980	0.6300	0.1900	0.3016	parametric		63.98	0.610
Peru (3)	8,940	0.5570	0.1560	0.2801	parametric	0.6000	69.18	0.660
Poland (1)	19,020	0.2710	0.0250	0.0923	parametric			0.430
Portugal (1)	24,710	0.2470	0.0300	0.1215	parametric			
Slovakia (1)	23,140	0.1320	0.0180	0.1364	parametric			0.370
Slovenia (1)	26,970	0.1040	0.0050	0.0481	parametric			0.520
South Africa (6)	10,280	0.6750	0.1690	0.2504	parametric	0.7055	58.09	0.440
Spain (1)	31,550	0.2160	0.0420	0.1944	parametric	0.4533		
Sweden (1)	39,600	0.1060	0.0120	0.1132	parametric	0.2125		0.400
Turkey (4)	14,580	0.3620	0.0948	0.2620	parametric			
Uganda (2)	1,230	0.4300	0.0400	0.0930	nonparametric		27.00	
UK (1)	36,580	0.2040	0.0420	0.2059	parametric	0.4760		0.310
US (7)	47,020	0.2200	0.0409	0.1860	semiparametric	0.4800		0.460

Notes: The source for inequality and IEO measures for each country is given in parentheses after the country's name, and refers to the studies below. GNI per capita is from the World Bank's World Development Indicators, for the year 2010, using PPP exchange rates for 2005. Total inequality is measured by the mean logarithmic deviation in all cases except those from source (2), which uses the Theil-T index. IEO indices are always based on the same inequality measure used for total inequality in that country. Sources for the numbers in the last three columns are given in the text.

Sources: (1) Checchi et al. (2010)

(2) Cogneau and Mesplé-Somps (2008)

(3) Ferreira and Gignoux (2011)

(4) Ferreira et al. (2011)

(5) Belhaj-Hassine (2012)

(6) Piraino (2012)

(7) Pistolesi (2009)

(8) Singh (2011)

Table 5.2 Comparing eight studies of ex-ante inequality of opportunity across 41 countries

	Number of references	Countries	Data sources	Outcome	Method	Circumstances	Types
1	Checchi et al. (2010)	Austria, Belgium, Czech Republic, Germany, Denmark, Estonia, Greece, Spain, Finland, France, Hungary, Ireland, Italy, Netherlands, Latvia, Lithuania, Norway, Poland, Portugal, Sweden, Slovenia, Slovakia, United Kingdom	EU-Silc 2005	posttax individual earnings	parametric	parental education, parental occupation, gender, nationality, geographical location	72
2	Cogneau and Mesplé-Somps (2008)	Ivory Coast, Ghana, Guinea, Madagascar, Uganda	Ivory Coast, EPAMCI 1985–1988; Ghana, GLSS 1998; Guinea, EICVM 1994; Madagascar, EPAM 1993; Uganda, NIHS 1992	per capita household consumption	nonparametric	three groups based on father's occupation and education, region of birth	6 (3 Uganda)
3	Ferreira and Gignoux (2011)	Brazil, Colombia, Ecuador, Guatemala, Panama, Peru	Brazil, PNAD 1996; Colombia, ECV 2003; Ecuador, ECV 2006; Guatemala, ENCOVI 2000; Panama, ENV 2003; Peru, ENAHO 2001	household per capita income	parametric	gender, ethnicity, parental education, father's occupation, region of birth	108 (54 Peru)
4	Ferreira et al. (2011)	Turkey	TDHS 2003–2004 and HBS 2003	imputed per capita consumption	parametric	urban/rural, region of birth, parental education, mother tongue, number of sibling	768

5	Belhaj-Hassine (2012)	Egypt	ELMPS 2006	total monthly earning	nonparametric	gender, father's education, mother's education, father's occupation, region of birth	72
6	Piraino (2012)	South Africa	NIDS 2008–2010	individual gross income	parametric	race, father's education	24
7	Pistolesi (2009)	United States	PSID 2001	individual annual earnings	semiparametric	age, parental education, father's occupation, ethnicity, region of birth	7,680
8	Singh (2011)	India	IHDS 2004–2005	household per capita earnings	parametric	father's education, father's occupation, caste, religion, geographical area of residence	108

countries are studied in each paper; the specific data sets (including survey year); the precise income and circumstance variables used; whether the estimation was parametric or otherwise; and the number of types included in each calculation. The table highlights a number of problems for comparability across these studies. First is the nature of the advantage variable (y) itself: whereas Checchi et al. (2010), Pistolesi (2009), Singh (2011), and Belhaj-Hassine (2012) use labor earnings, Ferreira and Gignoux (2011) and Piraino (2012) use incomes, Cogneau and Mesplé-Somps (2008) use consumption, and Ferreira et al. (2011) uses imputed consumption. And the definitions of earnings and incomes are not exactly the same across each of these papers either.

These distinctions are not immaterial: in a comparison of six Latin American countries, Ferreira and Gignoux (2011) found substantially higher estimates of IEO-R for consumption expenditure than for income distributions in the same countries.[9] They attributed this finding to the fact that income inequality measures are thought to contain greater amounts of measurement error, as well as transitory income components, which are less closely correlated with circumstances than permanent income or consumption might be. Bourguignon et al. (2007) also noted differences between estimates for individual earnings and for household per capita incomes, which they attributed to the fact that unequal opportunities affect the latter not only through earnings, but also through assortative mating, fertility decisions, and nonlabor income sources.

Second, the studies differ in the number of types used for the decomposition and, naturally, in the exact set of circumstances used in each case. On one extreme, the Cogneau and Mesplé-Somps study has a mere three types for Uganda, based on father's occupation and education levels, while on the other Pistolesi has 7,680 types, constructed on the basis of information on age (20 levels), parental education (4 levels for the mother and 4 for the father), occupational group of the father (6 categories), individual ethnic group (2 categories), individual region of birth (2 categories). There is, fortunately, a middle range of studies that account for most countries in the sample, with 72 to 108 types each. Nevertheless, results for Africa and the United States should certainly be interpreted with caution, in light of the number of types used in each case. Finally, a third comparability caveat, on which we have already dwelled, is the fact that some studies use nonparametric estimates while others use parametric ones.

Bearing these caveats in mind, table 5.1 nevertheless illustrates the substantial variation in inequality levels across countries—both in advantages and in opportunities. The mean log deviation for incomes (or the corresponding advantage indicator) ranges from 0.083 in Denmark to 0.675 in South Africa. Norway, Slovenia, and Sweden also have comparatively low levels of overall inequality, while Brazil and Guatemala stand out at the upper end. Inequality of opportunity levels (IEO-L) range from 0.003 in Norway and 0.005 in Slovenia to 0.199 in Guatemala and 0.223 in Brazil. In other words, the level of inequality in the distribution of *values of opportunity sets across types* (the smoothed distribution described in the second section) in Brazil is almost three times as large as the inequality (measured by the same index) in the distribution of actual incomes in Denmark. One can also observe substantial differences in IEO-L among countries at closer levels of development, and more methodologically comparable: Madagascar's level of inequality of opportunity is twice that of Ghana; those of the United States and the United Kingdom are ten times those of Norway's and almost four times higher than Denmark's.

The ratio of these two inequality measures, that is, the (lower-bound) share of the overall inequality due to inequality of opportunity (IEO-R), also varies substantially, from 0.02 in Norway to 0.34 in Guatemala. Slovenia also has a remarkably low inequality of opportunity ratio, at 0.05, while Brazil closely follows Guatemala in the upper tail, at around 0.32. Figure 5.1 shows the range of relative measures of inequality of opportunity graphically, for the entire sample, highlighting those countries where consumption (actual or predicted) was used instead of earnings or incomes.

It may be of interest to look at how these measures of inequality of opportunity correlate with some other important variables. Output per capita, overall income inequality, and measures of intergenerational mobility—a concept closely related to I.Op.—are natural candidates. Figures 5.2, 5.3, 5.4, and 5.5 depict the associations between the relative measure of inequality of opportunity (IEO-R) and four other variables—log per capita GNI, total inequality, the intergenerational elasticity of income, and the

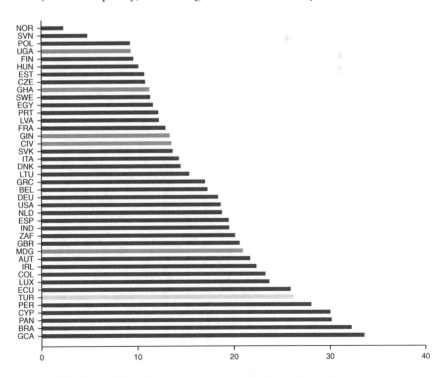

Figure 5.1 Inequality of economic opportunity: lower-bound estimates.

Note: Inequality of economic opportunity index (IEO-R).

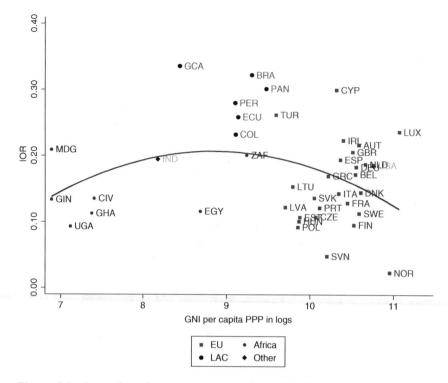

Figure 5.2 Inequality of economic opportunity and the level of development.

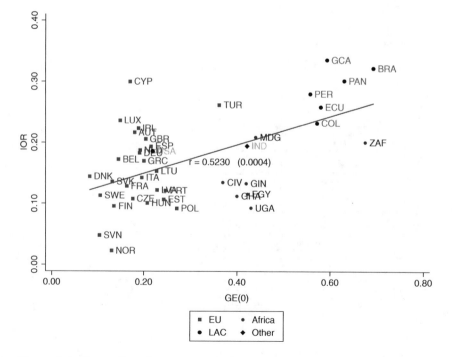

Figure 5.3 Inequality of opportunity and income inequality.

Note: Income inequality (mean logarithmic deviation)

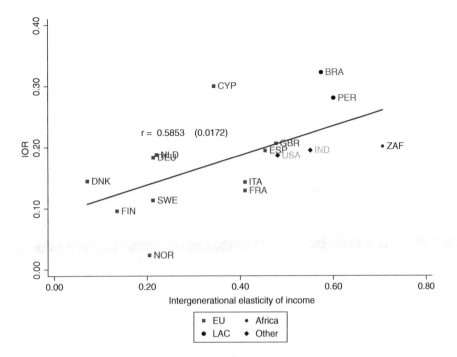

Figure 5.4 Inequality of opportunity and intergenerational mobility.

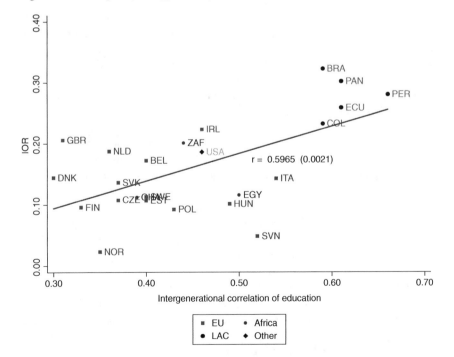

Figure 5.5 Inequality of opportunity and the intergenerational correlation of education.

intergenerational correlation of education. Figure 5.2 reveals a nonlinear relationship between inequality of opportunity and the level of development, as measured by log per capita income levels. In fact, the association appears to have an inverted-U shape, much as the "Kuznets curve" that used to be hypothesized for the relation between income inequality and the "level of development." The regression of IEO-R on a quadratic of log GNI is shown in the figure; the coefficient on the linear term is 0.32 (p-value: 0.05), and that on the quadratic term is -0.017 (p-value: 0.05).

A very similar relationship (not shown) is found between IEO-L and log per capita GNI (with a coefficient of 0.37 on the linear term, and on the square term of -0.02, both significant at the 1 percent level). While the poorest countries in this figure are all located in Africa, the middle-income countries near the turning point of the inverted-U include a number of Latin American countries, as well as Egypt, South Africa, and Turkey. The richer part of the sample is dominated by European countries and the United States. Although these tend to be more I.Op. egalitarian, there is still a considerable spread among them.

It is, of course, impossible to interpret this inverted-U pattern solely on the basis of the information available in our data. One can weave hypotheses: the nonlinearity might reflect two opposite effects at play, the relative strength of which changes as incomes grow. Perhaps at very low levels of development, new income opportunities are initially captured by a narrow privileged group—a few well-educated families, or a small ruling ethnic group. During that phase, disparities across types may grow even faster than overall income inequality. At some point, however, the grip of the elite on economic opportunities must weaken if growth is to continue. Such mechanisms have been modeled formally: the transition can occur when, at a certain point, the elite decides that the costs of expanding education to "the masses" (in terms of their own share of political power) is outweighed by the likely economic gains from a more skilled labor force (Bourguignon and Verdier 2000). Alternatively, the threat of revolution may impose the franchise and a broader sharing of political influence, even upon a less enlightened elite (Acemoglu and Robinson 2000). There is also some evidence that lower inequality of opportunity may be associated with faster growth, at least in richer countries (see, e.g., Marrero and Rodríguez 2010, for a sample of US states).

But these are only hypotheses consistent with the pattern in figure 5.2. It is equally possible, of course, that the pattern is spurious: other variables may cause inequality of opportunity first to rise, and then decline with GNI. As we have learned from work on the (income) Kuznets hypothesis, it would also be foolhardy to infer much about the time-series pattern in any given country from a simple cross-sectional association. At some level, in fact, it is probably fruitless to look for evidence of causal relationships between two variables at such a high order of aggregation. Both overall output levels (GNI) and inequality of opportunity are summary statistics, jointly determined by the full general equilibrium of the economy, including all of the key political economy processes that determine policy variables such as tax rates and spending allocations. It is likely that one can more easily find causality at the microeconomic level. From that vantage point, disentangling causality in the relationship depicted in figure 5.2 may well be pointless, even if the correlation between the two aggregate variables reflects genuine economic processes, which are both real and important.

Another question that naturally arises is whether there is any observable empirical relationship between inequality of opportunity and income inequality. Since the former is measured as a component of the latter, there is a mechanical aspect to the relationship in levels, but it is not obvious that there is any mechanical reason to expect a correlation between income inequality levels and the *relative* extent of inequality of opportunity. Figure 5.3 shows the association between overall inequality (in economic advantage) and the *share* of that inequality associated with inequality of opportunity. The correlation coefficient is 0.523 (p-value: 0.0004). A number of possible mechanisms might drive this correlation as well. One that appears eminently plausible is the notion that today's outcomes shape tomorrow's opportunities: large income gaps between today's parents are likely to imply bigger gaps in the quality of education, or access to labor market opportunities, among tomorrow's children (Ferreira 2001). Naturally, the reverse causality probably holds too: if opportunity sets differ a great deal among people, then individual outcomes are also likely to be unequal. Inequalities in income and opportunities are both endogenously determined: once again, the quest for causality at the aggregate level may be futile, even if the correlation reflects real underlying political and economic processes.[10]

The use of the links between parents' and children's incomes to describe an important manifestation of inequality of opportunity suggests that the concept should be closely related to intergenerational mobility. Indeed, if we wrote $y = \log y_c$ and $C = \log y_p$, equations (2) and (4) would be identical

suggesting that, if the set of observed circumstances becomes restricted to parental income, then our lower-bound measure of inequality of opportunity is very closely related to the commonest measure of intergenerational mobility, namely the IGE. It can easily be checked that the R^2 of (4) is identical to the IEO-R measure defined by (1) and (3) when the variance of logarithms is used as the inequality index.

Figure 5.4 documents the association between IEO-R and (inverse) economic mobility, as measured by the intergenerational elasticity of earnings (or incomes). The correlation across the 23 countries for which we have both variables is 0.5853 (p-value: 0.0172). Of course, the two measures are not exactly the same, in part because the vector of circumstances C used to partition types and generate IEO-R is not the same as a measure of parental income or earnings. In fact, C does not contain that variable for any of the 41 countries in table 5.1. It does, however, usually contain parental education (and in some cases parental occupation), which is itself a determinant of log parental income. And it often contains additional information, such as race or the region of the person's birth.

For these reasons, we expected the correlation in figure 5.5 to be strong, but not perfect. Given the likely correlation between most circumstances and parental economic well-being, it would be surprising if this association turned out to be weak. Given the isomorphism between the ex-ante measurement of inequality of opportunity and the measurement of intergenerational mobility, we find it intriguing that these comparisons do not appear to have been made before.

It should also be noted that figure 5.4 is close in spirit to Figure 2 in Corak (2012), which plots the IGE against income inequality (measured by the Gini coefficient) across countries.[11] Instead of plotting the estimates of IGE against overall inequality, we plot IGE against inequality of opportunity.

Reassuringly, a very similar correlation is found between the same measure of inequality of opportunity (IEO-R) and a different gauge for intergenerational (im)mobility, namely the correlation between parental and child schooling attainment. As noted earlier, the intergenerational correlations of education reported in table 5.1 come from Hertz et al. (2007), and use the average years of schooling completed by a person's mother and father as the measure of parental education. Figure 5.5 shows the scatter plot for the 23 countries for which data on both variables is available. The correlation coefficient is 0.5965 (p-value: 0.0021). So, IEO, as measured by IEO-R, is clearly negatively associated with two independent measures of intergenerational mobility (as opposed to persistence), one based on incomes and the other on educational attainment.

MEASURING DEVELOPMENT WITH A PENALTY FOR UNEQUAL OPPORTUNITIES

The country composition of table 5.1 was determined by the availability of information on measures of IEO and drew on the eight papers listed in table 5.2. The last column of table 5.1 contains estimates of the aggregate HOI, defined as a weighted average of the dimension-specific HOI.[12] This information was only available for 10 of the 41 countries in table 5.1, largely because the index has not been calculated in rich countries.

In table 5.3, however, we list the component (or dimension-specific) human opportunity indices for a larger set of countries, and for the following advantages (or "basic opportunities," or "services"): school attendance (10- to 14-year-olds); access to water; access to electricity; access to sanitation; and whether or not the child finished primary school on time (i.e., with zero grade-age delay). The indices are multiplied by 100, so the possible range is 0–100. The 39 countries included—all of them in either Africa or Latin America—is the full set available at the time of writing. As noted earlier, they come from Molinas Vega et al. (2011) for Latin America, and World Bank (2012a, 2012b) for Africa. Following the authors, the table also reports the simple average of the school attendance and primary school completion indices, as the HOI for education, and the simple average of the other three indices as the HOI for housing conditions. The simple average of these two numbers in turn yields the overall HOI reported in the last column of the table.

Table 5.3 The Human Opportunity Index for 5 service indicators and 39 countries

Country	Period	HOI school attendance (10–14 yrs)	HOI access to water	HOI access to electricity	HOI access to sanitation	HOI finished primary on time	HOI education	HOI housing conditions	HOI
Argentina	2008	96.80	97.30	100.00	64.40	82.60	89.70	87.23	88.47
Brazil	2008	97.30	82.50	96.40	78.20	34.90	66.10	85.70	75.90
Cameroon	2004	79.11	4.91	24.38	1.89	24.50	51.80	10.40	31.10
Chile	2006	98.40	93.90	99.20	86.10	82.00	90.20	93.07	91.63
Colombia	2008	93.00	54.00	100.00	77.00	70.00	81.50	77.00	79.25
Costa Rica	2009	95.50	95.40	98.80	92.80	66.40	80.95	95.67	88.31
Dem. Rep. Congo	2007	72.92	2.73	5.33	1.65	18.64	45.78	3.24	24.51
Dominican Republic	2008	96.50	70.10	95.40	48.80	53.40	74.95	71.43	73.19
Ecuador	2006	85.90	67.60	90.90	50.90	79.50	82.70	69.80	76.25
El Salvador	2007	89.40	18.30	83.00	18.60	42.50	65.95	39.97	52.96
Ethiopia	2011	69.09	0.93	5.61	0.14	15.75	42.42	2.23	22.32
Ghana	2008	84.59	4.90	36.70	3.91	42.26	63.42	15.17	39.30
Guatemala	2006	80.40	63.90	68.20	21.10	24.40	52.40	51.07	51.73
Honduras	2006	82.00	19.70	53.20	25.60	45.10	63.55	32.83	48.19
Jamaica	2002	95.00	23.40	85.40	35.70	93.00	94.00	48.17	71.08
Kenya	2008–09	93.34	8.36	4.92	1.53	47.31	70.32	4.93	37.63
Liberia	2007	59.10	1.03	1.04	4.70	8.45	33.78	2.26	18.02
Madagascar	2008–09	72.49	0.83	3.84	0.44	14.59	43.54	1.70	22.62
Malawi	2010	90.24	1.67	2.51	0.26	24.10	57.17	1.48	29.32
Mali	2006	39.32	3.17	6.14	1.08	10.85	25.09	3.47	14.28

Continued

Table 5.3 Continued

Country	Period	HOI school attendance (10–14 yrs)	HOI access to water	HOI access to electricity	HOI access to sanitation	HOI finished primary on time	HOI education	HOI housing conditions	HOI
Mexico	2008	92.50	80.30	98.30	72.00	86.70	89.60	83.53	86.57
Mozambique	2003	69.91	1.45	3.00	0.47	5.81	37.86	1.64	19.75
Namibia	2006–07	92.66	25.70	15.48	11.58	53.46	73.06	17.59	45.32
Nicaragua	2005	84.60	14.80	52.50	36.50	33.50	59.05	34.60	46.83
Niger	2006	29.98	1.03	2.54	0.17	5.88	17.93	1.25	9.59
Nigeria	2008	63.00	1.80	29.31	4.20	42.35	52.68	11.77	32.22
Panama	2003	90.80	50.20	60.20	31.40	70.60	80.70	47.27	63.98
Paraguay	2008	92.00	67.20	94.70	48.40	56.30	74.15	70.10	72.13
Peru	2008	95.00	42.60	64.40	54.40	74.10	84.55	53.80	69.18
Rwanda	2010	93.33	0.95	2.90	0.06	8.73	51.03	1.30	26.17
Senegal	2010–11	55.33	36.52	32.28	13.89	24.68	40.00	27.57	33.78
Sierra Leone	2008	65.73	2.37	3.24	0.61	24.41	45.07	2.07	23.57
South Africa	2010	98.72	20.57	78.82	24.95	50.74	74.73	41.44	58.09
Tanzania	2010	81.52	2.84	2.89	0.33	45.72	63.62	2.02	32.82
Uganda	2006	90.64	0.56	1.62	0.10	15.95	53.30	0.76	27.03
Uruguay	2008	94.80	89.30	98.20	96.60	78.40	86.60	94.70	90.65
Venezuela, R. B. de	2005	94.60	88.10	98.50	83.70	73.40	84.00	90.10	87.05
Zambia	2007	87.97	4.69	6.44	3.56	29.81	58.89	4.90	31.89
Zimbabwe	2010–11	92.05	8.48	12.63	7.58	78.00	85.03	9.56	47.30

Note: HOI education is the simple average of HOI for school attendance and HOI for finishing primary school on time. HOI housing conditions is the simple average of the other three individual HOIs. The last column is the simple average of the two preceding sub-aggregates. This follows the authors in the sources below.

Source: Molinas Vega et al. (2011) and World Bank (2012a)

The motivation behind the HOI, as initially proposed by Barros et al. (2009), was to measure the extent to which children in various developing countries have access to basic opportunities. Although the authors do not motivate it this way, one could view the index as an example of the ex-ante approach applied to a multidimensional advantage space, with each dimension corresponding to access to a particular service—such as water or schooling—and the valuation of the opportunity set of each type being given by the coverage of the service in that type. The particular inequality index applied to that smoothed distribution of probabilities is the dissimilarity index.

Although the dissimilarity index might therefore be seen as a measure of inequality of opportunity, the HOI itself clearly cannot.[13] It is intended—and defined—as a measure of average access, adjusted (or penalized) by inequality of opportunity. Unsurprisingly, therefore, it is closely correlated with other indicators of "level of development." This association is already clear in figure 5.6, which ranks the average HOI for all countries in table 5.3, ranging from 9.6 in Niger to 91.6 in Chile. There is almost no overlap in HOI between the African and the Latin American subsamples, and the correlation between the HOI and GNI per capita for these countries is 0.89 (p-value: 0.0005).

Perhaps more striking is the correlation with the UNDP's HDI, which is even higher (at 0.94) and highly statistically significant. Figure 5.7 presents the scatter plot. This is remarkable because the two indices are constructed

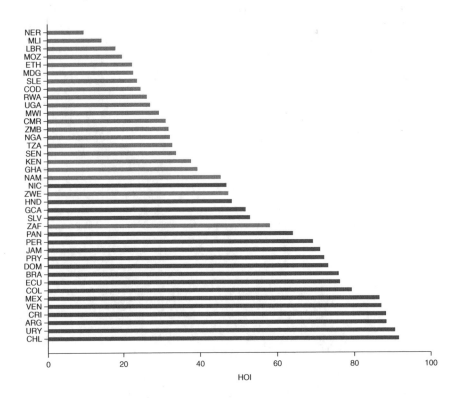

Figure 5.6 The Human Opportunity Index in Africa and Latin America.

on the basis of completely different data. Until 2010 (the year used in figure 5.7), the HDI was calculated as a simple average of three normalized indices in the dimensions of health, income, and education.[14] The income index used GNP per capita, and the health index was based on life expectancy at birth, while the education index combined information on literacy and the gross enrolment ratio. Of these four basic components, only one is close to the indicators used to construct the HOI, namely gross enrolment ratio, which is very near to the "school attendance" data used in the first column of table 5.3. The other four components of the HOI, listed above, do not enter directly into the computation of the HDI, and neither does the latter explicitly adjust for dissimilarity across types in any way. Conversely, life expectancy at birth, GDP per capita, and literacy do not enter the HOI explicitly.

A correlation of 0.94 between these two indices, albeit calculated only over a nonrepresentative sample of 39 countries in two of the world's regions, suggests two things. First, it suggests that the average coverage rates of services like access to water, electricity, etc. are highly correlated with the constituent elements of the HDI. Second, it suggests that the HOI is determined, to a very large extent, by these average coverage rates. In fact, the correlations between average coverage and the component-specific HOI in this sample are extremely high: they are greater than 0.99 for school attendance; access to water; access to electricity; and having finished primary school on time. It is 0.987 for access to sanitation. This implies, of course, that the penalty for inequality of opportunity, as measured by the dissimilarity index, accounts for a much smaller share of the variance in the HOI than mean coverage.

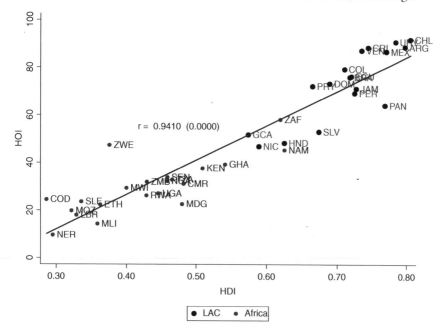

Figure 5.7   The Human Opportunity and Development Indices.

A final international comparison issue our data can shed light on is the association between the dissimilarity index (the measure of inequality of opportunity contained within the HOI) and the IEO-R. The dissimilarity index can be interpreted as the proportion of "basic opportunities" that is improperly allocated, relative to equal access across all types (Barros et al. 2011). In other words, it is a measure of how much redistribution in access to a particular service would be required to move from the observed allocation to one in which average access was the same across types. Subject to the caveat in endnote 11, this is a perfectly plausible measure of between-type inequality in a particular dimension (that of service j). IEO-R, on the other hand, measures inequality of opportunity as the between-type share of income (or consumption) inequality. How do these two measures correlate? Do they yield essentially the same country ranking, even though their information bases are quite different, as appears to be the case with the HDI and the HOI?

It is probably too early to answer this question in cross-country terms. The overlap between the country samples in table 5.1 (for which we have estimates of IEO-R) and in table 5.3 (for which we have estimates of the dissimilarity index) is only ten countries, six in Latin America and four in Africa. Very little can be said, even about descriptive correlations, on the basis of such a small and unrepresentative sample. Nevertheless, for what it is worth, figure 5.8 plots the IEO-R against the dissimilarity index, averaged across its five dimensions. The correlation is 0.6989 (p-value: 0.0245), suggesting that the two alternative approaches to measuring inequality of opportunity

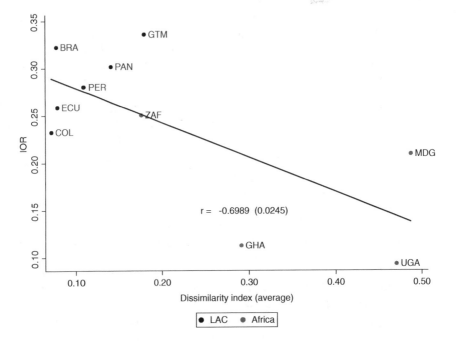

Figure 5.8 IEO-R and the dissimilarity index in the common subsample.

can yield very different country rankings. It is true, of course, that in this sample the negative correlation is driven primarily by a dichotomy between Africa and Latin America, where the latter has lower dissimilarity in access to services, but a higher income inequality share driven by unequal opportunities. Given that the IEO-R data for Africa in our sample is based on coarser partitions than in most other cases, one really should not read too much into this correlation. Nevertheless, it equally cannot be taken for granted that the IEO-R and the part of the HOI that seeks to capture inequality of opportunity are measuring the same things.

DISCUSSION

The data on inequality of economic opportunity presented in the third section for 41 countries shows that an important portion of income inequality observed in the world today cannot be attributed to differences in the levels of individual efforts and responsibility. On the contrary, it can be directly ascribed to exogenous factors such as family background, gender, race, place of birth, etc. Although the portion of exogenous inequalities, or inequality of opportunity, differs across countries, it generally represents a nonnegligible part of overall inequality—despite being a lower bound. As the distribution of exogenous circumstances is morally arbitrary, income inequalities based on them are morally unacceptable.

This evidence is of great importance to monitor social and economic progress and to aid in policy formulation. Monitoring how inequality of opportunity in a given country evolves over time can help to better understand the genesis of income inequalities. A reduction in inequality of opportunity can indicate a social improvement, *ceteris paribus*. Moreover, the analysis of inequality of opportunity can give clearer information on the priorities of a redistributive policy: once the key inequalities that are particularly unjust have been identified, it is necessary to concentrate efforts on reducing such inequalities.

Considering the evidence above, the importance of public sector interventions to progressively remove the obstacles that prevent groups and classes of individuals from undertaking investment and work, starting from interventions to protect early childhood, education policies, gender policies, and citizenship policies, becomes self-evident. More precisely, the equality of opportunities theory suggests targeted interventions on the exogenous factors that determine inequalities on the market.

These interventions can take the form of compensatory measures, focusing for instance on public expenditures in certain areas of the country or for certain categories of individuals, or focusing on active labor policies targeted toward specific groups and minorities in the population. Alternatively, or in addition, public policy can be oriented toward the ex-ante removal of inequalities of opportunities: for example, by ensuring the best possible access to childcare facilities, or by providing stronger income support to poor families with children. The provision and the promotion of public education,

since the very first years of life, is a prominent example of an ex-ante equality of opportunity policy. In the I.Op. perspective, public expenditure in education should also be designed to compensate for existing disparities among families in the resources devoted to the education of their children.[15] A selective type of intervention of this kind is also less vulnerable to the critique that public intervention would cause a distortionary effect and hence an efficiency loss: on the contrary, given its link to exogenous factors for reasons of equity, a redistributive intervention might well have desirable qualities even from an efficiency perspective.[16]

In addition to the considerations above, the data reveal a positive correlation between inequality of opportunities and income inequality. Countries with a higher degree of income inequality are also characterized by greater inequality of opportunity. This result is consistent with the empirical literature on social mobility, which considers only one exogenous circumstance (family background measured in terms of income or social status of the parents) and finds a negative correlation between inequality and mobility: less unequal countries are also those that have a higher degree of intergenerational mobility. In other words, the argument according to which inequality of results is the price to pay for a mobile society where the "social lift" works and where there is equality of starting points is not supported by the data. On the contrary, the empirical evidence suggests a negative correlation between income inequality and equality of opportunity: the greater the distance between individual outcomes and positions, the greater the difficulty in passing from one position to another from one generation to the next.

As suggested above, and with the appropriate *caveats*, a possible mechanism that might drive this correlation is via the private investment in education: bigger income gaps between today's parents are likely to imply bigger gaps in the quality of education among today's children, hence bigger income gaps among tomorrow's adults. This implies that even standard redistributive policies based on instruments such as progressive income taxation and cash transfers or public services toward poor families, by reducing income disparities among today's families, can be effective in reducing the future disparities in opportunities among citizens.

Conclusions

Inequality of opportunity is a complex concept that can be measured in a number of different ways. Most of these approaches have been applied to a single country or a very small group of countries, making cross-country comparisons impossible. Two exceptions are ex-ante measures of IEO, and the HOI. Our review of this empirical literature yielded (roughly) comparable measures of the IEO for 41 countries, and of the HOI for 39. Most countries in the first set are in Europe and Latin America, but there are examples from North America, Asia, Africa, and the Middle-East. The second set covers countries in Africa and Latin America exclusively, and the overlap between the two samples is ten countries.

There was considerable cross-country variation in the (lower-bound) relative measure of ex-ante inequality of opportunity, namely the share of overall inequality attributable to predetermined circumstances: Brazil's share (0.32) is 16 times as large as Norway's. Although there certainly is noise in these measures, and various comparability caveats, there appears to be some signal as well. The IEO-R measure is strongly positively correlated with total inequality, and negatively with two different measures of inter-generational mobility. These correlations are clearly related to the "Great Gatsby Curve" of Corak (2012), which shows a negative association between income inequality and economic mobility.

In fact, the IEO-R measure is strongly positively correlated with two different measures of intergenerational persistence (the converse of mobility): the intergenerational elasticity of income, and the correlation coefficient of parental and child schooling attainment. It bears emphasis that these measures of intergenerational transmission refer to different variables, collected in different data sets, and reported by different studies. This suggests that the cross-country association between IEO and intergenerational mobility is rather robust.

In a sense, this is not surprising: inequality of opportunity is the missing link between the concepts of income inequality and social mobility: if higher inequality makes intergenerational mobility more difficult, it is likely because opportunities for economic advancement are more unequally distributed among children. Conversely, the way lower mobility may contribute to the persistence of income inequality is through making opportunity sets very different among the children of the rich and the children of the poor.

We also found an inverted-U relationship, reminiscent of the old Kuznets curve for income inequality, between per capita GNI and inequality of opportunity. We argued that it is impossible to treat that relationship as causal (in either direction), but that this is due primarily to the order of aggregation of the two variables. It is quite possible that the relationship is underpinned by real economic processes, although it is likely that disentangling them requires looking for specific relationships among well-defined microeconomic variables.

Our international comparison exercise can also shed light on the differences between the IEO-R index and the HOI, even though both can be thought of as belonging to the ex-ante approach. These differences fall into at least three categories. First, the advantage space for the IEO index is unidimensional, and usually refers to a measure of economic well-being, such as income or consumption, while the HOI focuses on binary indicators of access to services. If it is constructed as a simple average of the measure for different services, it can be thought of as having a multidimensional advantage space (although aggregation across them is fairly ad-hoc).

Second, the HOI is deliberately constructed as a development index, with a functional form analogous to Sen's welfare index, with a mean penalized by an inequality measure. The HOI is not a measure of inequality of opportunity; it *contains* a measure of inequality of opportunities (in the space of access to services), which is the dissimilarity index. As we have seen, however, most of the cross-country variation in the HOI is driven by the mean coverage term, with correlations above 0.98 for each of the five main dimensions usually included. Partly as a result, the HOI is very highly correlated with the HDI, another famous aggregate development index, at least over the currently available sample of countries. It is not obvious that the extent of this correlation is well understood by the analysts working on either approach.

Third, over the (small and unrepresentative) sample of countries for which both measures are available, the dissimilarity index and the IEO-R—each an ex-ante measure of inequality of opportunity, albeit with respect to different advantage spaces—are actually negatively correlated. While sample size and comparability issues preclude taking this correlation too seriously, it may serve as a cautionary tale that different ways of measuring inequality of opportunity can measure (very) different things, and yield widely different country rankings.

We argued in our introduction that fairness matters to people, and affects individual behavior. There is also (anecdotal) evidence that measures of fair or unfair inequality matter to governments and international institutions like the World Bank increasingly use measures of inequality of opportunity in country dialogue. We hope that this simple description of how the two most commonly used measures vary across countries, and covary with related indicators, may both contribute to greater clarity in those discussions and help spur further analytical work.

Notes

1. This section is a much-abridged and simplified version of the conceptual section in the working paper version of this chapter: Brunori et al. (2012). See also two excellent and much more comprehensive surveys by Pignataro (2011) and Ramos and van de Gaer (2012).
2. Which factors belong to which category is a subject of considerable debate in the philosophical literature.
3. These basic principles can be formalized in various ways, and the theoretical literature has shown the existence of a basic tension between them (see Fleurbaey 2008).
4. The choice of the mean as the value of the opportunity set, in addition to being empirically justified by data availability and simplicity of computation, is rationalized by the I.Op. literature as the application of a specific "utilitarian" version of the reward principle, stating the complete neutrality with respect to inequalities due to effort and advocating a sum-maximizing policy among subgroups with identical circumstances.
5. Formally, in a discrete population of size n, let π_i^j denote the probability that person i has access to service j. $\bar{\pi}^j = \frac{1}{n}\sum_i \pi_i^j$ then denotes the expected coverage of service j in the population. In practice, probabilities are often estimated econometrically from binary data on access, and $\bar{\pi}^j$ can be interpreted as the average coverage of service j. Let this population

also be partitioned into k types. Denote the population share of type k by w_k and the average coverage of service j in type k as $\overline{\pi}^{jk} = \frac{1}{n_k}\sum_{i \in k}\pi_i^j$.

Then the HOI for service j is defined as: $H^j = \overline{\pi}^j(1 - D^j)$ where

$$D^j = \frac{1}{2\overline{\pi}^j}\sum_{k=1}^{K} w_k \left| \overline{\pi}^{jk} = \overline{\pi}^j \right| \cdot$$

6. However, see Ravallion (2011) on the potential pitfalls of such arbitrary aggregate indices or, as he calls them, "mashup indices" of development.

7. Ferreira and Gignoux (2011) refer to the corresponding measures that are obtained when the mean log deviation is used as the inequality measure I(.) as IOL and IOR. They also note that IEO-R is an application of a standard between-group inequality decomposition, which has long been familiar. See Bourguignon (1979).

8. Of course, this does not hold for the estimates of the individual coefficients $\hat{\beta}$. First, these coefficients are reduced-form, rather than structural, estimates. In addition, they are likely to be biased (upwards or downwards) even as reduced-form estimates, by the omission of unobserved circumstances. The lower-bound result applies only to the overall measures of inequality of opportunity, IEO-L and IEO-R.

9. Similarly, Singh (2011) finds a higher IEO-L for consumption than for earnings in India.

10. If an inverted U-shaped relationship is observed between income inequality and per capita GNI levels across countries—that is, if a cross-sectional "Kuznets curve" holds empirically—then the positive association between income inequality and IEO-R shown in figure 5.4 actually implies the inverted-U shape in figure 5.3. We are grateful to Branko Milanovic for pointing this out.

11. Corak's figure has rapidly become well known, in part because Alan Krueger, chairman of President Obama's Council of Economic Advisers, referred to it in a speech as "the Great Gatsby curve," relating the distance between the rungs of the economic ladder and the ease with which it is climbed.

12. The averaging procedure is the same suggested by Barros et al. (2011) for the HOI summary index: first calculate a HOI for education obtained as the mean of the two education components and a HOI for housing conditions (the mean of the other three components). Then obtain a summary HOI as a simple average of the two.

13. A possible caveat with viewing the dissimilarity index within the HOI as a measure of inequality of opportunity is that the index is typically calculated "for children." This justifies the use of certain variables—like geographic location or education of the adults in the household—as circumstances, which are clearly in the realm of choices for the adults. The argument is that the index applies to children, and these are circumstances from their perspective. But this then raises the issue of age of responsibility, and whether or not all inequalities in access to services for children below a certain age should not be considered inequality of opportunity. Under that view, unequal access to water or sanitation between five-year-olds within the same type (i.e., sharing identical observed circumstances) should also be counted as inequality of opportunity.

14. The correlation with the inequality-adjusted HDI introduced for the first time for 2011 is almost the same: 0.95.
15. For evaluations of educational policies from the equality of opportunity point of view, see Betts and Roemer (2007) and van de Gaer et al. (forthcoming).
16. For a discussion of the aspects linked to the efficiency of policies on equal opportunities, see Fleurbaey (2008) and World Bank (2006).

REFERENCES

Aaberge, Rolf, Magnus Mogstad, and Vito Peragine. 2011. "Measuring Long-Term Inequality of Opportunity." *Journal of Public Economics* 95(3–4):193–204.

Acemoglu, Daron and James A. Robinson. 2000. "Why Did the West Extend the Franchise? Growth, Inequality and Democracy in Historical Perspective." *Quarterly Journal of Economics* 115(4):1167–1199.

Arneson, Richard. 1989. "Equality of Opportunity for Welfare." *Philosophical Studies* 56:77–93.

Azevedo, Viniane M. R. and Cesar P. Bouillon. 2010. "Intergenerational Social Mobility in Latin America: A Review of Existing Evidence." *Revista de Analisis Economico* 25(2):7–42.

Barros, Ricardo, Francisco Ferreira, Jose Molinas, and Jaime Saavedra. 2009. *Measuring Inequality of Opportunity in Latin America and the Caribbean.* Washington, DC: World Bank.

Barros, Ricardo, Jose Molinas, and Jaime Saavedra. 2011. "Measuring Progress toward Basic Opportunities for All." *Brazilian Review of Econometrics* 30(2):335–367.

Belhaj-Hassine, Nadia. 2012. "Inequality of Opportunity in Egypt." *World Bank Economic Review* 26(2):265–295.

Betts, Julian R. and John E. Roemer. 2007. "Equalizing Opportunity for Racial and Socioeconomic Groups in the United States through Educational Finance Reform." In *Schools and the Equal Opportunity Problem.* Ludger Woessmann and Paul E. Peterson (eds.). Cambridge: MIT Press.

Bourguignon, François. 1979. "Decomposable Income Inequality Measures." *Econometrica* 47(4):901–920.

Bourguignon, François, Francisco Ferreira, and Marta Menendez. 2007. "Inequality of Opportunity in Brazil." *Review of Income and Wealth* 53(4):585–618.

Bourguignon, Francois and Thierry Verdier. 2000. "Oligarchy, Democracy, Inequality and Growth." *Journal of Development Economics* 62(2):285–313.

Brunori, Paolo, Francisco Ferreira, and Vito Peragine. 2012. Inequality of Opportunity, Income Inequality and Economic Mobility: Some International Comparisons. World Bank Policy Research Working Paper 6304.

Cappelen, Alexander W., Erik Ø. Sørensen, and Bertil Tungodden. 2010. "Responsibility for What? Fairness and Individual Responsibility." *European Economic Review* 54(3):429–441.

Cervini-Plá, María. 2009. Measuring Intergenerational Earnings Mobility in Spain: a Selection-Bias-Free. Working s No. wpdea0904, Department of Applied Economics at Universitat Autonoma of Barcelona.

Checchi, Daniele and Vito Peragine. 2010. "Inequality of Opportunity in Italy." *Journal of Economic Inequality* 8(4):429–450.

Checchi, Daniele, Vito Peragine, and Laura Serlenga. 2010. Fair and Unfair Income Inequalities in Europe. Working Papers 174. ECINEQ, Society for the Study of Economic Inequality.

Christofides, Louis N., Andros Kourtellos, Anna Theologou, and Konstantinos Vrachimis. 2009. Intergenerational Income Mobility in Cyprus. University of Cyprus, Economic Policy Research, Economic Policy Papers No 09–09.

Cogneau, Denis and Sandrine Mesplé-Somps. 2008. Inequality of Opportunity for Income in Five Countries of Africa. Working s DT/2008/04, DIAL (Développement, Institutions et Mondialisation).

Cohen, Gerry A. 1989: "On the Currency of Egalitarian Justice." *Ethics* 99(4):906–944.

Corak Miles. 2006. Do Poor Children Become Poor Adults? Lessons from a Cross Country Comparison of Generational Earnings Mobility. IZA Discussion Papers 1993, Institute for the Study of Labor (IZA).

———. 2012. "Inequality from Generation to Generation: The United States in Comparison." In *The Economics of Inequality, Poverty and Discrimination in the 21st Century.* R. Robert Rycroft (ed.). Santa Barbara: ABC-CLIO.

D'Addio, Anna Christina. 2007. Intergenerational Transmission of Disadvantage: Mobility or Immobility Across Generations? OECD Social, Employment and Migration Working Papers 52, OECD Publishing.

Dunn, Christopher E. 2007. "The Intergenerational Transmission of Lifetime Earnings: Evidence from Brazil." *The B.E. Journal of Economic Analysis & Policy* 7(2).

Dworkin, Ronald. 1981a. "What Is Equality? Part 1: Equality of Welfare." *Philosophy Public Affairs* 10(3):185–246.

——— 1981b. "What Is Equality? Part 2: Equality of Welfare." *Philosophy Public Affairs* 10(4):283–345.

Fehr, Ernst and Urs Fischbacher. 2003. "The Nature of Human Altruism." *Nature* 425:785–791.

Fehr, Ernst and Simon Gachter. 2000. "Cooperation and Punishment in Public Goods Experiments." *American Economic Review* 90(4):980–994.

Fehr, Ernst and Klaus M. Schmidt. 1999. "A Theory of Fairness, Competition and Cooperation." *Quarterly Journal of Economics* 114(3):817–868.

Ferreira, Francisco H. G. 2001. "Education for the Masses? The Interaction between Wealth, Educational and Political Inequalities." *Economics of Transition* 9(2):533–552.

Ferreira, Francisco H. G. and Jérémie Gignoux. 2011. "The Measurement of Inequality of Opportunity: Theory and an Application to Latin America." *Review of Income and Wealth* 57(4):622–657.

Ferreira, Francisco H. G., Jérémie Gignoux, and Meltem Aran. 2011. "Measuring Inequality of Opportunity with Imperfect Data: The Case of Turkey." *Journal of Economic Inequality* 9(4):651–680.

Ferreira Sérgio G. and Fernando Veloso. 2006. "Intergenerational Mobility of Wages in Brazil" *Brazilian Review of Econometrics,* 26(2):181–211.

Fleurbaey, Marc. 2008. *Fairness, Responsibility and Welfare,* 1st edition. Oxford: Oxford University Press.

Fleurbaey, Marc and Vito Peragine. 2012. "Ex Ante versus Ex Post Equality of Opportunity." *Economica* 80(317):118–130.

Grawe, N. D. (2004). "Intergenerational Mobility for Whom? The Experience of High- and Low-Earning Sons in International Perspective." In *Generational Income Mobility in North America and Europe.* Miles Corak (ed.). Cambridge, UK: Cambridge University Press.

Hertz, Tom, Tamara Jayasundera, Patrizio Piraino, Sibel Selcuk, Nicole Smith, and Alina Verashchagina. 2007. "The Inheritance of Educational Inequality:

International Comparisons and Fifty-Year Trends." *B.E. Journal of Economic Analysis and Policy* 7(2):1–46.

Hnatkovska, Viktoria, Amartya Lahiri, and Sourabh B. Paul. 2012. "Breaking the Caste Barrier: Intergenerational Mobility in India." Department of Economics, University of British Columbia, Canada, mimeo.

Hugalde, Adriana Sánchez. 2004. Movilidad intergeneracional de ingresos y educativa en España (1980–90). No 2004/1, Working Papers from Institut d'Economia de Barcelona (IEB), Universitat de Barcelona.

Kaldor, Nicholas. 1956. "Alternative Theories of Distribution." *Review of Economic Studies*, 23(2):94–100.

Kuznets, Simon. 1955. "Economic Growth and Income Inequality." *The American Economic Review* 45(1):1–29.

Marrero, Gustavo A. and Juan G. Rodríguez. 2010. Inequality of Opportunity and Growth. Working Papers 154, ECINEQ, Society for the Study of Economic Inequality.

Molinas Vega, Jose, Ricardo Paes de Barros, Jaime Saavedra Chanduvi, and Marcelo Giugale. 2011. *Do Our Children Have a Chance?* Washington, DC: World Bank.

Núñez E., Javier and Leslie Miranda. 2007. Recent Findings on Intergenerational Income and Educational Mobility in Chile. Working Papers 244, University of Chile, Department of Economics.

Pignataro, Giuseppe. 2011. "Equality of Opportunity: Policy and Measurement Paradigms." *Journal of Economic Surveys* 26(5):800–834.

Piraino Patrizio. 2007. "Comparable Estimates of Intergenerational Income Mobility in Italy." *The B.E. Journal of Economic Analysis & Policy* 7(2).

——— 2012. Inequality of Opportunity and Intergenerational Mobility in South Africa. Paper presented at the 2nd World Bank Conference on Equity. June 27, 2012. Washington, DC.

Pistolesi, Nicolas. 2009. "Inequality of Opportunity in the Land of Opportunities, 1968–2001." *Journal of Economic Inequality* 7(4):411–433.

Ramos, Xavi and Dirk van de Gaer. 2012. Empirical Approaches to Inequality of Opportunity: Principles, Measures and Evidence. Working Papers 259. ECINEQ, Society for the Study of Economic Inequality.

Ravallion, Martin. 2011. Mashup Indices of Development. Policy Research Working Paper 5432. Washington, DC: World Bank.

Roemer, John E. 1998. *Equality of Opportunity*. Cambridge, MA: Harvard University Press.

Singh, Ashish. 2011. "Inequality of Opportunity in Earnings and Consumption Expenditure: The Case of Indian Men." *Review of Income and Wealth* 58(1):79–106.

van de Gaer, Dirk, Joost Vandenbossche, and José Luis Figueroa. Forthcoming. "Children's Health Opportunities and Project Evaluation: Mexico's Oportunidades Program." *World Bank Economic Review*.

Voitchovsky, Sarah. 2009. "Inequality and Economic Growth." In *Oxford Handbook of Economic Inequality*. Wiemer Salverda, Brian Nolan, and Timothy M. Smeeding (eds.). London: Oxford University Press.

World Bank. 2006. *World Development Report: Equity and Development*. Washington, DC: World Bank.

——— 2012a. *Do African Children Have a Chance? A Human Opportunity Report for Twenty Countries in Sub-Saharan Africa*. Draft version June 2012.

——— 2012b. South Africa Economic Update. Issue 3. July 2012.

CHAPTER 6

Does Globalization Help to Overcome the "Crisis of Development?" Political Actors and Economic Rents in Central America and the Dominican Republic

Diego Sánchez-Ancochea

INTRODUCTION

Overcoming the productive, distributional, and environmental challenges discussed in this book does not only demand new policies, but also new politics. The promotion of structural change in developing countries, for example, requires more dynamic entrepreneurs with incentives to invest in new sectors and a more effective state with the power and capacity to create those incentives. Redistribution of income, meanwhile, is unlikely to happen unless workers and social movements can pressure for new labor and social policies—policies that can also contribute to new production models (see Thandika Mkandawire, this volume).

This paper explores the opportunities and constraints that globalization creates for a different type of politics in small developing countries.[1] Is globalization contributing to the emergence of "active citizens and effective states"—the two key ingredients to promote development for Oxfam's Head of Research Duncan Green (Green 2008:12)? In particular, does it strengthen or weaken those actors who may demand a sustainable expansion of real wages and redistributive social policies? Can globalization help to create the process of structural change and productivity growth that generates the resources needed to adopt those same policies (and that is discussed in Cimoli's chapter, this volume)?

To answer these questions, I concentrate on the cases of Central America and the Dominican Republic (CADR). Traditionally characterized by patrimonial states, rentist capitalist classes, weak trade unions, and primary specialization, CADR countries have witnessed dramatic transformations in political and economic structures in recent decades. While different processes have driven these changes (from the globalization of human rights to the global expansion of democracy and the increase in migration and finance), this chapter focuses on the impact of their growing participation in global production networks (GPNs) in sectors like apparel and, to a lesser extent, electronics.[2]

Without aiming to be exhaustive, the paper identifies three *political opportunities* created by new dependence on GPNs during the last two decades. First, the diffusion of corporate social responsibility (CSR) and consumer pressures in value chains forced suppliers to be more respectful of labor rights at the micro level. Second, the emergence of international labor alliances together with the existence of preferential trade arrangements (like the Caribbean Basin Initiative, CBI) created new pressures for labor-friendly legislation. Third, domestic suppliers within GPNs are being forced to continuously upgrade their operations and find new sources of competitive advantage. These new capitalists may be more inclined to support and even demand productivity-enhancing social spending than the traditional elite.

Yet the chapter argues that, unfortunately, these positive impacts are unlikely to consolidate over the medium run due to a set of *structural economic constraints*. As Kaplinsky (2005) shows, globalization has resulted in growing competition between developing countries for investment and, at the same time, oligopolistic concentration of buyers. These trends reduce the value added received by local suppliers in developing countries, which, in turn, respond by reducing labor costs and tax contributions.

The chapter is divided into four sections. The first section discusses the role of labor markets in overcoming the productive and distributional development challenges and highlights the changes that CADR has experienced in the last century. The following two sections concentrate on the political opportunities and structural constraints that participation in GPNs has generated for the creation of more positive interactions between workers, firms, and the state. The chapter concludes with some reflections on the policies at the national and international levels that can help to create more spaces for equitable development in Central America and beyond.

Equitable Development and Labor Markets in CADR and beyond

The labor market is at the heart of the process of economic development and a fundamental institution to explain the productive and distributional challenges developing countries face. Creating well-paying jobs is still the best way to reduce poverty and improve the standards of living of a majority of the population (Amsden 2010). Given the central role of payroll taxes in funding social programs, higher formal employment will also often have a positive effect on redistributive programs (Martinez Franzoni and

Sánchez-Ancochea 2013). The two main actors in the labor market (workers through trade unions and firms through business associations) also play a central role in shaping the type of social programs countries adopt (Hall and Soskice 2001, Huber et al. 2006).

Unfortunately, most developing countries have traditionally failed to create well-paying jobs for most of its citizens. Central America has not been an exception. Inequality in the distribution of land and the asymmetric power of the landowning elite within the capitalist class reduced the incentives for wage growth and the accumulation of skills (Bulmer-Thomas 1987, Huber 2003). According to Bulmer-Thomas (1983:270), in Central America "agrarian interests (the traditional oligarchy) exercise[d] preponderant influence over political affairs." Starting during the liberal revolutions of the late nineteenth century, the Central American economic model was driven by primary exports within a system of "coerced rural labor" (Baylora-Herp 1983:298). Since low wages and low taxes contributed to sustained profitability and the production process did not require skilled labor, there were little incentives to expand education and other social services. At the same time, agricultural production was based on latifundios, which "made independent peasant political organization difficult if not impossible" (Huber 2005:14).

The expansion of import substitution industrialization (ISI) did not change this pattern of state-society relations significantly. Contrary to the experience in larger countries, ISI in Central America took place "on top of" the primary export-led model (Bulmer-Thomas 1987). The landowning elite remained highly influential and avoided an excessive expansion of taxes on primary production, while manufacturing production was inefficient and dominated by monopolies. Skilled labor was more important than in previous periods and primary education and social security expanded in all countries, but social programs were concentrated in the urban sector and trade unions systematically persecuted. Costa Rica's success in developing universal social policies may have been exceptional, but even there trade union rights in the private sector were never protected (Martinez Franzoni and Sánchez-Ancochea 2013).

CADR's economic model has changed dramatically in the last two decades. The combination of civil wars and difficult economic conditions triggered a rapid growth of migration to the United States. Remittances have become the main source of foreign exchange in El Salvador, Guatemala, Honduras, and Nicaragua and are also important in the Dominican Republic. Tax incentives for nontraditional exports and tourism have contributed to a dramatic transformation of the region's export structure. Between 1990 and 2005, the share of traditional primary exports such as sugar, coffee, and cacao in total foreign income from goods and services decreased from 76 percent to 35 percent in Nicaragua, from 34 percent to 15 percent in Costa Rica, and from 31 percent to just 2 percent in the Dominican Republic.

Assembly of apparel, electronics, and medical equipment expanded rapidly due to a combination of internal and external factors between 1990 and the mid-2000s. All governments in the regions created new export processing zones (EPZs) and tried to maintain weak exchange rates. The region also benefited from US incentives within the Caribbean Basin Initiative (CBI) and from the search for new outsourcing bases by transnational corporations (TNCs). Between 2000 and 2006, manufacturing exports from the EPZs and related regimes grew by 5.7 percent per year in CADR (Padilla-Perez and Hernández 2010). By 2006, there were 155 EPZs in Mexico and the Caribbean Basin that were responsible for more than 5 million (mainly female) jobs (Singa Boyenge 2007).

New manufacturing exports have created some opportunities for upgrading, which so far only Costa Rica and the Dominican Republic have partly seized (Paus 2005, Sánchez-Ancochea 2011). The expansion of the EPZs has also created a new class of more dynamic firm owners in some countries and opportunities for North-South civil society alliances all over the region. Exploring the extent to which all these processes have shifted opportunities for development in the region is the aim of the rest of the chapter.

POTENTIAL POSITIVE EFFECTS OF THE GLOBALIZATION OF PRODUCTION ON LABOR

The increasing participation of CADR in GPNs has affected the relations between the state, the business elite, and trade unions and has triggered some processes that could potentially reshape the domestic political equilibrium in the long run. I concentrate on three different effects in this section, but this list is by no means exhaustive. First, transnational alliances have in some cases increased the bargaining power of workers at the firm level. Second, and more broadly, trade unions have used the threat of US trade sanctions to push for reforms in the labor code and other major legislation. Third, new exporters, who face intense competition to create new competitive capacities, may be more willing to support social spending in health and education than the traditional elite in countries like the Dominican Republic, El Salvador, or Guatemala—although the evidence of this trend is still patchy. The state remains at the centre of all these new processes and its reaction to the initial changes has commonly determined the ultimate trajectory of the country.

GPNs and the Power of Brands: Transnational Consumer Pressures and Corporate Social Responsibility

New transnational alliances of trade unions and social movements have emerged in parallel to the creation of GPNs. Trade unions and nongovernmental organizations (NGOs) from developed countries joined forces with their counterparts in developing countries to pressure companies involved in global production. According to Anner and Evans (2004:35), "the ties among 'workers of the world' are being replaced by 'workers and consumer activists of the world'. Growing labor-rights campaigns focus on brand-name images."

These transnational processes affect patterns of *domestic* state-society relations in at least two ways. By enforcing union rights at the firm level and promoting partnerships between trade unions and social movements, they can gradually increase the political influence of workers. By promoting codes of conduct and corporate social responsibility (CSR), they can also change the behavior and preferences of firms, reducing the incentives to maintain a "low road" to economic development. Both of these channels have been evident in various Central American countries in the last two decades. The region became a fertile arena for transnational collaboration in labor issues due to its closeness to the United States, the existence of preferential trade arrangements (particularly the CBI) and the historical weakness of unions. Campaigns have usually been organized around labor rights—including freedom of association—in specific factories and, in many occasions, have succeeded where exclusively domestic efforts failed.

The case of Mandarin International, a Taiwanese-owned apparel factory in El Salvador, is a good example (Anner 2003, Frundt 2002). Workers decided to organize in the early 1990s to fight against poor working conditions, including lack of drinking water and unpaid and mandatory overtime. The first two attempts to create a trade union, however, failed and led to massive firings. The third attempt resulted in the creation of a trade union, but the company responded by firing the union leaders. The conflict soon escalated beyond the factory as new actors got involved. A group of national NGOs began denouncing the situation in the maquila sector using the Mandarin problem as a showcase. When the US National Labor Committee (NLC) learnt about the case and found out that Mandarin was a supplier for The Gap, it launched a broad campaign on the issue in collaboration with Salvadorian trade unions. The campaign was ultimately successful and resulted in the rehiring of the union members and the creation of a monitoring mechanism—the first of its kind in El Salvador.

Collaboration between Central American (and Mexican) trade unions and NGOs and their US counterparts expanded rapidly during the 1990s. The Union of Needletrades, Industrial and Textile Employees (UNITE) became an active partner of maquila groups in Mexico, Honduras, and the Dominican Republic. Other social organizations like the United States-Guatemala Labour Education Project, Witness for Peace, the Support Committee for Maquiladora Workers, and the NLC promoted the creation of unions and the improvement of labor conditions all over Central America (Armbruster-Sandoval 1999). The student movement in US universities was also instrumental (Anner and Evans 2004) and United States against Sweatshops expanded to over 180 campuses, using its force to pressure university managers to buy ethically all over the world.

Most of these alliances have concentrated on securing freedom of association in specific companies and, ultimately, in all the EPZs. Yet consumer pressures have also forced TNCs to adopt a broader response. Through various codes of conduct and other voluntary initiatives, TNCs and international buyers have committed to secure labor rights in all stages of their value chain

(Gereffi 2005). They have also become responsible for effective monitoring of their suppliers in developing countries. As Auret Van Heerden, president of the Fair Labor Association (one of these initiatives), puts it, "One of the most powerful vehicles we have for ensuring the implementation of labor standards in global supply chains is the multinational enterprise."[3]

While both transnational social alliances and codes of conduct have been used effectively to promote labor rights at the micro level, they are unlikely to have macro impacts for at least three reasons. First, transnational collaborations involve complex interactions between different groups within and between countries. There are multiple opportunities for conflict because each group has a different agenda and responds to different constituencies. Disagreements between trade unions and other social movements in developing countries are common and may end up reducing the overall strength of workers. At the same time, relations between trade unions and their counterparts are still asymmetric and sometimes "weaker Southern actors find that their Northern counterparts tend to dominate campaigns strategies and agendas" (Anner and Evans 2004).

Second, the extent to which all these initiatives have really changed the distribution of power between workers and firms is unclear. Codes of conduct have sometimes been marketing operations with little impact on the behavior of firms. Large buyers and TNCs in the buyer-driven value chains have difficulties to monitor the behavior of their suppliers, which sometimes use sub-subcontracting to maintain exploitive labor conditions (Gereffi 2005). In an evaluation of the Ethical Trading Initiative—a transnational alliance that promotes codes of conduct—in the Vietnamese apparel and footwear sector, Barrientos and Smith find minor positive effects on labor conditions (IDS 2006). They also describe the difficulties to monitor the code because of the existence of an array of unaccountable subcontracting arrangements.

Probably the largest limitation of the approach based on targeting specific TNCs and specific unionization drives has been its limited macro effect. Even if workers succeeded in organizing trade unions in all apparel exporting firms in Central America, this would benefit a few thousand workers since most firms are not affected. This why efforts to influence labor regulation and enforcement may be more important.

GPNs, International Trade Agreements, and Labor Standards

A weak process of industrialization and the dominance of unequal relations in the agricultural sector conspired against strong trade unions in CADR during the period 1950–1985. Even in a democratic country like Costa Rica, workers in the private sector faced constraints to join unions: in 1971, the Secretary of Labor recognized that "trade union freedoms as such do not exist" (cited in Estado de la Nación 2001). By the mid-1970s, only 5 percent of private workers were members of trade unions compared to 43 percent in the public sector (Rottenberg and Bensión 1993).

Efforts to improve labor rights through institutional and legal reform during this period failed in all Central American countries. By the early 1980s, El Salvador had ratified only four International Labor Organization (ILO) conventions and Honduras 14, while the average in the rest of Latin America was 49 (Schrank and Piore 2007). In 1989, the Dominican Republic still used the 1951 Labor Code approved by the Trujillo dictatorship, despite a series of strikes demanding changes.

The situation changed dramatically during the 1990s when all Central American countries but Honduras introduced union-friendly reforms (Murillo and Schrank 2005). The Dominican experience constitutes a good example of how the combined role of GPNs and US incentives contributed to these changes.[4] After decades of resistance, the Dominican government finally decided to introduce a more progressive labor code in 1992. The new code included a "fuero sindical" (protection of trade union leaders against discrimination by firm owners), created a tripartite commission to set minimum wages (the "Comisión Nacional de Salarios"), and promoted the modernization of the Labor Courts and expanded firing compensation.

These new measures were primarily the result of international factors. In 1990, the ILO introduced a special reference to the Dominican Republic's labor violations in the report of the Conference Committee on the Application of Standards. In response to the report, the American Federation of Labor-Congress of Industrial Organization (AFL-CIO) requested the withdrawal of the Dominican Republic's preferential access to the US market, and European tour operators threatened with significant reductions in the number of tourists. Given the risk of losses in apparel and tourism—two growing sectors based on participation in GPNs—the Dominican government was forced to appoint a special commission that wrote a new labor code. Pressures from American trade unions and NGOs—in alliance with domestic actors— were also important for reforms in other Central American countries.

In principle, all the reforms should have facilitated union drives and strengthened the participation of trade unions in policy discussions, design, and implementation all over Central America. Yet the strength of this channel has partly depended on the governments' ability and willingness to enforce the new laws. Given the structural weakness of the labor movement, the creation of complementary institutions to sustain improvements in working conditions has become fundamental.

The state has, for example, been instrumental in contributing to a gradual improvement in labor regulation in the Dominican Republic. Since the mid-1990s, the secretary of labor used the civil service law to improve the professionalization and stability of its labor force. According to former minister Rafael Alburquerque, during his term in office (1991–2000) 60 percent of all workers in the Secretary became civil servants appointed through competitive examination—including most labor inspectors.[5] The subsequent secretary of labor, Milton Ray Guevara, maintained the same policy approach.

According to Schrank (2009), the professionalization of the labor inspectors triggered a virtuous circle of higher labor standards and increasing productivity. The new labor inspectors started pressuring firms in various sectors to respect labor regulations, while simultaneously assisting them in implementing technological upgrades to increase productivity. There are some signs that the Dominican Republic could be witnessing a simultaneous strengthening of trade unions at the national level and more positive collaboration between workers, firms, and the state—although this collaboration is by no means obvious in most sectors of the economy.

New Domestic Producers and the Accumulation of Human Capital

In the long run, survival in GPNs depends on a sustained upgrading of the firm capabilities—a point that is highlighted in other contributions of this book. According to Kaplinsky (2005:87), businesses competing in the global economy "need to develop a new way of working, not just with their existing labor force, but often recruiting new and different skills." As a result, some suppliers in GPNs are now demanding workers with at least some years of secondary education and, in some sectors, college training as well.

The Dominican experience gives again some indication of the competitive pressures that the new exporting elite faces and the *potential* effect that this can have on state-society relations. The expansion of EPZs since the beginning of the 1980s led to the emergence of some domestic suppliers, particularly in the Cibao region. Companies like D'Clase Corporation, Interamericana Products, Bratex Dominicana, and Grupo M were created after 1985—in many cases by former managers from foreign firms. They grew slowly in size and soon became some of the largest apparel exporters in the Caribbean Basin.

While initially specializing in basic assembly, by the mid-1990s, these leading companies were forced to move into full package.[6] According to managers from Bratex Dominicana and Grupo M, this decision was a response to new demands from international buyers who were no longer interested in participating in production. As a manager of Grupo M explained in 2002, "A few years ago our clients told us…'My area of expertise is marketing and design and I need someone that supplies me the rest'. For us then the decision was imposed because they told us 'If you do not supply me with all of this, we will move to Asia.'" Full package operations contributed to an increase in profits, but also increased the risk that Dominican companies had to bear and the working capital they required.[7] When the apparel sector faced problems to respond to competition from China after 2003, some of these same entrepreneurs began investing in other sectors. The owner of D'Clase, for example, invested in a call center and promoted alliances with Indian IT firms.[8] Peter Weinerth from Bratex Dominicana invested in the production of communication hardware within the new Technological Park of Santo Domingo.[9]

In order to sustain this gradual process of change, the new Dominican capitalists have collaborated with the government in various projects of human resource upgrading. A public-private alliance, for example, was behind the expansion of training programs delivered by the National Institute for Technical and Vocational Training. These programs have trained more than 74,000 workers from the EPZs and have contributed to the expansion of skills at the management level (Schrank 2006). More recently, the Dominican Association of Export Processing Zones (ADOZONAS) has also supported the expansion of education and new training projects. In a series of meeting with the government in September 2006, for example, members of ADOZONAS made clear that investment in human capital was a necessary condition for Dominican participation in GPNs of electronics and footwear.[10] Other countries are witnessing similar processes. In Costa Rica, for example, some TNCs like Intel are leading supporters of new programs in tertiary education (World Bank 2006).

The experience in the Dominican Republic, Costa Rica, and a few new entrepreneurs in neighboring countries illustrates the *potential* positive effect that participation in GPNs can have on the behavior of capitalists. Yet, like the rest of the channels discussed in this section, this process is still incipient and is in many ways problematic. The number of successful new capitalists is still low and their influence in the overall pattern of development limited. More importantly, relations between the state and the new capitalists are hindered by major coordination failures. Producers from the EPZs may demand higher social spending, but have been still reluctant to "pay the bill." They still demand new subsidies and tax exemptions that have limited the ability of the government to expand social services and improve their quality. Even when it has supported tax reforms, the Central American globalized business class has concentrated on value-added taxes and other relatively regressive income sources (Schneider 2012).

The influence of these new capitalists on development policy is also contradictory. While they may support some development-friendly measures, they have also promoted more problematic ones. In particular, suppliers of GPNs have enthusiastically lobbied for the approval of the Dominican Republic-Central America free trade agreement with the United States (DR-CAFTA), which could have negative effects on long-term technological upgrading (Shadlen 2005). Meanwhile, other actors with less political power and more to lose from new regulatory changes (such as stronger protection of intellectual property rights and new investment rules) have been left unprotected.

WHY GAINS DO NOT MATERIALIZE? STRUCTURAL CONSTRAINTS ON LABOR IMPROVEMENTS

In Central America, participation in GPNs may have opened some space for more dynamic and equitable relations between state and society—relations that are necessary to overcome the three development challenges discussed in this book. Transnational political alliances of different kinds can positively affect public policy and condition the behavior of TNCs and their suppliers. At the same time, competitive pressures on suppliers may increase their support for the accumulation of human capital through public social programs.

Yet the consolidation of more progressive interactions between labor, the private sector, and the state also faces structural obstacles created by the particular nature of global manufacturing value chains. Trade unions may create transnational alliances, but have to cope with the expansion of informal employment. Domestic suppliers may want to upgrade in the long run, but they first need to respond to increasing competition from China. Governments face new demands and growing constraints in their ability to raise taxes. This section shows that the potential positive effects of GPNs on state-society relations are thus unlikely to materialize due to the difficult global environment.

To evaluate these difficulties, the concept of rent—and how rents are distributed among actors in the global economy—constitute a good entry point. According to Kaplinsky (2005:62), "rent describes a situation where the parties who control a particular set of resources are able to gain from scarcity by insulating themselves from competition. This is achieved by taking advantage of or by creating barriers to entry of competitors." Rents thus can be seen as an income above competitive market profits and wages. They can be created by firms (through product and process innovation), by the state (through policies like protection of the domestic market), or by the general macro environment (e.g., quality of infrastructure, efficiency of the financial sector).

Berg (2005) offers a useful framework to analyze how the distribution of rents takes place along the value chain. She explores the division of rents in global value chains at three levels—the first two will be used for this analysis:

- Division of rents between firms in developed and developing countries, which determine the share of value added in GPNs that stays in the latter.
- Division of rents between firm owners and workers in developing countries, which explains the capacity for win-win situations.
- Division of rents between skilled and unskilled workers, which is determined by education policies and by the structure of the economy.

While she uses this approach to explain raising wage inequality in the Chilean economy, the same framework can be applied to the analysis of power constellations and state-society relations. My basic argument is that the specific nature of global value chains results in a reduction of the rents that accrue to supplier firms in developing countries. This generates immense pressures on both capital and labor, making the creation of more effective state-society relations particularly complicated. This section illustrates this point by discussing the first two levels in the division of rents within GPNs.

Division of Rents between North and South: Structural Constraints on Domestic Suppliers

In GPNs like apparel, there are significant asymmetries between lead firms and suppliers. While lead firms in developed countries are witnessing a process of consolidation, the number of suppliers from regions like Central America is growing and competition is intense. As a result, distribution of rents and thus value added among firms has been highly unequal.

Global marketers like Nike or Gap have succeeded in creating high barriers to entry by building desirable brands and sophisticated marketing campaigns. While the actual production of a pair of shoes may be simple, developing and selling new brands is complex and extremely expensive. Distributing and retailing mass consumption goods has also become difficult and capital intensive. As a result, the number of firms in direct contact with the consumer has gradually decreased and market concentration expanded. In 2010, Coca-Cola and Pepsi together controlled 71 percent of the soft drink market in the United States (Esterl 2011) and were also dominant in other parts of the world. In 2011, just three companies (Samsung, Apple, and Nokia) were responsible for more than half of all smartphones sold in the world (Ricknäs 2011). Sport footwear is increasingly dominated by only two firms (Nike and Adidas), which have made major purchases in the last decade (Nike bought Converse while Adidas merged with Reebok). Although oligopolistic competition between these firms is intense, they are still able to maintain high markup over costs (Milberg 2006).

At the same time, transport and communication costs have decreased rapidly, making access to developed countries from all over the world easier than ever before. The result has been a rapid increase in the number of suppliers from developing countries, each of which face increasing difficulties to protect their own market share—something that is particularly evident in the case of Central America. Figure 6.1 measures the market share of CAFTA countries in total US clothing imports. Costa Rica and the Dominican Republic were the first to integrate into the apparel GPNs and initially expanded their market share rapidly. The emergence of suppliers in Honduras and El Salvador, however, created significant pressures and the market share of the first comers went down. During the period 2004–2008, Nicaragua—the latest comer with lower wage costs—was the only country with a steady increase in its market share.[11]

Given the pressures that domestic suppliers face to reduce costs and their inability to create new technology rents, they are forced to pass on all productivity increases into price reductions. In this way, firms in Central America and other small developing countries are not in a position to lessen class conflicts through an adequate distribution of productivity gains—as countries in Northern Europe and, to a lesser extent, even East Asia did in the past.

Relations between suppliers in GPNs and the state are characterized by excessive short-terminism. While new domestic capitalists engaged in

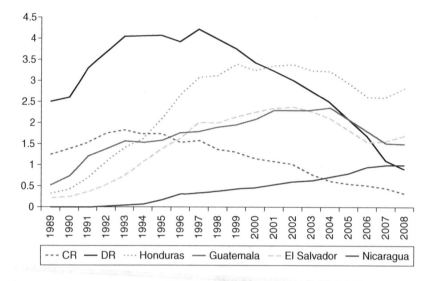

Figure 6.1 CAFTA. Market share in US clothing imports in US dollars, percent of total, 1989–2008.

Source: Authors own elaboration with data from the Office of Textiles and Apparel, US Department of Commerce (OTEXA).

GPNs know that their ultimate survival may require an expansion of public spending in infrastructure and education, they are also unwilling to pay the required tax increases. Most suppliers in manufacturing GPNs in Central America have benefited from tax incentives and have fought to maintain these incentives for as long as possible.

The situation in more capital intensive GPNs is somewhat different because of higher levels of productivity and profitability. Therefore, attracting foreign investment from companies like Intel—like Costa Rica has done in recent years—could potentially overcome some of the problems just described. Companies in high-tech activities have succeeded in sustaining high rents through product and process innovation. At the same time, competition among developing countries in high tech is lower than in apparel because the costs of entry are higher.

The problem, however, is that global production in these sectors is controlled by TNCs, and parent companies in developed countries determine the way profits are distributed among all subsidiaries. Companies like Intel or Apple make reinvestment decisions based on global not local conditions and thus have substantial bargaining power vis-à-vis small developing countries. In the case of Intel in Costa Rica, for example, decisions on what to do with profits do not depend on the subsidiary. They are made by a committee (a "virtual factory") with managers from factories all over the world. According to a manager from Intel-Costa Rica, investment plans "are considered at the macro level, there is little autonomy in this regard." Employment and wage levels, transfer prices, and most other strategic decisions are also centralized.[12] Other large TNCs in high-tech GNPs located in Costa Rica also follow a similar strategy (Paus 2005).

The importance of companies like Intel for a small economy like Costa Rica is immense and decisions on the reinvestment of its profits have a large macroeconomic effect. This gives TNCs significant political influence and direct and indirect access to the government. Intel's influence is sometimes positive (e.g., demand for better technical education and infrastructure), but has more questionable development impacts on other occasions. Intel was, for example, partly responsible for an increase in tax subsidies for high-tech firms and for a new push to liberalize the telecommunication system. According to Larraín et al. (2001:90), "the political balance among stakeholders in this realm [the liberalization of telecommunications] seems to have changed after Intel's arrival, and the reforms are more likely to take place." The Costa Rican Investment Board (CINDE) has also become a powerful lobbyist in favor of some neoliberal policies preferred by foreign firms but opposed by social movements—something evident in the debate on DR-CAFTA in the period 2004–2008.

Division of Rents between Firms and Workers: Difficulties to Consolidate Trade Unions

If domestic suppliers in Central America suffer from the asymmetric nature of GPNs, workers suffer even more as they confront simultaneous structural pressures at home and abroad. Neoliberal reforms have failed to reduce unemployment and subemployment and, as a result, several countries have witnessed an increase in the *domestic* reserve army of labor. At the same time, the entry of Eastern Europe, India, and China in GPNs has resulted in a rapid growth of global labor supply, thus expanding the *international* reserve army of labor.

This second effect has been particularly dramatic. During the 1990s, the world's labor force doubled as a result of the end of the Cold War and the spread of GPNs in more countries. Employment in the EPZs increased by 91 percent in only five years, from 22.5 million in 1997 to 43 million in 2002 (Gereffi 2005). Most new manufacturing workers came from China and other poor countries, where wages are low. In 2009, minimum hourly wages in apparel were $2.19 in Costa Rica, $1.21 in Guatemala, and $1.02 in Honduras compared to $0.93 in China—with even lower levels in interior providences—and just $0.21 in Bangladesh.[13]

The expansion of the international reserve army of labor has not simply been a onetime shock but may continue in the future. In China, for example, there is still between 100 and 150 million people working in low productivity, backward sectors who will likely move to export activities in the future (Kaplinsky 2005). This immense labor force—equivalent to more than 25 percent of the labor force in high income countries—will exert new pressures on labor markets all over the world, as they slowly enter into GPNs in the manufacturing and service sectors.

At the same time, Central American countries have generally failed to expand employment opportunities outside the EPZs. Unemployment and subemployment have remained high, and low-productivity jobs are still dominant in the economy. In the first decade of the 2000s, between 40 percent and 60 percent of Central American employees in the urban sector worked in low-productivity sectors. Domestic suppliers in the EPZs have access to a large pool of workers and thus face limited upward pressures on real wages.

Suppliers within GPNs can use the closure of factories to curtail workers' ability to negotiate better real wages and working conditions. In some cases, success in unionization drives has ultimately resulted in the shutting of factories. The experience of workers in the Guatemalan factory *Camisas Modernas* between 1992 and 1998 constitutes one of the most dramatic cases.[14] Workers from the factory created a legally recognized union in 1992, but did not succeed in forcing the owner (the US shirt producer Phillips-Van Heusen, PVH) to negotiate a collective agreement. Their failure to secure the support from the Guatemalan courts moved the new trade union to embrace a transnational strategy. Together with the US Guatemalan Labor Education Project and with UNITE, the Guatemalan workers launched a media campaign in the United States, which pressured both the company and its main buyer, J. C. Penney. After a long struggle, which even involved mediation from Human Rights Watch, PVH was forced to recognize the trade union and negotiate with it. The resulting collective agreement signed in 1997 resulted in a generous wage increase and some additional benefits (e.g., better medical services and subsidized transportation). As Armbruster-Sandoval (1999:119) argues, "The PVH workers and their allies defied the conventional wisdom about globalization and cross-border labor organizing and produced a stunning victory." The positive result was a great example of the development-friendly channel that I identified in the previous section. Yet the success was short-lived: in December 1998, PVH decided to close the plant and left all workers unemployed.

While capital mobility may be easier for foreign firms like PVH than for local ones, domestic suppliers are increasingly moving to cheaper neighboring countries as well. Nicaragua and Haiti are now favored destinations, given their low labor costs and geographical proximity. In the case of Haiti, for example, successful Dominican companies like Grupo M already moved the most labor-intensive activities to export zones across the border several years ago.

CONCLUSION

This chapter has mapped some of the political and economic consequences of Central America's participation in regional and global production networks. I have identified some processes that could result in positive change in labor markets. Growing links between suppliers in Central America and US corporations affected the way labor standards and industrial relations have been organized in Central America. Positive effects were maximized when the state used the external shocks to improve its regulatory capacity in the areas of industrial relations and social spending. Yet it seems evident that structural constraints are ultimately likely to prevent the consolidation of development-friendly state-society relations. When countries face difficulties to expand the value added they control, it is difficult to create better class compromises and secure more resources for the state. The growing difficulties of Central American countries to compete in the apparel sector and the negative impact of the global crisis on export growth are particularly illustrative of these economic obstacles to new politics.

How can these obstacles be overcome? What political changes and new policies are needed at the national, regional, and global levels? As politics is still local more than global, changes at the national level are particularly important. Countries need to slowly upgrade their social and firm-level capabilities to sustain productivity growth (Paus 2012). To do so, they may need to go beyond the East Asian model, which focused on state-capital relations and paid little attention to labor standards. Since most developing countries are unlikely to transform their economies as fast as East Asia did, they should find ways to strengthen labor rights and use wage growth to push technological learning and innovation in new sectors. The task will not be easy, given the temptation to compete only through labor costs and the pressures that governments face from traditional rentist elites.

At the regional level, social movements in the United States should find new, more creative ways to engage with developing countries and promote structural change. Shaming specific TNCs and its suppliers can promote some improvements at the micro level, but may only have limited effects at the national level. Demanding greater labor standards in regional agreements without simultaneously creating incentives for economic upgrading will not contribute to better living standards either. Social movements in the North should instead mobilize against poor behavior in global production networks and, at the same time, find ways to strengthen ties with social movements at the national level.

We should also gradually move the international agenda of development toward a more complex understanding of the links between political and economic transformation. Post–Washington Consensus reforms still focus on building an array of institutions to support free markets and formal democracy. The future agenda, however, must focus primarily on the creation of better jobs and more democratic labor relations. To do so, international institutions should focus on eliminating the most binding constraints that impede economic transformation in each country and should identify and strengthen those actors that can build more dynamic interactions between state and society. The task is not easy and change will be painfully slow but it is urgent if we want to overcome the productive and distributive challenge that most developing countries still face.

Notes

1. By globalization, I mean the growing cross-border flows of goods, people, and money as a result of which "economic developments in any one country are influenced to a significant degree by policies and developments outside its boundaries (Milberg 1998:71). This process has still continued despite the global financial crisis that exploded in 2008.

2. By doing so, I also hope to contribute to bringing politics to the literature on global value chains. As McDonald (2008:13) puts it, this literature has traditionally suffered from a "tendency to regard supply chains as part of the 'private' institutional domain—properly studied through primarily economic or sociological lenses—rather than as potential sites of *political* power, contestation and governance."

3. Testimony before the Congressional Human Rights Caucus "Human Rights and Brand Accountability: How Multinationals Can Promote Labor Rights," February 8, 2006. The FLA is a tripartite organization in charge of monitoring the implementation of a code of conduct among all member firms. The FLA was created by the Apparel Industry Partnership, an initiative promoted by the Clinton administration that brought together some companies, NGOs, trade unions, and the Department of Labor. At the moment, there are 31 participating companies as well as a substantial number of participating suppliers. See FLA (2006) and the FLA webpage www.fairlabor.org.

4. The following discussion is based on interviews that took place in Santo Domingo (Dominican Republic) in June and July 2002 with Rafael Alburquerque (secretary of labor from 1991 to 2000 and current vice president of the Republic) and trade union leaders from the trade union confederations Central General de Trabajadores (CGT), and the Confederación Sindical de Trabajadores Clasistas (CSTC). See also Murillo and Schrank (2005) and Schrank (2009).

5. Meeting with Rafael Alburquerque in Santo Domingo, Dominican Republic, June 2002.

6. Full package refers to the process by which firms find their own fabrics, cut them, sew them, add all the complements, and send the final product to the client.

7. Interviews with managers from Grupo M (Santiago de los Caballeros, Dominican Republic, June 2002) and Bratex Dominicana (Santo Domingo, Dominican Republic, July 2002).

8. Data provided by Andrew Schrank.

9. Secretaria de Estado de Economía de la República Dominicana "Inventores nacionales trabajan 14 proyectos en Parque Cibernético," www.stp.gov.do/noticias/noticia_inv_03042006.htm (accessed on August 8, 2007).

10. See ADOZONAS-Gobierno Dominicano "Presentación: Un Presente Forjando el Futuro," September 2006, www.adozona.org/manager/dlm/applications/DocumentLibraryManager/upload/PrADOZONA.pdf (accessed August 8, 2007).

11. The entry into force of CAFTA contributed to a small expansion of the market share in Honduras and El Salvador. Yet it was still more beneficial for Nicaragua, which has more flexible rules of origin and thus uses more East Asian inputs in the apparel process than neighboring countries.

12. Interview with a manager of Intel-Costa Rica, Rivera de Belen, September 2002.
13. Institute for Global Labour and Human Rights at www.globallabourrights. org/alerts?id=0297 (last accessed June 15, 2012).
14. The following discussion of the case is based on Armbruster-Sandoval (1999) and Anner (2003).

References

Amsden, Alice H. 2010. "Say's Law, Poverty Persistence and Employment Neglect." *Journal of Human Development and Capabilities* 11(1):57–66.
Anner, Mark. (2003). "Defending Labor Rights across Borders: Central American Export-Processing Plants." In *Struggles for Social Rights in Latin America*. Susan Eva Eckstein and Timothy P. Wickham-Crowley (eds.). New York: Routledge.
Anner, Mark and Peter Evans. 2004. "Building Bridges across a Double Divide: Alliances between US and Latin American Labour and NGOs." *Development and Practice* 14(1, 2):34–47.
Armbruster-Sandoval, Ralph. 1999. "Globalization and Cross-Border Labor Organizing: The Guatemalan Maquiladora Industry and the Phillips Van Heusen Workers' Movement." *Latin American Perspectives* 26(2):108–128.
Baloyra-Herp, Enrique A. 1983. "Reactionary Despotism in Central America." *Journal of Latin American Studies* 15(2):295–319.
Berg, Janine. 2005. *Miracle for Whom? Chilean Workers under Free Trade*. London: Routledge.
Bulmer-Thomas, Victor. 1983. "Economic Development of the Long Run: Central America since 1920." *Journal of Latin American Studies* 15(2):269–294.
———. 1987. *The Political Economy of Central America since 1920.* Cambridge, UK: Cambridge University Press.
Estado de la Nación. 2001. Séptimo informe del Estado de la Nación en Desarrollo Sostenible. *Informe 2000*. San José, CR: Proyecto Estado de la Nación.
Esterl, Mike. 2011. "Pepsi Thirsty for a Comeback." *Wall Street Journal*. March 18, 2011. http://online.wsj.com/article/SB10001424052748703818204576206653259805970.html (last accessed June 15, 2012).
Fair Labor Association (FLA). 2006. *2006 Annual Public Report*. Washington: FLA.
Frundt, Henry J. 2002. Central American Unions in the Era of Globalization. *Latin American Research Review* 37(3):7–53.
Gereffi, Gary. 2005. "The Global Economy: Organization, Governance and Development." In *The Handbook of Economic Sociology*, 2nd edition. Neil J. Smelser and Richard Swedberg (eds.). Princeton: Princeton University Press and Russell Sage Foundation.
Green, Duncan. 2008. *From Poverty to Power: How Active Citizens and Effective States Can Change the World*. Oxford: Oxfam.
Hall, Peter and David Soskice. 2001. "An Introduction to Varieties of Capitalism." In *Varieties of Capitalism: The Institutional Foundations of Competitiveness*. Peter Hall and David Soskice (eds.). Oxford: Oxford University Press.
Huber, Evelyne (ed.). 2003. *Models of Capitalism: Lessons for Latin America*. University Park: Pennsylvania State University Press.
———. 2005. Inequality and the State in Latin America. Paper prepared for the Conference of the APSA Task Force on Difference and Inequality in the Developing World, University of Virginia, April 22–23.

Huber, Evelyne, François Nielsen, Jenny Pribble, and John D. Stephens. 2006. "Politics and Inequality in Latin America and the Caribbean." *American Sociological Review* 71(6):943–963.

Institute of Development Studies (IDS). 2006. *Report on the ETT Impact Assessment 2006, Part 2b: Vietnam.* Brighton: IDS.

Kaplinsky, Raphael. 2005. *Globalization, Poverty and Inequality: Between a Rock and a Hard Place.* London: Polity Press.

Larraín Felipe B., Luis Felipe López-Calva, and Andrés Rodríguez-Clare. 2001. "Intel: A Case Study of Foreign Direct Investment in Central America." In *Development in Central America: Volume 1. Growth and Internationalization.* Felipe Larraín (ed.). Cambridge, MA: Harvard Studies in International Development.

Martinez Franzoni, Juliana and Diego Sanchez-Ancochea. 2013. "Can Latin American Production Regimes Complement Universalistic Welfare Regimes? Implications from the Costa Rican Case." *Latin American Research Review* 48(2): 148–173.

McDonald, Kate. 2008. The Politics of Global Supply Chains. Power and Governance beyond the State. DPhil diss. Oxford: St Antony's College.

Milberg, William. 1998. "Globalization and Its Limits." In *Transnational Corporations and the Global Economy.* Richard Kozul-Wright and Robert Rowthorn (eds.). New York: McMillan Press.

———. 2006. Pricing and Profits under Globalized Competition: A Post-Keynesian Perspective on US Economic Hegemony. SCEPA Working Papers, 2006–2005. New School for Social Research, New York.

Murillo, Victor and Andrew Schrank. 2005. "With a Little Help from My Friends: Partisan Politics, Transnational Alliances, and Labor Rights in Latin America." *Comparative Political Studies* 38(8):971–999.

Padilla-Perez, Ramón and René A. Hernández. 2010. "Upgrading and Competitiveness within the Export Manufacturing Industry in Central America, Mexico, and the Dominican Republic." *Latin American Business Review* 11(1):19–44.

Paus, Eva. 2005. *Foreign Investment, Development and Globalization. Can Costa Rica Become Ireland?* New York: Palgrave Macmillan.

———. 2012. "Confronting the Middle Income Trap: Insights from Small Latecomers." *Studies in Comparative International Development* 47:115–138.

Ricknäs, Mikael. 2011. Samsung Becomes Biggest Smartphone Vendor, as Android's Market Share Grows. *PC World.* November 15, 2011. www.pcworld.com/article/243861/samsung_becomes_biggest_smartphone_vendor_as_androids_market_share_grows.html (last accessed June 15, 2012).

Rottenberg, Simon and Alberto Bensión (eds.). 1993. *The Political Economy of Poverty, Equity and Growth: Costa Rica and Uruguay.* Oxford, UK: Oxford University Press for the World Bank.

Sanchez-Ancochea, Diego. 2011. Hacia un desarrollo superficial o los inicios del salto tecnológico? Exportaciones de maquilas y desarrollo económico en Costa Rica. LATN Working Paper 135, Buenos Aires.

Schneider, Aaron. 2012. *State-Building and Tax Regimes in Central America.* Cambridge: Cambridge University Press.

Schrank, Andrew. 2006. Labor Standards and Human Resources: A Natural Experiment in an Unlikely Laboratory. University of New Mexico, unpublished mimeo.

————. 2009. "Professionalization and Probity in a Patrimonial State: Labor Inspectors in the Dominican Republic." *Latin American Politics and Society* 51(2):91–115.

Schrank, Andrew and Michael Piore. 2007. Norms, Regulations and Labour Standards in Central America. *Serie Estudios y Perspectivas no 77.* CEPAL (Economic Commission for Latin America and Caribbean).

Shadlen, Kenneth. 2005. "Exchanging Development for Market Access? Deep Integration and Industrial Policy under Multilateral and Regional-Bilateral Trade Agreements." *Review of International Political Economy* 12(5):750–775.

Singa Boyenge, Jean-Pierre. 2007. ILO Database on Export Processing Zones (Revised). Sectoral Activities Programme. Working Paper 251. Geneva: International Labour Office (ILO).

World Bank. 2006. "The Impact of Intel in Costa Rica: Nine Years of the Decision to Invest." *Investing in Developing Countries Series.* Washington, DC: World Bank.

CHAPTER 7

From Authoritarianism to People Power in the Middle East and North Africa: Implications for Economic Inclusion and Equity

Eva Bellin

The developing world faces many challenges. These include the need to carry out substantial structural transformation, generate growth that is environmentally sustainable, and foster development that is economically inclusive. To balance the trade-offs inevitably generated by the simultaneous pursuit of these goals, many stakeholders have emphasized the importance of expanding the role of popular voice in the policy-making process. Augmenting the scope of *political* inclusion is considered pivotal especially with regard to advancing the goal of *economic* inclusion. By giving the (poor) majority greater political voice, it is argued, greater economic equity can be achieved.

If only it were so simple. As the experience of the Middle East and North Africa (MENA) suggests, political inclusion and economic inclusion may be less closely paired than many might think. Since the momentous events of the "Arab Spring" of 2011, this region, long an epicenter of authoritarianism, has begun a process of significant political opening. As such it presents a "natural experiment" for exploring the impact that expanded political inclusion may have on improving economic inclusion and equity.

Unfortunately, early observation of the region suggests that while democratic reform may deliver some measure of political empowerment to the people of the MENA, it may not necessarily have a positive impact in terms of delivering a better distribution of *economic* benefits to the demos. This is attributable to three factors. First, many regimes in the MENA had already established relatively commendable records in terms of economic inclusion, while still thoroughly authoritarian. Consequently, there are few "low-hanging fruit" for newly democratizing regimes to pick in terms of advancing economic inclusion. This weakens the linkage drawn between democratic advance and distributional gains. Second, the most pressing source of economic exclusion in the MENA today derives from the region's high level of unemployment. But it is not clear that augmenting the level of political inclusion will necessarily assist in delivering the most widely hailed remedy for unemployment—economic growth. Finally, to expand economic inclusion, regimes in the region must embrace public policies that are expressly redistributive as well as growth-oriented. Such policy initiatives require effective political mobilization of committed constituencies and policy makers. Unfortunately, effective mobilization is a political good that is not automatically guaranteed by political opening alone.

To clarify these points, this chapter explores the relationship between political inclusion and economic inclusion in the context of the MENA. First, the chapter will highlight the region's surprisingly strong past performance in terms of economic equity and distribution. The goal here is to show that political exclusion and economic exclusion are not necessarily a "matched pair" and to spotlight the comparatively high bar that democratizing regimes in the region must clear in order to register progress on economic inclusion. This high bar makes the linkage between economic and political inclusion less than automatic. Second, the chapter will identify the causal mechanisms that lead us to link political opening to economic inclusion (at least theoretically) and then present the mechanisms that thwart the pairing of these two goals in reality. Specifically, mobilizational failures by constituencies committed to distributive agendas prevent political opening from necessarily delivering on inclusionary goals. Third, the chapter will explore one of the most central development challenges faced by the region—unemployment— and consider the contribution political opening may make to meeting this challenge. The ambiguous role political opening plays in eliminating the key obstacles to job growth in the region (e.g., limited foreign investment, low integration into international trade) suggests the tenuousness of pairing political and economic inclusion in the MENA. Fourth, and more optimistically, the chapter will reflect on some of the positive models of paired political and economic inclusion that can be found among some key political and cultural referents for the region. Specifically, it will consider how success in Turkey, Indonesia, and Malaysia may gird the Arab world with the political inspiration and will to embrace the policies necessary to achieve dual inclusion simultaneously.

POLITICAL AND ECONOMIC INCLUSION/EXCLUSION— A MATCHED PAIR?

Analysts who are philosophically committed to the goals of both political inclusion and economic equity have long been susceptible to the persuasion that "all good things go together." That is, they have long been inclined to believe that the extension of political rights to ever-larger segments of society will result in a fairer sharing of society's bounty. Conversely, they tend to believe that *political* exclusion of major segments of society will also spell *economic* exclusion of the majority. Although there are valid analytic grounds for the pairing of political and economic inclusion (as will be explored below), the reality on the ground is often quite different.

Observers from the United States know this only too well. In terms of its formal political institutions, the United States is one of the most politically inclusive democracies in the world. And yet, the United States ranks as one of the least economically inclusive countries among its industrialized peers. Its performance on social indicators such as infant mortality and economic inequality place it in the company of countries that are much poorer and significantly less well endowed with democratic heritages (Bakalar 2011). Clearly, the provision of (formally) equal opportunities for political inclusion does not guarantee commensurate access to society's wealth.

The fact that political and economic inclusion and exclusion are not a matched pair is nowhere more evident than in the case of the Arab world. This is a region that has long been renowned for authoritarianism, exceptional in both its scope and endurance. Freedom House and the Polity Project have routinely ranked the Arab world as the world region that is the least free and the least politically inclusive. And yet the region's performance in terms of economic inclusion (i.e., sharing society's wealth among all segments of society) has been surprisingly strong. This is evident in terms of a number of indicators.

Most impressive is the Arab world's performance in terms of limiting levels of absolute poverty. The Arab world has long had the lowest level of absolute poverty of all developing regions in the world. That is, a smaller percentage of people live on less than $1 a day or even $2 a day in the Arab world than in Latin America, South Asia, Sub-Saharan Africa, or East Asia (see table 7.1 and figure 7.1). In this regard, the Arab world is "comparable to the super successful Asian countries" (Noland and Pack 2011:66). Among all Arab countries, only Yemen and Egypt have poverty levels that approach Third World levels (Noland and Pack 2011).

The Arab world's impressive performance in terms of economic inclusion is also evident in its performance on numerous human development / social welfare indicators. Between 1960 and 2000, the region registered considerable gains in terms of life expectancy, infant mortality, child immunization rates, child nutrition, and education rates. For example, by the early 2000s, life expectancy in most Arab countries had risen by 44 percent, nearly equaling that of the United States and surpassing the performance of comparably developed countries in East Asia and South Asia. Infant mortality rates had fallen dramatically, decreasing more than that of any other region. Child immunization rates had risen impressively, to the point that immunization became nearly universal. Educational opportunities increased dramatically with primary school education nearly universal in most Arab countries.[1] By some lights educational expansion had even gone too far, overproducing some tertiary education, if judged by the limited employment opportunities

Table 7.1 Population below the poverty line (%)

Country	Year	$1/day	$2/day
Middle East			
Algeria	1995	2.0	15.1
Egypt	2000	3.1	43.9
Jordan	2003	2.0	7.0
Morocco	1999	2.0	14.3
Tunisia	2000	2.0	6.6
Yemen	1998	15.7	45.2
Resource rich comparators			
Botswana	1993	23.5	50.1
Indonesia	2002	7.5	52.4
Nigeria	2003	70.8	92.4
Venezuela	2000	8.3	23.6
By region			
Middle East	2002	1.6	19.8
East Asia	2003	11.6	40.8
Latin America	2002	8.9	23.4
South Asia	2002	31.1	77.8
Sub-Saharan Africa	2002	44.0	74.9

Source: World Bank, cited in Noland and Pack (2011:68).

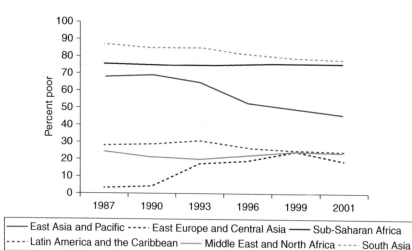

Figure 7.1 Comparative trends in regional poverty at $2/day line, 1987–2001.
Source: World Bank, cited in Iqbal (2006:8).

available to many university graduates (Iqbal 2006:21–22, Noland and Pack 2011:62–64). Table 7.2 illustrates these accomplishments.

Perhaps most surprisingly, the region's achievement in terms of economic inclusion is evidenced by its relatively strong performance in terms

Table 7.2 Human development in the Middle East and North Africa (1960–2000)

	1960	1980	2000
Years of education (average per person over 15)	0.9	2.6	5.5
Years of education (average per female over 15)	0.5	1.8	4.6
Child mortality (deaths per 1,000 births)	262	138	47
Life expectancy (years at birth)	47	58	68

Source: World Bank, cited in Iqbal (2006:22).

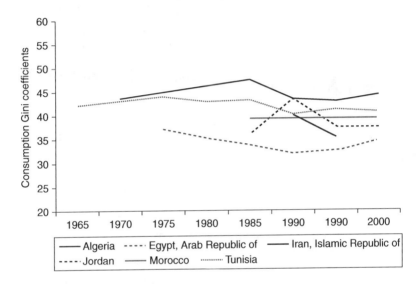

Figure 7.2 Trends in inequaltiy, 1965–2000.

Source: World Bank, cited in Iqbal (2006:8).

of income distribution. Looking at the ratio of the top fifth of the population versus the bottom fifth, income inequality in the Arab world is comparable to that of East Asia and South Asia, but well below inequality in Sub-Saharan Africa and Latin America (Noland and Pack 2011:64–68). And most Arab countries have seen an overall decline in income inequality since 1960, as illustrated in figure 7.2. This is most surprising given the fact that a sense of grievance over income inequality is widespread in many Arab countries.

How can this strong performance on "economic inclusion" be explained? At work are two elements: the combination of express public policy on the part of many Arab states and serendipitous economic and sociocultural factors in the region. Many states in the Arab world are the stewards of significant rent (oil, gas, transit, geo-strategic). Access to such rent has enabled them to carry out a variety of redistributive projects, including the provision of various public goods (immunization, education), the subsidization of basic consumer goods, and the expansion of the public sector. Growth of the public sector has proven especially important in terms of delivering employment to a significant segment of society and thereby providing many with a floor of subsistence (Adams and Page 2003).

But perhaps surprisingly, even states *without* large endowments of rent have often followed a distributive path. In the 1950s, 1960s, and 1970s, an ideological wave of "Arab Socialism" spread throughout the region and inspired many countries to embrace ambitious projects of inclusion. For the rent-poor states, these were often funded through debt, foreign aid, and the drawing down of currency surpluses accumulated during WWII. The appeal of Arab Socialism has certainly faded with time, but in many Arab countries, the institutional legacy of this ideology lives on in entrenched public sectors and social policies.

Besides these expressly redistributive policies on the part of the state, poverty in the region has also been reduced by access to employment opportunities in the oil-rich countries of the region. This has resulted in significant remittance earnings that buoy many poor families across the Arab world (Adams and Page 2003, Iqbal 2006:11). Finally, the region is endowed with strong sociocultural networks, some religiously based, some family based. These provide important safety nets to the poor and assist in alleviating some of the worst poverty in the region.

But whatever the explanation, the fact is that the Arab world has performed better in terms of economic inclusion than most other parts of the developing world. This in not to say that all is well in terms of economic equity. Serious levels of poverty persist in several Arab countries (e.g., in Egypt, 43% of the population still lives below $2 a day; and in Yemen, the level of absolute poverty is even worse; Noland and Pack 2011:68). Altogether, one out of every four or five people in the region still lives in poverty (Iqbal 2006:5). Moreover, there are significant disparities in development and wealth across the region, with pockets of severe regional poverty present even in relatively developed countries such as Tunisia or quite wealthy countries such as Saudi Arabia (Anon/IFAD 2003). Income distribution remains highly unequal in the MENA (Anon/IFAD 2003) and even if the region performs better than many other developing parts of the world in this regard (as measured by comparative Gini coefficients), there is a popular perception that, *within the region*, inequality has been increasing *over time*. Finally, the problem of unemployment has clearly gotten worse, especially among young people, a consequence of the demographic "youth bulge" experienced by the region during the past decade (Dhillon 2008). In short, there is significant basis for economic grievance in Arab society.

It is thus no surprise that "aish"—bread—was the first word of the three-term rallying cry that mobilized the crowds protesting during the Arab uprising of 2011.[2] Anger over economic grievances proved crucial to building up the popular steam that was decisive in overturning dictators during the Arab Spring. Failure in the domain of economic inclusion was, without question, an important factor in fueling the drive for regime change in the region.

Nevertheless, the relatively strong performance of the MENA region, at least compared to other developing parts of the world, provides compelling evidence that a region's level of authoritarianism does not covary with its level of economic exclusion. In short, political and economic exclusion (and inclusion) are not a matched pair. Consequently, the move toward political opening in the region may not necessarily result in immediate gains in economic inclusion. The low-hanging fruit of economic inclusion have already been picked (and to some degree over-picked). The relatively strong performance of the region's authoritarian regimes in terms of social welfare creates a high bar for newly liberalizing regimes to clear and surpass. This amplifies the political challenges these new regimes face and makes it that much harder for them to register gains in economic inclusion.

Analytic Linkage between Political and Economic Inclusion

Still, there are commonsensical reasons to assume that democracies will outperform authoritarian regimes in terms of economic inclusion and hence that democratization in the region will yield gains in this area. After all, the cardinal utility of bestowing people with the power of the vote is to force political regimes to be accountable to the popular will. Presumably, under these conditions, ruling elites will be obliged to direct resources toward constructive ends that benefit the commonweal rather than squandering scarce assets on vanity projects, corruption, and endeavors that benefit only the very few. In addition, freer political systems mean more space for the fourth estate (the media) and more space for civil society organizations to act as watchdogs. These institutions force the government to be more transparent and accountable in its use of public resources. Presumably this results in less waste and corruption as well as more focus on benefiting the commonweal. Finally, the wider distribution of political power across society should theoretically empower the poorer strata to impose a more distributive economic agenda on the state. This too should spell improved regime performance in terms of economic inclusion.

But reality is often quite different from plausible analysis. Even established democracies are routinely captured by special interests that siphon off resources for use in economically irrational ways. To push through a policy agenda that is economically distributive, the poorer strata must be politically well organized. Unfortunately, this is not a given in most democracies. To the contrary, privileged segments are often better positioned to dominate the political helm and its agenda. In addition, the less privileged are often effectively distracted from progressive economic agendas by countervailing appeals to identity politics. Think of the failure of progressive candidates to win the working-class vote in the United States (Haidt 2012). Add to this the myopia and short-term horizons that the electoral cycle imposes on political leaders and it is clear why democracies fail to outperform dictatorships in any consistent way, either in terms of economic growth or in terms of the distribution of material well-being (Bellin 2005:139–140; Clark et al. 2009:328; Przeworski and Limongi 1993).

This is not to say that democracy is bad for economic inclusion. Rather, democracy is neither necessary nor sufficient to deliver this outcome. Regime type is simply too blunt a variable to determine these results. Political variables such as leadership, party strength, organization of special interests, and the quality of the state bureaucracy, among others, often prove as important as regime type in determining economic outcomes—distributive or otherwise (Beinin and Herbst 1996, Haggard and Kaufmann 1992, Nelson 1994).

In short, one should not be overly optimistic about the distributive payoff from the Arab world's move toward greater political inclusion, at least not in the short term. Of course, transitioning out of authoritarianism should be valued in its own right, for the potential benefit it confers on society in terms of guaranteeing basic freedoms and human rights. But its impact on economic inclusion is indeterminate and wholly subject to effective political mobilization by the disadvantaged in society, among other factors.

The hope of such mobilization does not look terribly promising in the region today. As it stands, nowhere in the Arab world today has a party of popular consequence emerged that is devoted primarily to a progressive economic agenda. Even the leading Islamist parties, whether the Ennahda Party of Tunisia or the Muslim Brothers' Justice and Development Party in Egypt, have only vaguely defined economic agendas. Despite their broadly popular base, they have not made economic redistribution the centerpiece of their ambitions (Saif and Rumman 2012)

Major Development Challenges in the MENA: How to Advance Economic Inclusion

Given the region's relatively strong starting point in terms of economic inclusion (at least by standards of the developing world), making progress in this area means focusing less on guaranteeing a subsistence floor to most and more on lifting ever-larger numbers of people out of poverty. The most promising route to achieving this goal is to sop up the high levels of unemployment and underemployment that plague the region and consign so many to hopelessness. The level of unemployment in the Middle East and North Africa is one of the highest in the world; at nearly 14 percent, it is surpassed only by one other developing region (Sub-Saharan Africa—14.9%), and it is more than double that of East Asia and nearly double that of Latin America (World Bank 2006). But these numbers understate the incidence of unemployment borne by specific pockets of the population. For example, young people suffer unemployment rates that are more than double the general rate (clocking in at about 30%, but reaching levels as high as 40% for university graduates in some countries). Similarly, there are regional pockets in nearly every country that suffer from much higher unemployment rates than those captured by national averages. For example, central Tunisia suffers much higher rates of unemployment than those of the country's major cities or coastal areas. It is not surprising that Mohamed Bouazizi, the young fruit vendor whose self-immolation sparked the beginning of the Arab spring protests, hailed from Sidi Bouzid, a town in the central part of the country (30 percent unemployment). Finally, women are significantly underemployed in the region; with only 30 percent of Arab women employed outside the home, their level of employment is lower than that found in any other developing region in the world (UNDP 2006), though it is hard to parse the degree to which this is a consequence of cultural preference as opposed to limited opportunity. By any standard, unemployment levels in the region are intolerably high, and the lack of jobs constitutes a significant obstacle to effective economic inclusion.

To tackle the problem of unemployment, the region is obliged to focus on generating economic growth. As a leading Egyptian economist has said, without economic growth a politics of distribution simply means the distribution of poverty (Brookings Economic Forum, March 2011). In fact, the growth performance of the MENA region has been disappointing for the past two decades. Coming in at under 2 percent, the region registered the weakest real per capita growth of all regions in the world, with the possible exception of Sub-Saharan Africa (Bhattacharya and Wolde 2010:1–3). This growth problem needs to be tackled head on and to have the most distributive impact the region needs to focus especially on developing labor-intensive industries that will create jobs.

What are the obstacles to developing such industries? Economists identify a host of relevant factors but all agree that deficiencies in two areas are especially damning: (a) deficiencies in capital investment, both *foreign* (Foreign Direct Investment [FDI]) as well as investment by the *domestic* private sector; and (b) deficiencies in integration into the international economy, especially trade levels with the rest of the world. FDI in the region is extremely low by world standards, excluding natural resource–based sectors such as oil and gas (Noland and Pack 2011:111). The volume of trade (excluding fuels) is quite low as well (Noland and Pack 2011:103). These deficiencies are deleterious not only because they deny the MENA the necessary start-up capital for new industrial ventures, but also because lack of integration with foreign companies (i.e., low levels of intra-industry trade agreements) shut the region out of major sources of technology transfer and innovation as well as cost discipline (Henry and Springborg 2001:42–46, Page 1998:153). The latter is especially crucial to developing globally competitive (and hence sustainable) export industries.[3]

The MENA region has been unable to make progress in attracting FDI, local capital, and expanding intra-industry trade due to structural weaknesses such as inadequate infrastructure (especially underdeveloped transport and telecommunications) and the low level of labor skills and human capital compared to other countries with similar levels of per capita income (Bhattacharya and Wolde 2010). But another major reason why the MENA fails to attract investment and intra-industry trade is that the region's business environment is made unattractive by political factors. These include political instability ("capital is a coward"), dodgy political institutions (are property rights upheld in a timely fashion by the judiciary?), bureaucratic constraints (how difficult is it to get permits to start a business?), and corruption (how many officials must one pay off to get licenses and permits?). The World Bank's Business Enterprise Survey found that more than a quarter of all businesses polled identified licensing and customs as a major constraint on doing business in the MENA region and 54 percent identified corruption as a major constraint (Bhattacharya and Wolde 2010:20). Governance issues such as these constitute a major obstacle to economic progress in the region.

Of course other regions, notably China, have proven weak in some of these areas as well and yet these weaknesses have not proven to be a deterrent to investment. But unlike China, MENA countries do not offer the compensating benefits of a huge consumer market and extremely low wages. If anything, wage levels in the region are relatively high (in comparison to other developing areas) due to the impact of "Dutch disease" and the legacy of "Arab Socialism." Consequently, FDI and international integration of the Arab economies remains relatively low.

Is Political Inclusion the Remedy?

The question is whether progress on the political front, and specifically, progress toward political opening, is likely to improve the prospects for economic growth in the region. In the most optimistic of scenarios, it is plausible to see a link. Political liberalization could mean unseating the old political machines that long fueled corruption and maintained rent-creating distortions in the economy. Political opening might also mean an empowered fourth estate and civil society that might sustain a watchdog function, impose more political transparency, and reduce governmental corruption. Both factors would make the region a more attractive investment environment. In addition, greater freedom and reform might unleash new energy and optimism, reverse brain drain, and attract foreign investment and technology (Noland and Pack 2011:xiii).[4]

But just as political opening creates growth-enhancing opportunities, it also creates potential hazards. Perhaps the biggest hazard lies in the region's susceptibility to demagogues and populists. After years of political exclusion and pent-up demand for economic advance, the newly empowered demos may be ill-prepared for the material restraint necessary to truly spur growth. The temptation among inexperienced voters to elect politicians who promise them the moon may set off spending sprees that would only worsen the region's macroeconomic condition, not to mention its exchange rates. This prospect, along with the possibility of political instability, would only further discourage investment, growth, and job creation. Clearly this would not advance the cause of economic inclusion in any sustainable way.

Ray of Hope

There are, however, some reasons to be hopeful. And this is because there are a number of countries that, for reasons of cultural proximity, constitute important referents for the Arab world. And among those countries are several that have embraced both political opening as well as "globalization" and integration into the international economy, with significant success. Here I am referring to countries such as Turkey, Indonesia, and Malaysia. Each is a Muslim-majority country. Each has Islamist parties that have been central to political life. In Turkey, the Islamist-inspired Justice and Development Party (AKP) has led the government for over a decade. Each has pursued a strategy of export-oriented manufacturing as a crucial component of its growth plan. And each has experienced robust growth rates. These countries constitute an important model for the Arab world of a possible way forward. The importance of the demonstration effect should not be underestimated as it is one of the most important factors shaping a country's likelihood to embrace protest, democracy, or any number of other trends. Already, leaders of the Muslim Brothers in Egypt have conducted consultations with colleagues in these three countries to learn the "secrets" of their success. With the proven successes of these countries as a lure, the newly opening regimes of the Arab world may find the inspiration necessary to mobilize around policies (and discipline) necessary to fuel real growth.

Conclusion

Parts of the Arab world are on the threshold of a new era of political openness and inclusion. But whether this will spark greater equity and economic inclusion remains much more tentative. To advance this agenda requires, first and foremost, the creation of jobs. This, in turn, requires an increase in FDI, local capital mobilization, and greater integration of the region into the international economy. Political opening may create some of the conditions necessary to improve the attractiveness of the business environment in the Arab world. But this will require mobilization and self-discipline among both voters and politicians. With luck, the positive model of other Muslim-majority countries like Turkey and Indonesia will prove sufficiently compelling to direct the newly opening Arab countries on this track to growth, and ultimately, to the goal of greater economic inclusion.

Notes

1. Literacy rates for adult populations, however, continued to lag and a gender gap in educational attainment remained significant in many Arab countries (Noland and Pack 2011: 64).

148 ❖ EVA BELLIN

2. The slogan repeated by protesters across the region (but most consistently in Egypt) was "Aish, Hurriyah, Karama Insaniyya," that is, "Bread, Freedom, Human Dignity."

3. My colleagues in this volume, including Dani Rodrik, Mario Cimoli, and Jose Ocampo, also point to the importance of adopting expressly proactive policies (e.g., industrial policies and countercyclical policies) to fuel growth effectively. The absence of these has also contributed to low growth rates in many MENA countries.

4. In fact, the region witnessed such a surge of investment and reverse brain drain in the case of the Palestine Authority when a brief moment of optimism reigned in the late 1990s at the start of the "new regime" there. But as that case showed clearly, the window of opportunity is very short and such optimism can quickly be snuffed out.

References

Adams, Richard H. and John Page. 2003. "Poverty, Inequality and Growth in Selected Middle Eastern and North Africa Countries, 1980–2000." *World Development* 31(12):2027–2048.

Anon/IFAD. 2003. "Assessment of Rural Poverty: Near East and North Africa." International Fund for Agricultural Development.

Bakalar, Nicholas. 2011. "Childbirth: Neonatal Deaths Slow, but U.S. Still Lags." *New York Times*, September 5. www.nytimes.com/2011/09/06/health/research/06childbirth.html.

Beinin, Henry and Jeffrey Herbst. 1996. "The Relationship between Economic and Political Reform in Africa." *Comparative Politics* 29(1):23–42.

Bellin, Eva. 2005. "The Political-Economic Conundrum." In *Uncharted Journey: Promoting Democracy in the Middle East.* Thomas Carothers and Marina Ottaway (eds.). Washington, DC: Carnegie Endowment for International Peace.

Bhattacharya, Rina and Hirut Wolde. 2010. Constraints on Growth in the MENA Region. IMF Working Paper 10/30.

Clark, William Roberts, Matt Golder, and Sona Nadenicheck Golder. 2009. *Principles of Comparative Politics.* Washington, DC: CQ Press.

Dhillon, Navtej. 2008. "Middle East Youth Bulge: Challenge or Opportunity?" Brookings Address (May 22, 2008). www.brookings.edu/research/speeches/2008/05/22-middle-east-youth-dhillon.

Haggard, Stephen and Robert Kaufmann. 1992. *The Politics of Economic Adjustment.* Princeton: Princeton University Press.

Haidt, Jonathan. 2012. "Why Working Class People Vote Conservative." *The Guardian*, June 5.

Henry, Clement and Robert Springborg. 2001. *Globalization and the Politics of Development in the Middle East.* New York: Cambridge University Press.

Iqbal, Farrukh. 2006. *Sustaining Gains in Poverty Reduction and Human Development in the Middle East and North Africa.* Washington, DC: World Bank.

Nelson, Joan. 1994. *A Precarious Balance: Democracy and Economy Reforms in Eastern Europe.* San Francisco: ICS Press.

Noland, Marcus and Howard Pack. 2011. *Arab Economies in a Changing World, 2nd Edition.* Washington, DC: Peterson Institute.

Page, John. 1998. "From Boom to Bust and Back." In *Prospects for Middle Eastern and North African Economies*. Nemat Shafik (ed.). New York: St. Martin's Press.

Przeworski, Adam and Fernanco Limongi. 1993. "Political Regimes and Economic Growth." *Journal of Economic Perspectives* 7(3):51–69.

Saif, Ibrahim and Muhammad Abu Rumman. 2012. The Economic Agenda of the Islamist Parties. Carnegie Paper (May), Carnegie Endowment for International Peace.

UNDP (United Nations Development Programme). 2006. *Arab Human Development Report 2006*. New York: United Nations Development Programme.

World Bank. 2006. *World Development Indicators 2006*. Washington, DC: World Bank.

PART III

Making the Environment Count

CHAPTER 8

The Macro- and Mesoeconomics of the Green Economy

*José Antonio Ocampo**

INTRODUCTION

Under the influence of the United Nations, particularly the United Nations Environment Programme (UNEP), the concepts of "green economy," "green growth," and "global green new deal" have emerged in the global policy debate (Barbier 2010, UNEP 2011a, 2011b).[1] There is no unique definition of the concept of the "green economy," but the term itself underscores the *economic* dimensions of sustainability. Thus, UNEP has argued that the concept responds to the "growing recognition that achieving sustainability rests almost entirely on getting the economy right" (UNEP 2011a:2). It also emphasizes the crucial point that economic growth and environmental stewardship can be complementary strategies, thus countering the view that still holds a strong influence that there are significant trade-offs between these two objectives.

Responding to concerns by many countries and analysts (e.g., Khor 2011), it has been made clear that the concept should be seen as consistent with the broader and older concept of sustainable development. The specificity of the broader concept is associated with both its *holistic* character, as it encompasses the three pillars of development—economic, social, and environmental—, and its particular focus on *inter*generational equity, which derives from its original formulation under the Brundtland Commission as development "that meets the need of the present without compromising the ability of future generation to meet their own needs" (World Commission on the Environment and Development 1987:8).

What is essential to the concepts of green economy and green growth is, therefore, the understanding that the benefits of environmental sustainability outweigh the costs of investing in and protecting the ecosystems, so that it is possible to have a win-win or "double dividend" strategy of growth with environmental sustainability, and even win-win-win or "triple dividend" strategy that also includes poverty reduction.

This chapter focuses on two aspects of the green economy: its *macro*economic dimensions, which refer to the effects of sustainability on overall economic performance, and the *meso*economic dimensions, understood as the processes of structural change that characterize all processes of economic growth, but those particularly required to meet the challenges of the green economy. These emphases depart from the main focus of the massive literature on the links between the economy and the environment, which generally deal with its *micro*economic dimensions and, particularly, the role of externalities and different options to correct them (regulations, taxes and/or emissions trading, and subsidies), or with its sectoral dimensions, particularly the links between the energy system and climate change, but also forests, water systems, agriculture, fisheries, mining, and waste management, et cetera.

One way to divide the set of the specific economic and associated policy issues is to classify them under four different headings. The *first* one relates to how the welfare of future generations is taken into account in savings and investment decisions today, and thus with the social discount rate that should be applied for investments in environmental sustainability. The *second* refers to aggregate supply and (the much less common) aggregate demand analyses that incorporate environmental investments and constraints. The *third* is the analysis of economic growth as a process of structural change—that is, as a process that involves significant changes in the structure of production and consumption, which is largely driven by technological change. The *fourth* one relates to the debates on financing the green economy, particularly of developing countries' participation in global initiatives in this area.

It is also important to emphasize that the macro- and mesoeconomic analyses are deeply embedded in distributional debates. They relate again to not only the intergenerational character of sustainable development, but also to how the opportunities and costs of the green economy are shared between developed and developing countries. There are also many other subordinate distributional issues associated with the micro and sectoral dimensions, such as who is affected by carbon taxation or high hydrocarbon prices, by the composition of spending, by policies aimed at administering different sectoral policies, et cetera. For reasons of space, this chapter will only make passing reference to these issues.

The international equity dimensions have been made more difficult by the overexploitation of ecosystems by industrial countries in the past. This is particularly challenging in relation to climate change, as the *accumulated* emissions of greenhouse gases (GHGs), largely generated by industrial countries in the past, imply that there is no solution that is viable today that does not involve the active participation of developing countries. In the words of the proponents of the Greenhouse Development Rights Framework, "it is too late to talk of emissions reductions of Annex I countries alone. It is now necessary to secure significant cuts in emissions in the growing nations of the developing world" (Baer et al. 2008:5)—where, they add, there are still high levels of poverty.[2]

This implies, in fact, that we face the task of reducing massive climate risks and other major environmental disruptions, but doing so while reducing the accumulated international inequalities. This is the particular challenge that is derived from the principle of "common but differentiated responsibilities." In the words of the UN Department of Economic and Social Affairs: "The active participation of developing countries is now required and such participation can occur only if it allows economic growth and development to proceed in a rapid and sustainable manner" (United Nations 2009:v).

The "common" part of the responsibilities is derived, in any way, from the fact that, despite the fact that per capita emissions continue to be much lower than those of industrial countries, developing countries contributed 78.5 percent of the growth of CO_2 emissions between 1973 and 2008 and represented 44.3 percent of current emissions in the latter year.[3] Similarly, although industrial countries affected their ecosystems much earlier, the responsibility of developing countries derives from the fact that they hold in their territories the most mega-diverse ecosystems and the largest remaining natural forests. This also implies that the global community has to compensate them with adequate payment for the global environmental services they provide. In turn, in areas such as the quantity and quality of water resources, the fertility of land, or the access to clean air in the cities, the responsibility of the developing countries is clearly to their own populations.

The following four sections survey the existing literature, organized around the four issues highlighted before. The last section draws policy conclusions.

Valuing the Welfare of Future Generations

The first approach can best be discussed in terms of the debate on the Stern Review on Climate Change (Nordhaus 2007, Stern 2007, 2009, Weitzman 2007), but it has precedents in similar debates in the past.[4] In technical terms, the fundamental question is how to maximize a social welfare function that is the discounted value of the utility of consumption of current and future generations in a growth process that takes into account the links between the economic and the climate systems. The debate relates to the social discount rate that should be used to estimate the present value of future costs and benefits of alternative environmental and economic policies.

The major policy implication of the debate is whether the strategy to combat climate change requires a gradual tightening strategy by which investment in mitigation and carbon prices are progressively increased (a "climate policy ramp," to use Nordhaus's terminology), or stronger action today to avoid damages that will be experienced in the future as global temperature rises, and as insurance against extreme events (catastrophes).

The debate formally uses the Ramsey-Koopmans-Cass model, which indicates that the social discount rate that should be used to estimate the present value of future benefits and costs of climate change should take into account three factors: (i) the pure rate of time preference or, better, the intergenerational rate of time preference; (ii) the elasticity of substitution between consumption in different periods, which in intergenerational terms may be interpreted as the willingness of the current generation to sacrifice its consumption today to benefit future generations; and (iii) the expected growth in per capita consumption, which in this model that involves long-term horizons may be said to basically depend on productivity growth.[5] The discount rate will therefore be higher if the rate of time preference and productivity growth are higher, or if the elasticity of substitution is lower (i.e., if current generations are less willing to benefit future generations).

The importance of this issue is derived from the fact that discount rates have enormous implications for cost-benefit analysis involving very long time periods. For example, an adverse effect of climate change (or any other environmental damage) of $100 half a century from now is worth $49.90 today using the Stern Report's discount rate of 1.4 percent but only $5.43 to $6.88 using the alternative rates preferred by its critics (6 percent and 5.5 percent, respectively). So, the use of higher discount rates significantly reduces the social profitability of actions on mitigation today that have no guaranteed high rates of return.

A central issue here is that implicit or explicit ethical choices are always involved in selecting the discount rate (Stern 2009, Chapter 5, TEEB 2010a). So, it can be said that intergenerational equity requires a zero rate of time preference (i.e., total neutrality among generations). A similar equity principle should also be applied, though more controversially so, to the second factor (the elasticity of substitution between consumption in different periods), as the neutrality among generations could be said to imply that the rate of substitution between consumption today and that of future generations should be one (i.e., increasing or sacrificing a proportion of consumption of the current generation should be equivalent to increasing or sacrificing the consumption of a future generation by the same proportion). Interestingly, if we adopt both criteria, the intergenerationally equitable rate of discount is the rate of expected productivity growth.[6]

The major criticism of this conclusion is that such a rate is inconsistent with both observed market parameters (returns on risk-free financial instruments are closer to it but those of riskier assets are much higher) as well as with savings behavior. The first is not a relevant issue in this context, as market returns do not take into account environmental externalities, and financial markets are ripe with market imperfections. In relation to the latter, it implies that *all* capital income should be saved.[7] Another way of looking at this issue is that adopting market rates of returns on capital and current savings behavior may bias decisions in favor of the current generation, as they undervalue the consumption of future generations and, therefore, lead to levels of savings that are less than desirable for those generations to enjoy higher consumption levels.[8]

Two caveats are in place. The first one is that using low discount rates for very long time horizons may give a weight to hypothetical events too far in the future (say two centuries from now), so perhaps a long but limited time horizon may be preferable. The second is that other ethical principles could be adopted aside from the intergenerational equity, particularly a principle that would aim at maximizing the welfare of the poorest generation (Nordhaus 2007). The latter may be interpreted also as an argument for developing countries using a higher social discount rate, which is consistent also with the fact that their productivity growth has to be higher to guarantee convergence of income levels with those of industrial countries. However, this does not take into account the fact that ecosystem constraints are of a *global* character. So, a more appropriate approach would be exempting the poor from making commitments to achieve global climate change objectives. This is precisely the approach of the Greenhouse Development Rights Framework, which exempts individuals under a certain poverty line from making commitments in the area of climate change.[9] This approach does not necessarily apply in relation to other environmental issues, such as biodiversity, land fertility, or water management, as in those cases, green policies will directly increase the income of the poor (TEEB 2010b, UNEP 2011b).

Aside from the issues regarding the choice of a social discount rate, there are others associated with *risk* and *uncertainty*, including the effects of the deterioration of the ecosystem on productivity levels. The difference between these two concepts is crucial. The first refers to choices that we can make based on known parameters—or, to be precise, on parameters that can be inferred from past behavior of the economy and the ecosystem. The second refers to decisions that have to be made with imprecise or even lack of information ("known unknowns"), and thus without knowledge of the adequate parameters. It is here that the "precautionary principle" of the 1992 Earth Summit fully applies.

The most important cases are catastrophic events that could lead to irreversible processes beyond a certain threshold, which may also be known only with a high level of imprecision or belong to the "known unknowns." Such catastrophic events are present in some of the future climate change scenarios, but are already happening in the area of biodiversity (rapid extinction of species) and may be close to happening with fisheries and some water systems. Another and, in a sense, closely interlinked case refers to the fact that the likely probability of very adverse environmental events is higher than that of very favorable events. This is what most climate change scenarios project and it is certainly true of biodiversity.

Risk should, of course, lead to precaution, and thus to lower discount rates, the higher the level of risk aversion—which, again, implies that society should weigh more heavily the welfare of future generations. However, the phenomenon of uncertainty is the one that should be our major concern. This includes uncertainty about the benefits and costs of future events and even of what the appropriate discount rate should be. The former include not only uncertainty about future events but also our incomplete knowledge of the ecosystems (as reflected, for example, in the multitude of climate change scenarios) and of the damage they can inflict on the economy. In economic terms, the precautionary principle should lead to a policy that insures against extreme events. For Martin Weitzman, a critic of the Stern Review, this is the best defense of strong action in the area of climate change: "Spending money now to stop global warming should not be conceptualized primarily as being about optimal consumption smoothing so much as an issue about how much insurance to buy to offset the small chance of a ruinous catastrophe that is difficult to offset by ordinary savings" (Weitzman 2007:704–705, see also Weitzman 2010).

Finally, although the policies adopted to correct the negative externalities and to promote activities with positive externalities have a rationale of their own, they may also have macroeconomic and sectorial effects. They imply that state intervention has to increase, which aside from active regulation may also (though not necessarily) mean that a larger fraction of world GDP may end up going through state budgets, as both revenue and spending. Some may fear that larger states could have negative effects on aggregate supply, though there is conflicting evidence on this subject that will not be surveyed here. The new revenues, particularly those from higher direct or indirect taxation on carbon, also provide opportunities for changing the structure of governments' revenues. In turn, the sectorial effects are associated with the fact that investment decisions involve very different time horizons, and the likely negative effects of environmental problems also play unevenly through time in different sectors.

Aggregate Supply and Demand Analysis

A second family of macroeconomic effects is those that green economy policies have on aggregate supply and demand. Aggregate supply effects have been abundantly explored in the existing literature, particularly in relation to climate change. Aggregate demand effects are less commonly analyzed but have occupied a central place in recent stimulus packages and in demand-driven growth models in the Keynesian tradition.

The supply effects can be conceptualized in two different but complementary ways. The first one is to include a stock of natural capital that affects aggregate production together with other capital stocks—physical and human, as well as intangible ones like institutional and social capital. A problem with this approach is that measurement problems are monumental. The second is to view the damage to the ecosystems as a constraint on aggregate supply, or eventually as a productivity loss or a rising aggregate cost curve.

The contrast between these approaches is useful to differentiate two basic ways of understanding the relations between the macroeconomy and the ecosystems. The first, which has been suggested by the World Bank (2006), considers development as a "process of portfolio management," in which the resource rents from exhaustible natural resources can be transformed into other assets through investment. From here the Bank derives a measure of "adjusted net savings," which takes into account investments in all forms of capital as well as depreciation of physical capital and depletion of natural capital. This analysis carries the correct message that countries—developing countries, in particular—should fully save the rents from natural resources. But it also incorrectly implies that the scarcity of resources should not be regarded as a bottleneck, as investments in physical and human capital can compensate for depletion of natural resources—a concept that has come to be called "weak sustainability." So, this concept is only useful in a limited sense to understand the macroeconomics of the green economy.

The alternative approach, which comes from ecological economics, rather views the macroeconomy as an open subsystem within the finite natural ecosystem. Its major conclusion is that capital cannot substitute for resources, as they perform different functions, and at least some of those functions cannot be duplicated by humans. This leads to the concept of "strong sustainability," which posits that there are ecological limits that can constrain economic growth.

A recent survey of macroeconomic models that analyze the links between the macroeconomy and environmental sustainability indicate that the dominant link analyzed is the one that goes from the economy to energy, and then to climate change (or the environment in general), with few feedbacks, the main one being taxation. It also concludes that the linear relations that those models use are appropriate for the analysis of marginal changes, but not to events that are nonlinear, such as thresholds generated by deep depletion of resources or the rising probability of catastrophes. The models also generally assume, in a way that is consistent with the concept of "adjusted net savings," that physical capital can substitute for the depletion of natural capital. Technology is generally treated as an exogenous variable, and uncertainty is almost always left aside (Cambridge Econometrics and Sustainable Europe Research Institute 2010).

One common use of these models is the analysis of policies to confront climate change—which is termed the "costs of action." More stringent action to mitigate climate change will increase the costs of energy, which will then have adverse effects on global output. According to the survey by the Intergovernmental Panel on Climate Change (IPCC 2008, Chapter 3), costs in 2030 consistent with emissions trajectories toward stabilization between 445 and 535 ppm CO_2 equivalent represent a maximum loss of 3 percent in global GDP (a loss in the growth rate of 0.12% a year). They reach a maximum of 5.5 percent of GDP in 2050 (equivalent again to a reduction in growth rates by 0.12% a year) based on a portfolio of existing technologies and those that are expected to become profitable. Costs are higher, the more stringent the objective, and differ by region. They can be reduced substantially if an efficient portfolio of interventions is adopted and if revenues are used to promote low-carbon technologies or reform existing taxes. Models that assume induced technological change also give lower costs but require larger upfront investments. There are, however, large uncertainties about both cost estimates far into the future and the optimal path to achieve the required level of mitigation.

These costs of action obviously have to be confronted with the "costs of inaction": the disruptions generated by environmental damages, which in this context can be interpreted as a reduction in the aggregate productivity of the economy. The IPCC reports the large divergence of views on these damages as well as the difficulty in costing nonmarket damages in economic terms. A cost-benefit analysis should then compare these costs with those of taking action. It is here that the discount rate plays a critical role. The Stern Review comes to the conclusion that mitigation costs of around 1 percent of GDP are highly worthwhile to limit damage costs of around 5 percent of world GDP by 2050 (which could be significantly higher). However, costs can be higher if they rise rapidly after some point, including the rising probability of catastrophes.

A broader analysis of the macroeconomic implications of environmental protection is provided by UNEP's recent Green Economy Report (UNEP 2011b:Chapter 13). According to the simulations provided, investing in the green economy $1.3 trillion, equivalent to 2 percent of world GDP or one-tenth of global investment, may lead to slower growth for a few years (relative to the scenario in which those resources are invested according to past patterns), as renewable natural resources are replenished, but will result in faster growth after 5–10 years. Aside from the fact that the green economy can deliver in the long term more growth, it also reduces downside risks associated with climate change, energy shocks, water scarcity, and loss of ecosystem services, increases employment (as green investments are generally more employment intensive) and has direct benefits in terms of poverty reduction (particularly through improvements of agricultural productivity of rural smallholders). Relative to business-as-usual, this scenario reduces energy demand by 40 percent by 2050 (largely through reduced power, and transport efficiency), which is increasingly supplied by renewables production, and also decreases water demand by 22 percent and the ecological footprint by 48 percent.

These simulations as well as those of all supply-driven models may underestimate the potential short-term as well as long-run benefits from an ambitious investment drive in this area, particularly in industrial countries that require new demand impulses given the high levels of unemployment that have prevailed since the 2007–2008 global financial crisis. This idea was behind some of the stimulus packages approved during the crisis. The share of green investments in the packages was particularly large in Korea, some European countries, and China, but only 15 percent of global stimulus spending (Barbier 2010). There has been a weakening of the commitment of most countries to this strategy since 2010, but it should remain on the agenda.

If this strategy is successful in igniting a new wave of investments and thus increasing aggregate demand, it also has the long-term effects suggested by Keynesian growth models in which investment plays the dual role of increasing domestic demand in the short run and of accumulating assets that are essential for long-term growth.[10] To the extent that investment is embodied in new equipment or leads to learning-by-doing, higher investment also induces technological change, further reinforcing long-term growth. Indeed, some of the positive effects of the structural dynamics that we will consider in the next section work through the induced technological change.

Whether an aggregate supply or demand framework is used, it is important to emphasize that the macroeconomic effects of green growth are closely linked with sectorial and microeconomic effects. This is behind the "expanded Keynesianism" suggested by Harris (2009), as well as the Green or Sustainable New Deal proposed by the United Nations (2009) and Barbier (2010). What this approach implies is that the demand stimulus should be accompanied by changes in the composition of investment and consumption. Some of this additional spending should thus be aimed at environmental conservation, research, and development in new technologies, creating the infrastructure necessary to increase energy efficiency (e.g., public transport, subsidizing new consumer spending on residential energy conservation, etc.) and, more broadly, at forms of public infrastructure investment that "lock in" patterns of private investments that are beneficial for environmental sustainability. To the extent that the strategy includes limits to population, it should take into account that the transition to a stable population is also to a transition to an aging population, which increases the demand for social security and medical expenses. In short, the strategy should mix Keynesian demand management with green taxes and redistribution of demand toward environmentally sounder areas of spending, thus combining macroeconomic policy with microeconomic incentives.

GREEN GROWTH AS A PROCESS OF STRUCTURAL CHANGE

A major weakness of growth analysis that looks only at the dynamics of macroeconomic aggregates is that it ignores that the growth process is always accompanied by major changes in production structures: variations in sectoral contributions to GDP, employment, investment, and patterns of international specialization. The implicit assumption is that these transformations are just a side effect of growth. But the alternative "structuralist" view is that these changes are not just a by-product of growth but rather are among the prime movers: that development is nothing else than the capacity of an economy constantly to generate new dynamic activities (Ocampo 2005, Ocampo et al. 2009). New activities are generally accompanied by the decline of others, in the process that Schumpeter (1962) correctly characterized as "creative destruction," and thus have distributive implications.

For industrial countries, the main engine of this process is technological change. Since technology generation is highly concentrated at the world level, it generates a global "center-periphery" pattern. In developing countries, the process leads to the lagged transfer from industrial countries of those activities that mature in technological terms and, with a shorter lag, they respond to demands for natural-resource intensive goods from the leading economies. A handful of successful dynamic developing countries are now playing a more active, though still subsidiary, role in the generation of technology and new economic activities.

This structuralist view carries, of course, major policy implications. Because production structure must change if growth and development are to proceed, conscious choice of policies that will drive the transformation of the system toward new dynamic activities can play an essential role for long-term economic expansion.

The relevance of this issue for the subject of this chapter is that the full development of the green economy involves no less than a technological revolution and major changes in production and consumption patterns. This technological revolution is likely to differ from previous processes of this sort in at least three major ways. First of all, government policy is going to play a more central role than in past industrial revolutions. Second, given the level of integration of the world economy today and the fact that the revolution is responding to veritable global challenges, it is going to be essentially global in character, with international institutions playing a fundamental role in coordinating international cooperation. The latter include those that are at the center not only of negotiations and enforcement of global environmental agreements, but also of trade rules and the financing facilities that developing countries are likely to require. Third, it will take place under the prevalence of intellectual property rights that are stronger and enjoy global protection under the TRIPS Agreement (Trade-Related Aspects of Intellectual Property Rights) of the World Trade Organization (WTO), and additional protection in many bilateral and plurilateral free trade agreements.

The process of creative destruction can have distributive impacts, across and within countries. The essential issues here are who benefits from technological change, in terms of being at the center of research and development efforts, and generating new economic activities and demand effects (linkages) with the rest of their economies, and who will be negatively affected by the activities for which there will be reduced demand. Given the center-periphery character of the process of technology generation and diffusion, a crucial question is whether this process will generate new forces for international inequality associated with the uneven technological capacities that already exist, both between industrial and developing countries but now also among developing countries (and perhaps also among industrial countries). Past industrial revolutions generated unequalizing trends, and the ongoing industrial revolution will be no different. However, the fact that this time international cooperation is at the center of this process creates the opportunity to reduce these unequalizing forces.

Issues associated with the nature of the new technologies, capacities to both generate and absorb technology, and intellectual property rights are crucial in this regard. The first refers to how much technology is embodied in equipment or inputs, or in easily transferable blueprints versus in tacit (or informal) knowledge that is much less readily transferable to other firms and for which such transfer tends to take place, if at all, via foreign direct investment. In relation to the second issue, we know that, aside from the very large disparities in capacities to generate technology, technological absorption on the recipient side is always an active learning process. It requires mechanisms to transfer technology, such as agricultural extension services for green agricultural technologies and similar mechanisms to disseminate to households and construction firms knowledge of better building practices, and energy-saving technologies to small- and medium-sized manufacturing firms, to just mention a few. It also requires the development of public/private/academic research centers, as well as engineering teams in larger firms that buy equipment and/or technological packages.

In turn, intellectual property raises well-known questions about the conflict between the public good character of knowledge and the incentives that may be needed to induce private investments in innovation and to transfer the technology to third parties, but which generate distortions of their own (creation of temporary private monopolies). These distortions would have limited effects if there is competition among firms generating new technology.

The evidence available indicates that most innovation in climate-mitigating technology does take place in Organization for Economic Cooperation and Development (OECD) countries and that, therefore, firms from those countries are the main holders of intellectual property rights. According to optimistic assessments, however, there is enough competition—though clearly of an oligopolistic character—within and across technologies to guarantee that developing countries should be able to obtain licenses on reasonable terms (Barton 2007, Copenhagen Economics and the IPR Company 2009, Lee et al. 2009). A few developing countries, notably China, hold a minority but growing proportion of patents, particularly in solar photovoltaic (PV) and wind technologies. Ethanol and biodiesel industries exist in several developing countries (e.g., Brazil, China, India, Pakistan, Thailand, Malaysia), indicating that this sector is characterized by low barriers to entry.

In any case, given the fact that most developing countries will be technology followers, there is a need to generate global institutional arrangements that create incentives to increase international cooperation in research and development in all areas relevant for green growth and accelerate the transfer of those technologies to developing countries. These should include a large component of open innovation systems and publicly financed innovations and prizes. The model of the green revolution and the network of research institutions under the Consultative Group on International Agricultural Research (CGIAR) could be replicated. Technology initiatives should also include designing a "model" R&D cooperation agreement, global demonstration programs, knowledge-sharing platforms, and a global database on freely available technologies and best practices in licensing.

Reforms of the global regime of intellectual property regime are also necessary, including broader room for compulsory licensing (replicating this and other aspects of the WTO Doha 2001 agreement on intellectual property rights and public health) and strengthening patenting standards, particularly of breadth and novelty (Henry and Stiglitz 2010, Lee et al. 2009). They should also allow innovators to use patented knowledge to generate new innovations.

The nature of the linkages generated by the new activities also plays a critical role in disseminating or not the benefits of the new technological revolution to developing countries. In this regard, trade rules must facilitate access of developing countries that are active in the production of green technologies to the markets of industrial countries. More broadly, protectionist policies should not be used with environmental objectives. Furthermore, aside from avoiding border carbon adjustments, which would operate in practice as an additional import tariff, any GHG emission targets set should be consumption rather than production based, in order to avoid discriminating against production in developing countries (Dervis 2008).

The management of subsidies for green technologies and activities in the international trade regime also requires careful scrutiny and possibly new rules. In this regard, it is clear that subsidies should be allowed, but also that those regimes that do so (such as the WTO agricultural regime) tend to benefit industrial economies. This could be compensated in part by the ability of developing countries to access global funds to finance some of their subsidies in this area.

In turn, some natural-resource intensive exports from developing countries may be adversely affected. This "destructive" part of the technological revolution must therefore lead to support for these countries for the development of alternative dynamic activities as part of necessary adjustment in their production structures.

Finally, and perhaps most fundamentally, the speed required to put the technological revolution in place and to guarantee that its benefits are shared equitably requires a much larger role for state action than has been typical in recent decades, involving regulation, taxes and subsidies, and mixing both market and nonmarket measures. This is true even of industrial countries but even more so of developing countries.

For this reason, an investment-based strategy is essential to manage the transition to the green economy in the case of developing countries. The two keys to such a strategy are public investment and production sector (industrial) policies that induce strong private-sector responses. The latter should include a strong technology policy with a focus on adaptation and dissemination of green technologies, treatment of green economy activities as "infant industries" that requires appropriate support (time-bound subsidies and/or protection), and government procurement policies that mainstream environmental criteria. The former should include public sector investments that support these industrial policy efforts and build the necessary public sector infrastructure, as well as access targets for basic energy and water and sanitation services for the poor.

FINANCING DEVELOPING COUNTRIES' GREEN ECONOMIES

The resources required to finance the transition to a green economy have been subject to widely diverging estimates.[11] UNEP's Green Economy

Report summarizes estimates for investment needs (public and private) for the green economy, placing them in the range of 1.6 to 4 percent of world GDP in 2011. It then builds its scenarios for the impact of these investments on the basis of a figure of 2 percent of world GDP ($1.3 trillion). Close to three-fifths of this sum would be invested in energy efficiency (particularly in buildings, industry, and transport) and in renewables; the remainder would be invested in tourism, water, agriculture, fisheries, waste management, and a small amount in forestry. The resources allocated to energy (slightly over 1% of GDP) are broadly consistent with Stern's estimates of mitigation costs for a scenario for emissions of 450 ppm CO_2 by 2050, and with full abatement costs by McKinsey for 2030.

Over half of the estimated needs will come from developing countries, particularly in the area of energy, where the greatest expansion of energy demands is projected. Compared with these needs, those of adaptation are of a much smaller order of magnitude: 0.04–0.15 percent of world GDP in 2030 according to estimates by the United Nations Framework Convention on Climate Change (UNFCCC 2008:Table 5).[12] Similarly, the financing of access to basic services for the poor represent very limited amounts.[13]

In this context, the commitment reached in the 2009 UNFCCC Conference of the parties held in Copenhagen of mobilizing $100 billion a year by 2020 for a global climate fund to address the needs of developing countries looks encouraging, though at the low end of existing estimates, whereas the target of $30 billion as fast start in 2010–2012 is clearly low. According to the Report of the Secretary-General's High-Level Advisory Group on Climate Change Financing (United Nations 2010), the $100 billion target is "challenging but feasible," using resources from a wide variety of sources.[14] It could also generate $30–50 billion in carbon market flows, but they are really a substitute for domestic mitigation commitments that firms have to meet in industrial countries. For this reason, they should be excluded as contributions to the financing of the mitigation and adaptation needs of developing countries.

The criteria proposed by the Advisory Group to select the desired resources are revenue capacity, efficiency (whether a given instrument has a "double dividend" by also helping to correct externalities), equity, incidence on developed versus developing countries (only net flows from the former to the latter are included), reliability (predictability of revenue stream), practicality (feasibility of implementation), and political acceptability. They add that these resources should be clearly additional to development assistance as such, though in practice the two are mixed.

Aside from the required scale of financing, which is the issue these estimates refer to, there are many additional questions regarding the financing strategy. Most importantly, priority should be given to the poorest countries, which according to most estimates are also those more likely to be affected by climate change and should absorb a significant share of adaptation funds and international support to countries that are affected by associated disasters (hurricanes, floods, and desertification). There are, in this regard, large synergies between poverty alleviation and associated green economy projects, most particularly in sustainable agriculture, water, and sanitation.

However, beyond these allocations to the poorest countries and those most likely to suffer major environmental disruptions, a strong case can also be made for transfer-like resources for *middle-income* countries to help them contribute to the global public good of climate stability (Dervis 2008). Indeed, again, one possible criterion is to extend the Greenhouse Development Rights Framework to the allocation of climate change funds (see again Baer et al. 2008). To this we should add the protection of natural forests and biodiversity, as some of the remaining natural wealth in these two areas (which is, of course, interlinked) is located in middle-income countries. Indeed, the best solution in this case is clearly the payment for the value of the associated environmental services.

Throughout the developing world, priority should be given to public sector infrastructure investments that are critical to the transition to the green economy, notably public transportation systems, and efficient water and sewage systems and electricity grids. Infrastructure investments are, of course, critical for "crowding-in" private investments and "locking" them in the direction of green investments. Due attention should also be given to the allocation of funds among private agents between firms and households. In particular, since there are large benefits associated with improved building standards (insulation, lighting systems, air conditioning, and water heating), a major share in the associated funds should be channeled to improve household dwellings (Enkvist et al. 2007, IEA 2006:Chapter 8). The best mechanism is this regard may be a subsidy on energy-saving building standards and appliances financed by a tax on energy consumption.

In macroeconomic terms, two issues should be at the center of the design of the financing mechanisms. The first is related to the fact that a net transfer of resources requires that recipient countries should be running a *current-account* deficit in their balance of payments,[15] which they may be unwilling to run if they increase the risk of a financial crisis. Under these conditions, additional *external* financing is not what these countries require, and would only lead to larger reserve accumulation without any effect on investment. Developing countries may be particularly reluctant if the additional financing comes in the form of lending, but they could respond in a similar way to additional transfers, as they may also generate appreciation pressures. They may be even more reluctant to receive the transfer in the form of subsidized imports if the imports of goods and services compete with domestic production. The major implication of this is that priority should be given to financing programs that generate strong synergies with domestic efforts. Perhaps the most important are global financial efforts that facilitate the free or low-cost access to technology: global financial technology funds that create knowledge that is freely available, public sector purchase of relevant technology to also make it freely available, technical assistance in building technological capabilities, and human capital formation.

The second macroeconomic issue relates to the features of domestic versus external financing, particularly the fact than in most countries domestic financing has a short-term bias, so that it may not be adequate to finance the long-term needs associated with the green economy. One possible way would be to use the capitalization of multilateral development banks to expand considerably their bond issuance and lending in the domestic currencies of developing countries, and to support domestic financial development in these countries, particularly the efforts of domestic development banks to extend the maturities of available domestic financing.

This is not the place to analyze in detail sectorial priorities, but the foregoing analysis provides some clues. Priority should be given to investments with "double" or "triple dividends" in terms of poverty alleviation in the poorest countries of the world, including access to basic services. Global disaster relief and associated insurance facilities should also be in the agenda. Given again their limited costs and large benefits in terms of both biodiversity and climate mitigation, natural forest protection should be on the agenda, possibly through payment of their associated environmental services. To these we should add two areas that could have large positive impacts on developing countries, given their resource endowments: research into tropical agriculture (a large under-researched area) and environmentally friendly exploitation of coal reserves, particularly carbon storage and sequestration.

Policy Conclusions

The analysis of the macro- and mesoeconomics of the green economy involves four different issues. The first one relates to the inter-temporal welfare and, particularly, to the social discount rates that should be used in a cost-benefit analysis involving future generations—an issue that is closely linked with ethical debates on intergenerational equity. In this regard, it can be argued that the social discount rates used in this analysis should be below (indeed well below) market rates, and that savings and investment today must be increased to benefit future generations. This is particularly so of actions that may be interpreted as insuring against the asymmetric and nonlinear effects that certain actions can have on the ecosystem, including the rising likelihood of extreme events (catastrophes).

The second issue relates to the effects of green investments on aggregate supply and demand. A strategy of reallocating investment toward the green economy may lead to slower potential economic growth (aggregate supply capacities) for a few years, as renewable natural resources are replenished, but will result in the long run in faster growth. It also reduces downside risks associated with climate change, energy shocks, water scarcity, and loss of ecosystem services, increases employment and has direct benefits in terms of poverty reduction (particularly through improvements of agricultural productivity of rural smallholders). Such investments can also help increase aggregate demand in the short run; this demand effect may prevail in the short run over the adverse effects on aggregate supply. In turn, higher investment will induce productivity growth through learning-by-doing and other effects, reinforcing again long-term growth. Demand stimulus must be accompanied by changes in the composition of investment and consumption: certain types of consumption and investment must be restricted to avoid excessive resource depletion and waste, but environmentally friendly investment and consumption can expand.

Third, the transition to the green economy involves no less than a technological revolution and will have deep impacts on production structures, as well as on consumption patterns. Since the production structure must change if growth and development are to proceed, production sector strategies are called for to drive the transformation of the system toward new dynamic green activities. In developing countries, this requires an investment-led strategy with two essential elements: public investment and active production sector (industrial) policies, aiming to encourage in both cases a strong private-sector response. The transformation can also generate losers, which implies the need to put in place appropriate support for those natural-resource intensive developing countries that may have to experience a significant transformation of their production structures.

Finally, the analysis of financial flows required to support developing countries' green economies involves a cluster of issues. UNEP estimates indicate that the scale of financing required at the global level should be at least 2 percent of world GDP ($1.3 trillion at current prices). In turn, existing international commitments state that at least $100 billion dollars should be contributed to a proposed green climate fund. Priority in the allocation among developing countries should obviously be given to the poorest countries and to those more likely to be affected by climate change (which may be the same countries). However, a strong case can also be made for transfer-like resources for middle-income countries to help them contribute to the provision of global public environmental goods. In the allocation of funds across different economic agents in recipient countries, priority should be given to public sector infrastructure investments that are critical to the transition to the green economy. Households should also be a major target of financing, particularly to support energy-efficient housing, including subsidies that could be financed with a tax on energy use.

In macroeconomic terms, given the reluctance of several developing countries to run current-account deficits, priority should be given to financing programs that generate strong synergies with domestic efforts and avoid rising costs associated with green growth. This includes, as pointed out below, free or low-cost access to technology. In addition, the global financing strategy should help improve the availability and term structure of domestic financing available for green economic activities in developing countries. Actions of multilateral development banks in support of domestic development banks can be critical in this regard.

A common theme of both the analysis of structural transformations and financing is the central role of technology. It is essential in this regard to guarantee the adequate participation of developing countries in the generation of the new technologies. However, since most developing countries will be technology followers, there is a need to accelerate the transfer of those technologies to these countries through open innovation systems, publicly financed innovations, as well as global demonstration programs, knowledge-sharing platforms, and a global database on freely available technologies and best practices in licensing. The technological regime should also include reforms of the global regime of intellectual property regime, including broader room for compulsory licensing, strengthening patenting standards, and allowing innovators to use existing patented knowledge to generate new innovations. On the financing side, this calls for a global technology fund to support the creation of knowledge that would be disseminated as a public good, public sector purchases of relevant technology to make it freely available, technical assistance in building technology efforts, and human capital formation.

Notes

* This is a revised version of a paper written for the UN Department of Economic and Social Affairs (UNDESA), the United Nations Environmental Programme (UNEP), and the United Nations Conference on Trade and Development (UNCTAD) as part of the preparations for the United Nations Conference on Sustainable Development (Rio+20). The author is professor of the School of International and Public Affairs and fellow of the Committee on Global Thought at Columbia University, and formerly undersecretary general of the United Nations for Economic and Social Affairs, executive secretary of the Economic Commission for Latin America and the Caribbean, and minister of finance of Colombia. I am grateful to Sir Nicholas Stern and David O'Connor for many useful comments, and to Nicole Ngo for her support in the background research.

1. See also OECD (2010) and, for the origins of the term Pearce et al. (1989).
2. Annex 1 countries are industrialized countries and transition economies.
3. Estimated from data from IEA (2010:45). Out of the total, China represents about half of the emissions from developing countries in 2008 and slightly over half of the increase in 1973–2008.
4. See, for example, the debate on global warming in the 1990s between Cline (1992) and Nordhaus (1994).
5. Formally, maximization of inter-temporal welfare using this model leads to a discount rate that is expressed as $r = \delta + \eta\pi$, where δ is the intergenerational rate of time preference, η is the inverse of the elasticity of substitution between consumption in different time periods, and π is productivity growth, which determines the evolution of per capita consumption through time. The effects of δ and π in this equation are easy to understand, but that of η is more difficult. A higher η (a lower elasticity of substitution between consumption in different time periods) implies that people are less willing to accept variations in their consumption through time, which in intergenerational terms means that the current generation is less willing to sacrifice their consumption today to increase the consumption of future generations. A major implication of the model is that the higher the time preference and the lower the elasticity of substitution, the lower the savings rate should be.

6. Formally $\delta = 0$ and $\eta = 1$, so that $r = \delta + \eta\pi = \pi$.

7. Indeed, an interesting implication of $\delta = 0$ and $\eta = 1$ is that all capital income should be saved (or that aggregate savings should be equivalent to capital income). This is, in fact, consistent with the "golden rule" in a Solow-Swan growth model—that is, that which maximizes per capita consumption through time. In a macroeconomic model in the tradition of Michal Kalecki or Nicholas Kaldor, among others, if all savings come out of profits, this is also consistent with profits being entirely saved.

8. The "calibration" of parameters used in simulations can have this effect. So, for example, Nordhaus (2007) assumes $\delta = 0$ but then calibrates the model according to market parameters and obtains $\eta = 3$, which implies a very low willingness by current generations to substitute their current consumption with that of future generations.

9. See again Baer et al. (2008). Please notice that their proposal refers to persons, but of course the proportion of poor persons is much larger in poor countries. They define a "development threshold" (poverty line) of $20 per day ($7,500 year), which encompasses 70 percent of the world's people, but who only account for about 15 percent of emissions.

10. This tradition is associated with the pioneering contributions of Michal Kalecki, Nicholas Kaldor, and Joan Robinson, among others. See, for example, Kaldor (1978:Chapters 1, 2, and 4).

11. We will concentrate here on the broader calculations of green investments by UNEP (2011b) and the estimates on climate change mitigation by Stern (2009), McKinsey (Enkvist et al. 2010), and the summary of different projections made by United Nations (2009:Chapter VI). Alternative estimates are available from UNDP (2008:Chapter 3) and World Bank (2009).

12. The magnitudes have been translated to proportions of world GDP in 2030 on the basis of world economic growth of around 3 percent per year.

13. UNEP uses as a reference estimates by Hutton and Bartram of $18 billion to meet the Millennium Development Goals (MDG) target of halving the number of people without access to water and sanitation by 2015 and a $50 billion cost estimate by McKinsey of meeting the world's water needs.

14. They include a share in carbon taxes raised in developed countries for transfers to developing countries; carbon pricing of international aviation and shipping; redeployment of fossil fuel subsidies; some form of financial transaction tax; additional capital for multilateral development banks that generates a grant equivalent through its financing; direct budget contributions; and net transfers associated with a reduced return (by 2%) of private capital flows.

15. This point comes from the well-known macroeconomic identity according to which a transfer of resources that allows investment to exceed domestic savings requires that there should be a current-account deficit (imports larger than exports).

References

Baer, Paul, Tom Athanasiou, Sivan Kartha, and Eric Kemp-Benedict. 2008. *The Greenhouse Development Rights Framework: The Right to Development in a Climate Constrained World*, revised 2nd edition. Berlin: Heinrich Böll Foundation, Christian Aid, EcoEquity and Stockholm Environmental Institute.

Barbier, Edward B. 2010. *A Global New Deal: Rethinking the Economic Recovery.* Cambridge: Cambridge University Press and UNEP.

Barton, John H. 2007. *Intellectual Property and Access to Clean Energy Technologies in Developing Countries: An Analysis of Solar Photovoltaic, Biofuel and Wind Technologies.* ICTSD Trade and Sustainable Energy Series Issue Paper No. 2, December. Geneva: International Centre for Trade and Sustainable Development.

Cambridge Econometrics and Sustainable Europe Research Institute. 2010. *A Scoping Study of the Macroeconomic View of Sustainability.* Final Report for the European Commission, DG Environment, July 29.

Cline, William R. 1992. *The Economics of Global Warming.* Washington, DC: Institute for International Economics.

Copenhagen Economics and the IPR Company. 2009. *Are IPR a Barrier to the Transfer of Climate Change Technology?* Copenhagen: Copenhagen Economics, January 19.

Dervis, Kemal. 2008. *The Climate Change Challenge: WIDER Annual Lecture 11.* Helsinki: United Nations University World Institute for Development Economics Research.

Enkvist, Per-Anders, Jens Dinkel, and Charles Lin. 2010. *Impact of the Financial Crisis on Carbon Economics: Version 2.1 of the Global Greenhouse Abatement Cost Curve.* McKinsey and Company.

Enkvist, Per-Anders, Tomas Nauclér, and Jerker Rosander. 2007. "A Cost Curve for Greenhouse Gas Reduction." *The McKinsey Quarterly* 1:35–45.

Harris, Jonathan. 2009. "Ecological Macroeconomics: Consumption, Investment and Climate Change." *Real-World Economics Review* 50:34–48.

Henry, Claude and Joseph E. Stiglitz. 2010. "Intellectual Property, Dissemination of Innovation and Sustainable Development." *Global Policy* 1(3):237–251.

Intergovernmental Panel on Climate Change (IPCC). 2008. *Climate Change 2007: Mitigation of Climate Change.* Cambridge: Cambridge University Press.

International Energy Agency (IEA). 2006. *World Energy Outlook 2006—The Alternative Policy Scenario.* Paris: IEA.

———. 2010. *Key World Energy Statistics 2010.* Paris: IEA.

Kaldor, Nicholas. 1978. *Further Essays on Economic Theory.* London: Duckworth.

Khor, Martin. 2011. "Challenges of the Green Economy Concept and Policies in the Context of Sustainable Development, Poverty and Equity." In *The Transition to a Green Economy: Benefits and Challenges from a Sustainable Development Perspective, Report of a Panel of Experts.* United Nations Department of Economic and Social Affairs (UNDESA), United Nations Environment Programme (UNEP), and UN Conference on Trade and Development (UNCTAD) (eds.). New York: United Nations.

Lee, Bernice, Ilian Iliev, and Felix Preston. 2009. *Who Owns Our Low Carbon Future? Intellectual Property and Energy Technologies.* London: Chatam House.

Nordhaus, William D. 1994. *Managing the Global Commons: The Economics of Climate Change.* Cambridge: MIT Press.

———. 2007. "A Review of the 'Stern Review' on the Economics of Climate Change." *Journal of Economic Literature* 45(3):686–702.

Ocampo, José Antonio. 2005. "The Quest for Dynamic Efficiency: Structural Dynamics and Economic Growth in Developing Countries." In *Beyond Reforms: Structural Dynamics and Macroeconomic Vulnerability.* José Antonio Ocampo (ed.). Palo Alto: Stanford University Press, ECLAC and World Bank, Chapter 1.

Ocampo, José Antonio, Codrina Rada, and Lance Taylor. 2009. *Growth and Policy in Developing Countries: A Structuralist Approach.* New York: Columbia University Press.

Organization for Economic Cooperation and Development (OECD). 2010. *Interim Report of the Green Growth Strategy: Implementing Our Commitment for a Sustainable Future: Meeting of the OECD Council at Ministerial Level,* May 27–28. Paris: OECD.

Pearce, David, Anil Markandya, and Edward B. Barbier. 1989. *Blueprint for a Green Economy.* London: Earthscan.

Schumpeter, Joseph. 1962. *Capitalism, Socialism and Democracy,* 3rd edition. New York: Harper Torchbooks.

Stern, Nicholas. 2007. *The Economics of Climate Change: The Stern Review.* Cambridge: Cambridge University Press.

———. 2009. *The Global Deal: Climate Change and the Creation of a New Era of Progress and Prosperity.* New York: PublicAffairs.

The Economics of Ecosystems and Biodiversity (TEEB). 2010a. *Mainstreaming the Economics of Nature: A Synthesis of the Approach, Conclusions and Recommendations of TEEB.* New York: UNEP.

———. 2010b. *The Economics of Ecosystem and Biodiversity: Ecological and Economic Foundations.* London: Earthscan.

United Nations. 2009. *World Economic and Social Survey 2009: Promoting Development, Saving the Planet.* New York: United Nations.

———. 2010. Report of the Secretary-General's High-Level Advisory Group on Climate Change Financing. November 5.

United Nations Development Program (UNDP). 2008. *Human Development Report 2007/8: Fighting Climate Change.* New York: UNDP.

United Nations Environment Program (UNEP). 2011a. *Towards a Green Economy: Pathways to Sustainable Development and Poverty Eradication. A Synthesis for Policy Makers.* New York: United Nations.

———. 2011b. *Towards a Green Economy: Pathways to Sustainable Development and Poverty Eradication.* New York: United Nations.

United Nations Framework Convention on Climate Change (UNFCCC). 2008. Investments and Financial Flows to Address Climate Change: An Update, Technical Paper. FCCC/TP/2008/7, November 26.

Weitzman, Martin L. 2007. "A Review of the 'Stern Review' on the Economics of Climate Change." *Journal of Economic Literature* 45(3):703–724.

———. 2010. GHG Targets as Insurance against Catastrophic Climate Damage. Working paper available at: www.economics.harvard.edu/faculty/weitzman/papers_weitzman.

World Bank. 2006. *Where Is the Wealth of Nations? Measuring Capital for the 21st Century.* Washington, DC: World Bank.

———. 2009. *World Development Report 2010: Development and Climate Change.* Washington, DC: World Bank.

World Commission on Environment and Development (Brundtland Commission). 1987. *Our Common Future.* Oxford: Oxford University Press.

CHAPTER 9

Environmental Sustainability and Poverty Eradication in Developing Countries

*Edward Barbier**

INTRODUCTION

Land use change in developing countries is critically bound up with their pattern of economic development. Most of these economies, and certainly the majority of the populations living within them, depend directly on natural resources. Primary product exports account for the vast majority of the export earnings of many developing economies, and one or two primary commodities make up the bulk of exports (Barbier 2005:Chapter 1). Agricultural value added accounts for an average of 40 percent of GDP, and nearly 80 percent of the labor force is engaged in agricultural or resource-based activities (World Bank 2008). Further adding to these disparities, by 2025, the rural population of the developing world will have increased to almost 3.2 billion, placing increasing pressure on a declining resource base (United Nations Population Division 2008).

In developing economies, cropland area has continued to expand at the expense of forest and woodland (Barbier 2011, FAO 2006, Fischer and Heilig 1997, Ramankutty and Foley 1999). In the developing regions of Africa, Asia, and Latin America, tropical forests were the primary sources of new agricultural land in the 1980s and the 1990s (Gibbs et al. 2010). Almost one-fifth of new-crop production in developing countries from 1990 to 2050 is expected to rely on expanding cultivated area, and two-thirds of this new land will come from conversion of forests and wetlands (Fischer and Heilig 1997). In some regions, such as tropical Latin America, livestock grazing is also projected to cause extensive deforestation in the near future (Wassenaar et al. 2007). Although historically such land use changes may have been associated with successful resource-based development, this is less likely for most developing countries today (Barbier 2011). The main reason is that the current process of land use and expansion has two unique structural features.

First, considerable land expansion in ecologically fragile areas is serving mainly as an outlet for the subsistence and near-subsistence needs of the rural poor (Barbier 2005, 2010). A substantial proportion of the population in low- and middle-income countries is concentrated in marginal areas and on ecologically fragile land, such as converted forest frontier areas, poor quality uplands, converted wetlands, and so forth (Molden 2007, World Bank 2003). Households on these lands not only face problems of land degradation and low productivity but also tend to be some of the poorest in the world. Yet, population increase and other economic pressures are driving many of the rural poor to bring yet more marginal land into production (Chen and Ravallion 2007, United Nations Population Division 2008). The result is that such marginal land expansion continues to be the main basis for absorbing the growing number of the rural poor in developing economies (Barbier 2011, Carr 2009, Coxhead et al. 2002, Pichón 1997).

Second, marginal land expansion may be an important outlet for the rural poor, but it may not be the main cause of overall land use change in developing countries. Recent evidence suggests that the main agents of tropical deforestation globally are commercially oriented economic activities, such as plantation owners, large-scale farmers, ranchers, timber concerns, and mining operations, assisted by government policies (Boucher et al. 2011, Chomitz et al. 2007, DeFries et al. 2010, FAO 2001, 2003, 2006, Rudel 2007). These activities rely on large-scale capital investments that often result in export-oriented extractive enclaves with little or no forward and backward linkages to the rest of the economy (Barbier 2005, 2011, Bridge 2008, van der Ploeg 2011). Such development promotes substantial resource conversion, especially the expansion of the agricultural land base through the conversion of forests, wetlands, and other natural habitat, while simultaneously ensuring that developing economies remain highly dependent on the exploitation of natural resources and are unable to diversify.

The purpose of this paper is, first, to explain the economic and poverty implications of these two structural features of resource-based development in low- and middle-income economies, and, second, to suggest policies to change this inimical pattern of development. The interconnection between natural resources and economic development provides an opportunity to design better development policies for poverty eradication. Overcoming the linkages between resource-based development and poverty in poor economies will also require new mechanisms of funding the necessary financial and technical support to help instigate such change.

Resource-Based Development and Poverty in Poor Economies

Since 1950, the estimated population in developing economies on "fragile lands" has doubled (World Bank 2003). These fragile environments are prone to land degradation, and consist of upland areas, forest systems, and drylands that suffer from low agricultural productivity, and areas that present significant constraints for intensive agriculture. Today, nearly 1.3 billion people—almost a fifth of the world's population—live in such areas in developing regions (Barbier 2011:Table 9.10). Almost half of the people in these fragile environments (631 million) consist of the rural poor, who throughout the developing world outnumber the poor living on favored lands by two to one (Molden 2007:Table 15.1).

Figure 9.1 illustrates that rural poverty is correlated with the fraction of the population in developing countries found on fragile lands. As the figure indicates, for a sample of 92 low- and middle-income economies, the incidence of rural poverty rises with the share of the total population concentrated on marginal lands. Although the average poverty rate across all economies is 45.3 percent, the rate falls to 36.4 percent for those countries with less than 20 percent of their population in fragile environments. For those with more than 50 percent of their populations in marginal areas, however, the incidence of rural poverty rises to 50 percent or more.

The tendency for the rural poor to be clustered in the most marginal environments is also supported by studies at the regional and country level, although important differences exist within and between countries. For example, researchers from the World Bank have examined the "poverty-environment nexus" in three of the poorest countries in Southeast Asia—Cambodia, Laos, and Vietnam (Dasgupta et al. 2005, Minot and

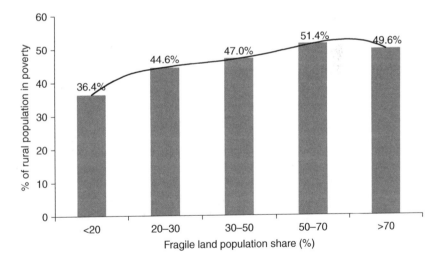

Figure 9.1 The rural poor and population on fragile lands in developing economies.

Notes: Developing economies are all low- and middle-income economies with 2009 per capita income of $12,195 or less, following World Bank (2012).

Percentage of rural population in poverty is from World Bank (2012).

Percentage of population on fragile land is from World Bank (2003).

Number of observations = 92 countries, of which 13 (<20% of population on fragile land), 32 (20–30%), 33 (30–50%), 9 (50–70%), and 5 (> 70%). The average rural poverty rate across all countries is 45.3 percent, and the median is 46.6 percent.

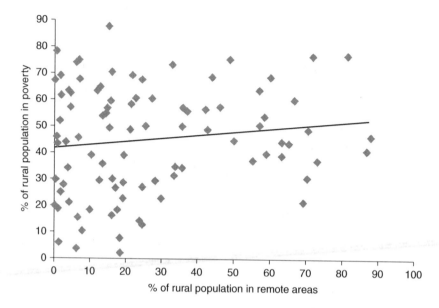

Figure 9.2 The rural poor and population in remote areas of developing economies.

Notes: Developing economies are all low- and middle-income economies with 2009 per capita income of $12,195 or less, following World Bank (2012).

Remote areas are locations with poor market access, requiring five or more hours to reach a market town of 5,000 or more.

Percentage of rural population in poverty is from World Bank (2012).

Percentage of rural population in remote areas is from World Bank (2008).

Number of observations = 91 countries. Average (median) share of rural population in remote areas is 26.9 percent (19.0%). Average (median) share of rural population in poverty is 45.2 percent (46.5%). Correlation coefficient *r* = 0.15.

Baulch 2002). In Cambodia, the core poor in rural areas appear to be located in areas that are already heavily deforested; on the other hand, poor populations tend to be more concentrated in the lowlands rather than steeply sloped lands. In Laos, the poorest provinces in the north and northeast also have the highest incidence of poor rural populations. These individuals are located mainly in forested areas and the highlands. In Vietnam, large poor populations confined to steep slopes exist in the provinces comprising the Northern and Central Highlands, but extensive rural poverty is also found along the North Central Coast and the Red River Delta.

The rural poor of developing economies also tend to be concentrated in remote areas, locations with poor market access and that require five or more hours to reach a market town of 5,000 or more (see figure 9.2). Around 430 million people in developing countries live in such distant rural areas, and nearly half (49%) of these populations are located in less favored areas, which are arid and semiarid regions characterized by frequent moisture stress that limits agricultural production (World Bank 2008). As indicated in figure 9.2, developing countries that have a larger share of their rural population located in remote rural areas also display higher rural poverty rates. Across 91 developing countries, the average (median) share of rural population in remote areas is 26.9 percent (19.0%), whereas the average (median) share of rural population in poverty is 45.2 percent (46.5%).

Developing economies with high concentrations of their populations on fragile lands and in remote areas not only display high rates of rural poverty but also are some of the poorest countries in the world today. The relationship between GDP per capita, rural poverty, and the share of populations concentrated in fragile and remote areas is summarized in table 9.1. The table includes 89 developing economies that have, on average, at least 20 percent of their population located on fragile lands and 30 percent of their rural population in remote areas. Across all economies, the average real GDP per capita is $1,613 and the rural poverty rate is 47.3 percent. In addition, several important trends emerge from the table. First, more than half (48) of the countries are low-income economies with real GDP per capita of less than $1,000. Second, none of the economies with a GDP per capita greater than $4,000 have more than 50 percent of their population located in fragile areas. Finally, the table confirms that lower-income economies generally have more of their populations concentrated in fragile and remote rural areas and higher rural poverty rates.

The rural poor will continue to be clustered on marginal lands, fragile environments, and remote areas, given current global rural population and poverty trends. First, despite rapid global urbanization, the rural population of developing regions continues to grow, albeit at a slower rate in recent years. From 1950 to 1975, annual rural population growth in these regions was 1.8 percent, and from 1975 to 2007 it was just over 1.0 percent (United Nations Population Division 2008). Second, around three-quarters of the developing world's poor still live in rural areas, even allowing for the higher cost of living facing the poor in urban areas. In general, about twice as many poor people live in rural than in urban areas in the developing world (Chen and Ravallion 2007).[1]

Developing economies that are extremely resource dependent, that is, where primary exports account for a large share of total merchandise exports, also have more of their population living in "fragile" environments (see figure 9.3). Developing countries with around 60 percent of their exports from primary products typically have around 20–30 percent of their populations in marginal areas. But as resource dependency rises further, countries have more of their people concentrated in fragile environments, reaching 70 percent or more for those low- and middle-income countries with a primary products' share of 79 percent. Resource-dependent developing economies also have a higher share of their rural populations living in remote areas (see figure 9.4). This trend is especially notable for economies once the primary products' share in total exports exceeds 60 percent. At over 65 percent of primary product share, developing countries have 15 to 30 percent of their

Table 9.1 Population in fragile and remote areas, rural poverty, and GDP per capita

	Share of population on fragile land > 50% (in %)	Share of population on fragile land 30–50% (in %)	Share of population on fragile land 20–30% (in %)
GDP per capita less than $1,000 (Avg. $409)	Afghanistan (55, 38) Burkina Faso (1, 52) Congo Dem. Rep. (49, 76) Eritrea (60, 69) Mali (4, 58) Niger (4, 64) Papua New Guinea (87, 68) Somalia (64, NA) Sudan (42, NA) Yemen (59, 40) Zimbabwe (65, 44)	Benin (6, 46) Cameroon (14, 55) Central African Rep. (22, 69) Chad (21, 59) Comoros (NA, 49) Ethiopia (63, 39) Gambia (0, 68) Guinea (4, 63) Haiti (15, 88) Kenya (21, 49) Kyrgyz Rep. (57, 51) Lao PDR (33, 32) Lesotho (67, 61) Mauritania (23, 61) Nepal (36, 35) Nigeria (12, 64) Pakistan (17, 49) Rwanda (57, 64) Senegal (2, 62) Sierra Leone (0.4, 79) Tajikistan (43, 49) Tanzania (73, 37) Uganda (25, 27) Uzbekistan (13, 30)	Burundi (44, 69) Cambodia (4, 35) Côte d'Ivoire (13, 54) Ghana (10, 39) Guinea-Bissau (2, 69) India (2, 28) Liberia (24, 68) Madagascar (33, 74) Mongolia (88, 47) Mozambique (42, 57) Togo (6, 74) Vietnam (10, 19) Zambia (72, 79)
GDP per capita $1,000–$4,000 (Avg. $2,066)	Bhutan (70, 31) Cape Verde (NA, 44) Egypt (0.2, 30) Namibia (71, 49) Niger (66.0) Swaziland (7, 75)	Algeria (16, 30) Angola (85, NA) Belize (3, 44) Guatemala (16, 71) Guyana (34, 35) Iran (60, NA) Morocco (24, 15) Solomon Islands (NA, NA) South Africa (30, 23) Syria (6, NA) Tunisia (6, 4) Turkmenistan (61, NA) Vanuatu (NA, NA)	Azerbaijan (18, 19) Bolivia (81, 77) China (18, 3) Congo (46, 58) Ecuador (36, 56) El Salvador (0.5, 47) Honduras (13, 65) Indonesia (16, 17) Jamaica (2, 25) Jordan (1, 19) Kazakhstan (69, 22) Peru (58, 64) Sri Lanka (6, 16)

Continued

Table 9.1   Continued

	Share of population on fragile land > 50% (in %)	Share of population on fragile land 30–50% (in %)	Share of population on fragile land 20–30% (in %)
GDP per capita over $4,000 (Avg. $5,992)		Botswana (50, 45) Costa Rica (19, 23) Equatorial Guinea (20, NA) Grenada (NA, NA) St. Vincent & Gren. (NA, NA)	Dominican Rep. (15, 57) Malaysia (18, 8) Mexico (27, 61) Panama (16, 35) Trinidad & Tob. (0, 20)

Notes: GDP per capita ($2,000) is from World Bank (2012). Share of population on fragile land is from World Bank (2003). First figure in parenthesis is the percentage share of rural population in remote areas, from World Bank (2008). Second figure in parenthesis is the percentage of the rural population in poverty, from World Bank (2012). Total countries = 89, of which 48 with GDP per capita less than $1,000 (average share of rural population in remote areas = 31.1%, average rural poverty rate = 54.4%), 31 with GDP per capita between $1,000 and $4,000 (30.4%, and 37.5%), and 10 with GDP per capita greater than $4,000 (20.7%, 35.5%). Across all 89 countries, average GDP per capita is $1,613, average share of rural population in remote areas is 29.9 percent, and average rural poverty rate is 47.3 percent.

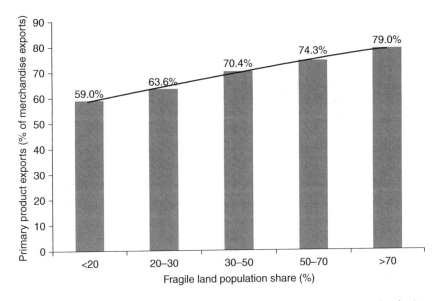

Figure 9.3   Resource dependency and population on fragile lands in developing economies.

Notes: Primary product export share is the percentage of agricultural raw material, food, fuel, ore, and metal commodities to total merchandise exports, latest year (average = 67.9%, median = 77.5%), from World Bank (2012).

Share of population on fragile land is from World Bank (2003). Fragile land is defined in World Bank (2003:59) as "areas that present significant constraints for intensive agriculture and where the people's links to the land are critical for the sustainability of communities, pastures, forests, and other natural resources."

Number of observations = 101, of which 5 (> 70%), 11 (50–70%), 40 (30–50%), 31 (20–30%), and 13 (< 20%).

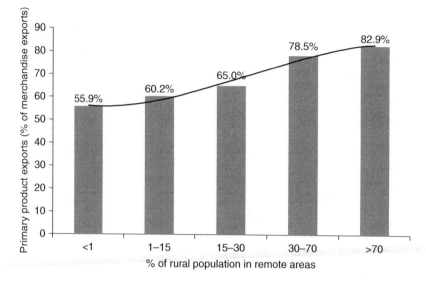

Figure 9.4 Resource dependency and population in remote areas of developing economies.

Notes: Primary product export share is the percentage of agricultural raw material, food, fuel, ore, and metal commodities to total merchandise exports, latest year (average = 67.8%, median = 78.6%), from World Bank (2012).

Remote areas are locations with poor market access, requiring five or more hours to reach a market town of 5,000 or more, from World Bank (2008).

Number of observations = 103, of which 8 (> 70%), 28 (30–70%), 26 (15–30%), 33 (1–15%), and 8 (< 1%).

populations located five or more hours from a market town of 5,000 or more. Economies with over 75 percent of primary product share have 30 to 70 percent of the rural population in remote areas, and countries with over 80 percent of resource-dependent exports have more than 70 percent of their rural population living in regions with poor market access.

Toward a New Resource-Based Development and Poverty Eradication Strategy

To summarize, a distinct pattern of natural resource use and rural poverty has emerged in developing economies since 1950. Many low- and middle-income economies display both a high degree of resource dependency that coincides with the concentration of a large segment of the population in fragile environments and in remote areas with poor market access, and rural poverty. Moreover, there appears to be a correlation of this pattern of resource use with poor economic performance: those developing countries that are highly resource dependent and whose populations are concentrated in fragile environments and remote areas tend not only to have a high incidence of rural poverty but also are some of the poorest economies in the world.

To eradicate such persistent problems of rural poverty in developing economies will require a structural transformation of resource-based development in many low- and middle-income countries. Such a change in development strategy will require two key policy elements.

First, natural resource management must become the central focus of sustainable economic development. New policies must be developed to target the main primary production activities of an economy to improve their competitiveness, attain their export potential, limit resource overexploitation and waste, and generate increase returns and revenues. The financial returns and funds generated from primary production activities must in turn be reinvested in the industrial activities, infrastructure, health services, education, and skills necessary for long-term economic development.

However, designing and implementing policies for more efficient and sustainable resource-based development is necessary but not sufficient. In addition, specific policies need to be targeted at the poor where they live, especially the rural poor clustered in fragile and remote areas. This will require direct financing, such as through involving the poor in payment for ecosystem services (PES) schemes and other measures that enhance the environments on which the poor depend, targeting investments directly to improving the livelihoods of the rural poor, thus reducing their dependence on exploiting environmental resources, and tackling the lack of access of the rural poor in less favored areas to well-functioning and affordable markets for credit, insurance and land, and the high transportation and transaction costs that prohibit the poorest households in remote areas to engage in off-farm employment.

Policies for More Efficient and Sustainable Resource-Based Development

Since 1950, few low- and middle-income economies with abundant endowments of land, mineral, and fossil fuel resources have achieved successful resource-based development (Barbier 2005, 2011, van der Ploeg 2011). For example, Gylfason (2001) has examined the long-run growth performance of 85 resource-rich developing economies since 1965. Only Botswana, Malaysia, and Thailand managed to achieve a long-term investment rate exceeding 25 percent of GDP and long-run average annual growth rates exceeding 4 percent, which is a performance comparable to that of high-income economies. Malaysia and Thailand have also managed successfully to diversify their economies through reinvesting the financial gains from primary production for export. Botswana has yet to diversify its economy significantly but has developed favorable institutions and policies for managing its natural wealth and primary production for extensive economy-wide benefits.

In addition, there are signs that four large emerging-market economies, Brazil, China, India, and Russia—the "BRIC" economies—, are beginning to reap economy-wide benefits from exploiting their vast sources of land and natural resources, as well as through instigating economic reforms and growth-promoting policies. But these economies are unusual compared to most developing countries because of the sheer scale of their populations, economies, and resource endowments. Although the economic growth performance of the BRIC countries over the past two decades has been impressive, it is unclear how much of this recent economic development is the result of successful and sustainable management of their large natural resource endowments, or simply due to the having such large endowments to command for economic development (Barbier 2011). All four countries have expanded the production and consumption of their strategically important mineral endowments as their economies have grown. Russia and China have also made extensive use of their domestic fossil fuel resources to promote energy-intensive industrialization. Brazil has engaged in extensive frontier agricultural land expansion, and, along with China and India, has harnessed its freshwater resources for agricultural, industrial, and hydro-electric uses. Overall, it appears that the successful resource-based development of the BRIC economies has more in common with the type of development pursued by the resource abundant and populous United States during its long phase of economic boom from the late nineteenth century onwards than with the typically smaller resource-rich developing economies (Barbier 2011).

In sum, although there have been few examples of a successful resource-based development strategy for many developing economies perhaps as a guide to such a strategy, policy makers should look to the three successful, resource-rich small open economies identified by Gylfason (2001)—Botswana, Malaysia, and Thailand. Although these countries still face problems in managing their natural resources and overcoming dualism and poverty, several lessons for improving the sustainability of other small resource-dependent developing economies can still be learned from these three country examples.[2]

First, the type of natural resource endowment and primary production activities is not necessarily an obstacle to implementing a successful strategy. Botswana's economy is largely dependent on minerals, Thailand started out as almost exclusively an agricultural-based food exporter, and Malaysia built its success first on mineral and timber reserves, then plantation tree crops, and finally, by developing a highly diversified economy. All three countries are testament to the fact that neither the abundance of natural resources nor the type of resources exploited for primary production are inherently a "curse" or a "blessing" on economic development (Barbier 2005, 2011, Gylfason 2001, Sarraf and Jiwanji 2001, van der Ploeg 2011). It is the institutions and policies of an economy that determines whether or not resource-based development will be successful in the long run. Or, as Sarraf and Jiwanji (2001:3) have argued, "The natural resource curse is not necessarily the fate of resource abundant countries...sound economic policies and good management of windfall gains can lead to sustained economic growth."

Second, because resource endowments, primary production activities, and the historical, cultural, economic, and geographic circumstances of each country are different, the type of successful development strategy adopted will also vary for different economies. For example, Thailand and Malaysia initially embarked on similar strategies to encourage sustainable primary production and resource use, but the primacy of agriculture in Thailand plus differing economic and social conditions meant that its diversification strategy eventually diverged from that of Malaysia.

Third, the development strategy has to be comprehensive. The success of Malaysia and Thailand in diversifying their economies, and Botswana in sustaining growth, suggests that reliance on primary product exports is not necessarily an obstacle to development. But it must be accompanied by specific policies to improve the competitiveness and export potential of the main primary production activities of the economy, while limiting resource overexploitation and waste. In addition, the resulting increased returns and revenues generated from primary production activities must be reinvested in the industrial activities, infrastructure, health services, and the education and skills necessary for long-term economic development.

Finally, no strategy is perfect. In all three economies, important sectors and populations have yet to gain significantly from improving the sustainability of the main primary producing sectors. In Malaysia, there is concern about the continuing destruction of forests, especially in the more remote Sabah and Sarawak Provinces, and the expansion of oil palm plantations. In Thailand, the loss of mangroves, growing pollution problems, and the failure to instigate development in upland regions are major issues. Botswana has still to grapple with a stagnant agricultural sector, large numbers of people living in fragile environments, and widespread rural poverty. Finding ways to broaden the economy-wide benefits and improve the sustainability of resource-dependent economies is an ongoing challenge for such small open economies.

Policies for Targeting Poverty Alleviation in Less Favored and Remote Areas

However, encouraging more efficient and sustainable resource-based development in developing economies may not on its own eliminate the persistent problem of widespread rural poverty. Specific policies need to be targeted at the poor where they live, especially the rural poor clustered in fragile environments and remote areas. Even developing economies that have pursued successful resource-based development, such as Botswana, Malaysia, and Thailand, are still grappling with these structural poverty problems. For example, as indicated in table 9.1, Botswana has 30 to 50 percent of its population located on fragile land and nearly 60 percent of its rural population living in poverty. Malaysia has 20 to 30 percent of its population in less favored areas and rural poverty rate of around 16 percent. Around 18 percent of Thailand's rural population is located in remote areas, and 14 percent of the rural population lives in poverty (World Bank 2008, 2012).

A targeted strategy for the rural poor in remote and less favored areas will require the following components:

- Provide financing directly, through involving the poor in PES schemes and other measures that enhance the environments on which the poor depend.
- Target investments directly to improving the livelihoods of the rural poor, thus reducing their dependence on exploiting environmental resources.
- Improve access of the rural poor in less favored and remote areas to well-functioning and affordable markets for credit, insurance, and land .
- Reduce the high transportation and transaction costs that prohibit the poorest households in remote areas to engage in off-farm employment.
- Provide effective institutions and governance in support of poor communities use of common-pool resources.

If policies are to be targeted to improve both rural livelihoods and protect the fragile environments on which many poor people depend, such a strategy must take into account many important factors influencing households' behavior, including lack of income opportunities or access to key markets for land, labor and credit, and the availability and quality of natural resources, including land, to exploit (Barbier 2010). Nevertheless, there are several ways in which a strategy could be developed to target improving the livelihoods of the poor.

The first is to provide financing directly, through involving the poor in PES schemes and other measures that enhance the environments on which the poor depend.[3] Payments for the conservation of standing forests or wildlife habitat are the most frequent type of compensation programs used currently in developing countries, and they have been mainly aimed at paying landowners for the opportunity costs of preserving natural landscapes that provide one or more diverse services: carbon sequestration, watershed protection, biodiversity benefits, wildlife protection, and landscape beauty (Grieg-Gran et al. 2005, Pagiola et al. 2005, Wunder 2008). Wherever possible, the payment schemes should be designed to increase the participation of the poor, to reduce any negative impacts on nonparticipants while creating additional job opportunities for rural workers, and to provide technical assistance, access to inputs, credit and other support to encourage poor smallholders to adopt the desired land use practices. More effort must be devoted to designing projects and programs that include the direct participation of the landless and near landless.

Even in a poor African economy, such as Tanzania, a correctly designed PES program can provide an important source of funding for sustainable land use practices in agriculture while leading to greater watershed protection (Branca et al. 2011). In the upstream catchment area of the Ruvu River, poor farmers face financial and technical obstacles to adopting sustainable land management that reduce soil erosion and enhance downstream water quality. By providing institutional, technical, and financial support to farmers, a PES scheme for watershed protection delivers on these environmental goals while at the same time boosting crop productivity from improved soil conservation and fertility and thus raising farm incomes. The PES scheme is now trying to enhance sustainability by investing in an appropriate legal and institutional framework for long-term financing and expansion of sustainable land management among farmers to improve watershed management.

A second objective is to target investments directly to improving the livelihoods of the rural poor, thus reducing their dependence on exploiting environmental resources. For example, in Ecuador, Madagascar, and Cambodia, poverty maps have been developed to target public investments to geographically defined subgroups of the population according to their relative poverty status, which could substantially improve the performance of the programs in terms of poverty alleviation (Elbers et al. 2007). A World Bank study that examined 122 targeted programs in 48 developing countries confirms their effectiveness in reducing poverty, if they are designed properly (Coady et al. 2004).

Targeting the poor is even more urgent during major economic crises, which occur frequently in developing economies (Ravallion 2008). Underinvestment in human capital and lack of access to financial credit are persistent problems for the extreme poor, especially in fragile environments. Low-income households generate insufficient savings, suffer chronic indebtedness, and rely on informal credit markets with high short-term interest rates. Two types of policies and investment programs targeted to the poor are essential in these circumstances. The first is a comprehensive and targeted safety net that adequately insures the poor in time of crisis. The second is the maintenance, and if possible expansion, of long-term educational and health services targeted at the poor. Unfortunately, during financial and economic crises, publicly funded health and education services are often the first expenditures reduced by developing country governments.

Ultimately, however, it is the lack of access of the rural poor in less favored areas to well-functioning and affordable markets for credit, insurance, and land, and the high transportation and transaction costs that prohibit the poorest households in remote areas to engage in off-farm employment, which are the major long-run obstacles that need to be addressed. Such problems lie at the heart of the poverty-environment trap faced by many poor people in remote and less favored areas (Barbier 2010). For example, Carter and Barrett (2006:195) note that the existence of a poverty trap threshold "depends on the degree to which the household is excluded from inter-temporal exchange through credit, insurance or savings, whether formally or through social networks. A household with perfect access to capital over time and across states of nature would not face a critical threshold." Similarly, Shively and Fisher (2004:1366) maintain that "policies to reduce deforestation should focus on increasing returns to off-farm employment, strengthening rural credit markets, and ensuring farmers have secure tenure over existing agricultural land."

Finally, in many developing countries, the current legal framework and formal institutional structures for resource management do not allow local communities any legal rights to establish and enforce control over the ecosystem goods and services on which the livelihoods of these communities depend.[4] Establishing an improved institutional framework does not necessarily require transferring full ownership of natural resources to local communities, but could involve comanagement by governments and local communities that would allow, for example, for the participation of the communities in decisions concerning the long-term management, development, and utilization of these resources. Without such institutional involvement of local communities, multiple problems can arise from competing interests among stakeholders, undeveloped or inappropriate governance structures, poor science, or lack of political will, which can ultimately undermine well-intentioned efforts to improve poor people's livelihoods (Aswani et al. 2012, Chhatre and Agrawal 2008).

New Financing of Environment and Development Assistance

To provide the necessary financial and technical support for more sustainable resource-based development and eradicating rural poverty, low- and middle-income economies will need new sources of assistance (Barbier 2012). Existing sources of aid are simply inadequate for the task. For example, the cost of funding the UN Millennium Development Goals of reducing global poverty requires additional development assistance of $83 billion annually by 2010, whereas from 2001 to 2008, developing countries received only $37 billion in extra aid for this purpose (Atkinson 2006, UNCTAD 2010).

Table 9.2 outlines actual and potential funding mechanisms for environment and development assistance. Three alternatives have been widely proposed to conventional sources of assistance: environment and development funds; creating global markets for carbon and environmental payments; and revenues from global trade and financial transactions.

Existing environment and development funds have met with limited success. One established fund, the Global Environmental Facility (GEF), started in 1991, has elicited $10 billion from direct donor contributions, supplemented by more than $47 billion in cofinancing from additional supplementary aid from governments, for over 2,900 projects in 165 developing economies.[5] That seems a lot, yet the facility is clearly underfunded: since 1994, its total budget allocation has declined in real terms by 10 percent, while its range of environment and climate projects continues to expand (Clemençon 2006). A newer initiative, the Adaptation Fund, finances adaptation investments in developing countries that are parties to the Kyoto Protocol on climate change. This fund is financed with 2 percent of the Certified Emission Reduction credits issued for projects of the Clean Development Mechanism and from other sources. Currently, the Adaptation

Table 9.2 Financing mechanisms for environment and development assistance

Mechanism	Description	Actual/potential funds
Global Environmental Facility (GEF)	A multi-donor global mechanism to meet the additional costs of developing countries in achieving global environmental benefits from biological diversity, climate change, international waters, ozone layer depletion, reduced land degradation, and abatement of persistent organic pollution.	$57 billion total
Adaptation Fund	A fund financing adaptation projects and programs in developing countries; funded with 2% of the Certified Emission Reduction credits issued for projects of the Clean Development Mechanism and from other sources.	$286 million total
International payment for ecosystem services (IPES)	A global mechanism for raising and distributing funds from beneficiaries of ecosystem services to those who conserve them.	None currently other than REDD+
Reduced emissions from deforestation and forest degradation (REDD+) scheme	A specific IPES aimed at reducing GHG emissions from deforestation and forest degradation in developing countries.	$120 million total
Global carbon cap and auction system	A cap and auction scheme for GHG emissions; funds are raised by auctioning the initial emission permits.	Unknown, depends on auction scheme
Global carbon tax	Taxes applied to carbon-equivalent GHG emissions.	$500 billion/year
International Finance Facility (IFF)	Mobilize financing from international capital markets by issuing long-term bonds repaid by donor countries.	$10 billion/year
Sovereign wealth fund (SWF)	A proportion of a country's foreign exchange reserves set aside for investment purposes.	$40 billion/year
Financial transaction tax (FTT)	Tax applied to the sale of specific financial assets, such as stock, bonds, or futures.	$48 billion/year
Currency transaction tax (CTT or Tobin tax)	Tax applied to currency exchange transactions.	$400 billion/year
Airline travel tax	Tax applied to international airline ticket sales.	Unknown
Aviation or shipping fuel tax	Tax applied to international aviation and shipping fuel use.	$27 billion/year
Arms trade tax	Tax applied to international exports of armaments.	$5 billion/year
Tobacco excise tax	Tax applied to sales of tobacco products, a proportion of which is allocated to global funds.	$11 billion/year

Source: Based on Barbier (2012).

Fund has raised only $286 million; to adapt to climate change, developing countries will need $70 to $100 billion a year in additional assistance from 2010 to 2050.[6]

International payment for ecosystem services (IPES) has emerged as a possible new source of financing environment and development schemes. The only such scheme operating is the nascent mechanism to reduce emissions from deforestation and forest degradation (REDD+). This initiative has the capacity to make a huge difference, although it is costly. A 50 percent decline in global deforestation through REDD+ would reduce global greenhouse gas (GHG) emissions by 1.5 to 2.7 Gt[7] (3 to 6% of total annual emissions), but cost $17.2 to $28 billion per year (Kindermann et al. 2008). Financing REDD+ through carbon markets could earn developing countries $2.2–13.5 billion annually—not nearly enough to match the costs (Ebeling and Yasué 2008). A pilot initiative established by several UN agencies in 2008, UN-REDD, has $120 million in funds—not nearly enough to make up the shortfall.[8] The sums cannot be made to add up, even including bilateral initiatives such as the Amazon Fund ($57.5 million), the Congo Basin Forest Fund ($165 million), and Norway's International Climate and Forest Initiative ($517 million).[9] Negotiations to expand global funding of REDD+ have stalled over concerns with verifying deforestation rates and carbon emissions, losses in timber and agricultural revenues, and corruption, fraud, and governance.

A global cap and auction system for GHG emissions or a global carbon tax could in theory raise substantial funds. Harmonized carbon taxes, which are more efficient and easier to administer globally, could raise $318 to $980 billion annually by 2015 (in 2005 prices) and $527 to $1,763 billion by 2030 (Hyder 2008). But political considerations, especially in the United States, seem to have ruled the option out. The alternative—raising revenues from global trade and financial transactions—is more appealing.

An International Finance Facility (IFF) mobilizes resources from international capital markets by issuing long-term bonds that are repaid by donor countries over 20 to 30 years. By selling the bonds in capital markets, these long-term government pledges are converted into funds for immediate investment. An IFF for Immunization (IFFIm), launched in 2006, has so far raised $3.6 billion through bonds, which it is using for immunization programs and vaccine purchases in 70 developing countries.[10] Unlike other global financing mechanisms, an IFF can be started by a handful of donor countries without the need of an international agreement involving many countries, and can be implemented through existing aid institutions, such as the World Bank. However, the amounts raised through bonds are most likely to be in the tens, rather than hundreds of billions of dollars. This suggests that an IFF is best suited for a specific health or infrastructure investment, such as immunization, clean energy, or improved sanitization.

Alternatively, the United Nations Conference on Trade and Development (UNCTAD 2011) has proposed that developing economies invest 1 percent of their sovereign wealth funds (SWFs) in regional development banks, which could in turn facilitate a wide range of sustainable development initiatives. Such funds are routinely created by countries, when they set aside for investment purposes a proportion of their foreign exchange reserves accumulated from buying and selling goods and services in world markets. About $4.3 trillion in global foreign exchange reserves, including $3.5 trillion in developing countries, are held in such funds. Allocating just 1 percent from G20 countries would raise at least $40 billion annually for global environment and development investments (Gates Foundation 2011).

A financial transaction tax (FTT) is another possible long-term funding source for major sustainability initiatives. An FTT is a tax collected on the sale of specific financial assets, such as stock, bonds, or futures. A very small FTT collected on the sale of financial assets, such as stock, bonds, or futures, would have a negligible impact on liquidity or overall financial transactions, but could raise substantial funds globally. For example, a small tax of 0.10 percent on equities and 0.02 percent on bonds could bring in about $48 billion from G20 member states (Gates Foundation 2011). The European Union proposed an FTT at the G20 summit in Cannes, France, in November 2011. Although favorably received by many G20 countries, the proposal failed to receive full G20 back, due to opposition from the United States, the United Kingdom, and Canada worried about its added burden to their banks.

A variant on the FTT is a currency transaction tax, or Tobin tax, named after the economist James Tobin who first proposed it in the 1970s. This is a tax applied to any foreign currency exchange transaction. Foreign exchange transactions total around $800 trillion annually, which means that a Tobin tax of only 0.05 percent could raise $400 billion in revenues for aid to poor economies, climate change mitigation, and ecosystem conservation (Spahn 2010). Such small tax rates would not deter financial speculation, but they could raise substantial revenues for global initiatives.

Alternatively, taxes could be imposed on anything from the arms trade to airline travel. A 10 percent tax on global arms exports, for example, has been estimated to raise up to $5 billion annually (Brzoska 2004). Additional tobacco sales taxes in G20 and other European Union countries could generate $10.8 billion, global aviation fuel taxes an extra $27 billion, and shipping fuel taxes $37 billion (Gates Foundation 2011).

The problem with any of these taxes is that they would require a negotiated international agreement involving many countries. Revenues should probably flow directly to a global fund, to prevent nations from collecting and siphoning the funds into their own national expenditures. But negotiating and establishing such a mechanism would be difficult. Perhaps more problematically, taxing tobacco and arms could just lead to more black market activity, driving trade for light weapons underground. Yet despite these obstacles, a report by the Gates Foundation (2011) to the G20 argued that along with a FTT, extra duties on these traded "bads" will be the most effective and equitable way of raising funds for global development efforts. This powerful message—the need to think creatively about financing sustainable development—is likely to remain on the agenda of the international community for some time.

CONCLUSION

Overcoming the problem of widespread poverty in low-developing economies without jeopardizing the environment will require new strategies for resource-based development and poverty eradication. Polices to make resource-based development more efficient and sustainable should target the main primary production activities of developing economies to improve their competitiveness, attain their export potential, limit resource overexploitation and waste, and generate increase returns and revenues. The increased financial returns and funds generated from primary production activities must be reinvested in the industrial activities, infrastructure, health services, education, and skills necessary for long-term economic development. Policies to eradicate poverty need to be targeted at the poor where they live, especially the rural poor clustered in fragile environments and remote areas. The specific elements of such a strategy include involving the poor in PES schemes and other measures that enhance the environments on which the poor depend, targeting investments directly to improving the livelihoods of the rural poor, thus reducing their dependence on exploiting environmental resources, and tackling the lack of access of the rural poor in less favored areas to well-functioning and affordable markets for credit, insurance, and land, and the high transportation and transaction costs that prohibit the poorest households in remote areas to engage in off-farm employment.

Such strategies for sustainable resource-based management and poverty eradication will require additional financial and technical support from the world community. Unfortunately, conventional sources of development assistance are insufficient for this task. The international community must become serious about designing new financial mechanisms for channeling assistance to the developing world, such as financial transactions taxes and other innovative instruments, if these new strategies for sustainable development are to succeed.

NOTES

* I am grateful for comments provided by Eva Paus on an earlier version of this paper.

1. For example, Chen and Ravallion (2007) note that $1-a-day rural poverty rate of 30 percent in 2002 is more than double the urban rate, and although 70 percent of the rural population lives on less than $2 a day, the proportion in urban areas is less than half that figure.
2. For further discussion of the long-run natural resource management and development strategies of Botswana, Malaysia, and Thailand, see in particular Barbier (2005, 2011), Coxhead and Jayasuriya (2003), Iimi (2007), Lange and Wright (2004), Sarraf and Jiwanji (2001), and Vincent et al. (1997).

3. See, for example, Alix-Garcia et al. (2008), Barbier (2010), Bulte et al. (2008), Grieg-Gran et al. (2005), Pagiola et al. (2005), Wunder (2008), and Zilberman et al. (2008).
4. See, for example, Aswani et al. (2012), Barbier and Sathirathai (2004), Chhatre and Agrawal (2008), Ferraro and Kiss (2006), and Jindal et al. (2008).
5. From www.theGeF.org, January 18, 2012.
6. From www.climatefundsupdate.org/, March 30, 2012.
7. A gigatonne (GT) is 1 billion tons.
8. From www.climatefundsupdate.org/, March 30, 2012.
9. From www.climatefundsupdate.org/, March 30, 2012.
10. Information on the IFFIm can be obtained from its website www.iff-immunisation.org.

REFERENCES

Alix-Garcia, Jennifer, Alain De Janvry, and Elisabeth Sadoulet. 2008. "The Role of Deforestation Risk and Calibrated Compensation in Designing Payments for Environmental Services." *Environment and Development Economics* 13(3):375–394.

Aswani, Shankar, Patrick Christieb, Nyawira A. Muthigac, Robin Mahond, Jurgenne H. Primaverae, Lori A. Cramerf, Edward B. Barbierg, Elise F. Granekh, Chris J. Kennedyi, Eric Wolanskij, and Sally Hackerk. 2012. "The Way Forward with Ecosystem-Based Management in Tropical Contexts: Reconciling with Existing Management Systems." *Marine Policy* 36(1):1–10.

Atkinson, A. B. 2006. "Funding the Millennium Development Goals: A Challenge for Global Public Finance." *European Review* 14(4):555–564.

Barbier, Edward B. 2005. *Natural Resources and Economic Development.* Cambridge, UK: Cambridge University Press.

——— 2010. "Poverty, Development and Environment." *Environment and Development Economics* 15(6):635–660.

——— 2011. *Scarcity and Frontiers: How Economies Have Developed through Natural Resource Exploitation.* Cambridge, UK: Cambridge University Press.

——— 2012. "Tax 'Societal Ills' to Save the Planet." *Nature* 483:30.

Barbier, Edward B. and Suthawan Sathirathai (eds.). 2004. *Shrimp Farming and Mangrove Loss in Thailand.* London: Edward Elgar Publishing.

Boucher, Doug, Pipa Elias, Katherine Lininger, Calen May-Tobin, Sarah Roquemore, and Earl Saxon. 2011. *The Root of the Problem: What's Driving Tropical Deforestation Today?* Cambridge, MA: Union of Concerned Scientists.

Branca, Giacomo, Leslie Lipper, Bernardete Neves, Dosteus Lopa, and Iddi Mwanyoka. 2011. "Payments for Watershed Services Supporting Sustainable Agricultural Development in Tanzania." *Journal of Environment & Development* 20(3):278–302.

Bridge, Gavin. 2008. "Global Production Networks and the Extractive Sector: Governing Resource-Based Development." *Journal of Economic Geography* 8(3):389–419.

Brzoska, Michael. 2004. "Taxation of the Global Arms Trade? An Overview of the Issues." *Kyklos* 57(2):149–172.

Bulte, Erwin H., Randall B. Boone, Randy Stringer, and Philip K. Thornton. 2008. "Elephants or Onions? Paying for Nature in Amboseli, Kenya." *Environment and Development Economics* 13(3):395–414.

Carr, David. 2009. "Population and Deforestation: Why Rural Migration Matters." *Progress in Human Geography* 33(3):355–378.

Carter, Michael R. and Christopher B. Barrett. 2006. "The Economics of Poverty Traps and Persistent Poverty: An Asset-Based Approach." *Journal of Development Studies* 42(2):178–199.

Chen, Shaohua and Martin Ravallion. 2007. "Absolute Poverty Measures for the Developing World, 1981–2004." *Proceedings of the National Academy of Sciences* 104(43):16757–16762.

Chhatre, Ashwini and Arun Agrawal. 2008. "Forest Commons and Local Enforcement." *Proceedings of the National Academy of Sciences* 105(36):13286–13291.

Chomitz, Kenneth, Piet Buys, Giacomo De Luca, Timothy S. Thomas, and Sheila Wertz-Kanounnikoff. 2007. *At Loggerheads? Agricultural Expansion, Poverty Reduction, and Environment in the Tropical Forests.* Washington, DC: World Bank.

Clemençon, Raymond. 2006. "What Future for the Global Environmental Facility?" *Journal of Environment & Development* 15(1):50–74.

Coady, David, Margaret Grosh, and John Hoddinott. 2004. "Targeting Outcomes Redux." *World Bank Research Observer* 19(1):61–85.

Coxhead, Ian and Sisira Jayasuriya. 2003. *The Open Economy and the Environment: Development, Trade and Resources in Asia.* Northampton, MA: Edward Elgar Publishing.

Coxhead Ian, Gerald Shively, and Xiaobing Shuai. 2002. "Development Policies, Resource Constraints, and Agricultural Expansion on the Philippine Land Frontier." *Environment and Development Economics* 7(2):341–363.

Dasgupta, Susmita, Uwe Deichmann, Craig Meisner, and David Wheeler. 2005. "Where Is the Poverty-Environment Nexus? Evidence from Cambodia, Lao PDR, and Vietnam." *World Development* 33(4):617–638.

DeFries, Ruth S., Thomas Rudel, Maria Uriarte, and Matthew Hansen. 2010. "Deforestation Driven by Urban Population Growth and Agricultural Trade in the Twenty-First Century." *Nature Geoscience* 3:178–801.

Ebeling, Johannes and Maï Yasué. 2008. "Generating Carbon Finance through Avoided Deforestation and Its Potential to Create Climatic, Conservation and Human Development Benefits." *Philosophical Transactions of the Royal Society Series B* 363(1498):1917–1924.

Elbers, Chris, Tomoki Fujii, Peter Frederik Lanjouw, Berk Özler, and Wesley Yin. 2007. "Poverty Alleviation through Geographic Targeting: How Much Does Disaggregation Help?" *Journal of Development Economics* 83(1):198–213.

Ferraro, Paul J. and Agnes Kiss. 2006. "Direct Payments to Conserve Biodiversity." *Science* 298(5599):1718–1719.

Fischer, Günther and Gerhard K. Heilig. 1997. "Population Momentum and the Demand on Land and Water Resources." *Philosophical Transactions of the Royal Society Series B* 352(1356):869–889.

Food and Agricultural Organization (FAO) of the United Nations. 2001. *Forest Resources Assessment 2000: Main Report.* FAO Forestry Paper 140. Rome: FAO.

——— 2003. *State of the World's Forests 2003.* Rome: FAO.

——— 2006. Global Forest Resources Assessment 2005, Main Report. Progress Towards Sustainable Forest Management. FAO Forestry Paper 147. Rome: FAO.

Gates Foundation. 2011. *Innovation with Impact: Financing 21st Century Development.* A Report by Bill Gates to G20 leaders, Cannes summit, November

2011. www.thegatesnotes.com/Topics/Development/G20-Report-Innovation-with-Impact

Gibbs, Holly K., A. S. Ruesch, F. Achard, M. K. Clayton, P. Holmgren, Navin Ramankutty, and Jonathan A. Foley. 2010. "Tropical Forests Were the Primary Sources of New Agricultural Lands in the 1980s and 1990s." *Proceedings of the National Academy of Sciences* 107(38):16732–16737.

Grieg-Gran, Maryanne Ina Porras, and Sven Wunder. 2005. "How Can Market Mechanisms for Forest Environmental Services Help the Poor? Preliminary Lessons from Latin America." *World Development* 33(9):1511–1527.

Gylfason, Thorvaldur. 2001. "Nature, Power, and Growth." *Scottish Journal of Political Economy* 48(5):558–588.

Hyder, Pat. 2008. "Recycling Revenue from An International Carbon Tax to Fund An International Investment Programme in Sustainable Energy and Poverty Reduction." *Global Environmental Change* 18(3):521–538.

Iimi, Atsushi. 2007. "Escaping from the Resource Curse: Evidence from Botswana and the Rest of the World." *IMF Staff Papers* 54(4):663–699.

Jindal, Rohit, Brent Swallow, and John Kerr. 2008. "Forestry-Based Carbon Sequestration Projects in Africa: Potential Benefits and Challenges." *Natural Resources Forum* 32(2):116–130.

Kindermann, Georg, Michael Obersteiner, Brent Sohngen, Jayant Sathaye, Kenneth Andrasko, Ewald Rametsteiner, Bernhard Schlamadinger, Sven Wunder, and Robert Beach. 2008. "Global Cost Estimates of Reducing Carbon Emissions through Avoided Deforestation." *Proceedings of the National Academy of Sciences* 105(30):10302–10307.

Lange, Glenn-Marie and Matthew Wright. 2004. "Sustainable Development and Mineral Economies: The Example of Botswana." *Environment and Development Economics* 9(4):485–505.

Minot, Nicholas and Bob Baulch. 2002. The Spatial Distribution of Poverty in Vietnam and the Potential for Targeting. Policy Research Working Paper 2829. Washington, DC: World Bank.

Molden, David (ed.). 2007. *Water for Food, Water for Life: A Comprehensive Assessment of Water Management in Agriculture.* London: Earthscan and International Water Management Institute, Colombo, Sri Lanka.

Pagiola, Stefano, Agustin Arcenas, and Gunars Platais. 2005. "Can Payments for Environmental Services Help Reduce Poverty? An Exploration of the Issues and the Evidence to Date from Latin America." *World Development* 33(2):237–253.

Pichón, Francisco J. 1997. "Colonist Land-Allocation Decisions, Land Use, and Deforestation in the Ecuadorian Frontier." *Economic Development and Cultural Change* 45(4):707–744.

Ramankutty, Navin and Jonathan A. Foley. 1999. "Estimating Historical Changes in Global Land Cover: Croplands from 1700 to 1992." *Global Biogeochemical Cycles* 13(4):997–1027.

Ravallion, Martin. 2008. Bailing out the World's Poorest. Policy Research Working Paper 4763. Washington, DC: World Bank.

Rudel, Thomas K. 2007. "Changing Agents of Deforestation: from State-Initiated to Enterprise Driven Process, 1970–2000." *Land Use Policy* 24(1):35–41.

Sarraf, Maria and Moortaza Jiwanji. 2001. Beating the Resource Curse: The Case of Botswana. Environment Department Working Paper 83, Report 24753. Washington, DC: The World Bank Environment Department.

Shively, Gerald E. and Monica Fisher. 2004. "Smallholder Labor and Deforestation: A Systems Approach." *American Journal of Agricultural Economics* 86(5):1361–1366.

Spahn, Paul Bernd. 2010. "a Double Dividend." *The Broker,* October/November 22:8–14.

United Nations Conference on Trade and Development (UNCTAD). 2010. *The Least Developed Countries Report 2010: Towards a New International Development Architecture for LDCs.* New York: United Nations.

——— 2011. *The Least Developed Countries Report 2011: The Potential Role of South-South Cooperation for Inclusive and Sustainable Development.* New York: United Nations.

United Nations Population Division. 2008. *World Urbanization Prospects: The 2007 Revision: Executive Summary.* New York: United Nations.

van der Ploeg, Frederick. 2011. "Natural Resources: Curse or Blessing?" *Journal of Economic Literature* 49(2):366–420.

Vincent, Jeffrey R., Razali M. Ali, and Associates. 1997. *Environment and Development in a Resource-Rich Economy: Malaysia under the New Economic Policy.* Cambridge, MA: Harvard Institute for International Development.

Wassenaar, T., P. Gerber, P. H. Verburg, M. Rosales, M. Ibrahim, and H. Steinfeld. 2007. "Projecting Land Use Changes in the Neotropics: The Geography of Pasture Expansion into Forest." *Global Environmental Change* 17(1):86–104.

World Bank. 2003. *World Development Report 2003: Sustainable Development in a Dynamic World.* Washington, DC: World Bank.

——— 2008. *Word Development Report 2008: Agricultural for Development.* Washington, DC: World Bank.

——— 2012. *World Development Indicators 2012.* Washington, DC: World Bank.

Wunder, Sven. 2008. "Payments for Environmental Services and the Poor: Concepts and Preliminary Evidence." *Environment and Development Economics* 13(3):279–297.

Zilberman, David, Leslie Lipper, and Nancy McCarthy. 2008. "When Could Payments for Environmental Services Benefit the Poor?" *Environment and Development Economics* 13(3):255–278.

CHAPTER 10

Environment as an Element of Development: The Growing Role of Energy Efficiency and Environmental Protection in Chinese Economic Policy

Deborah Seligsohn

The developmental issues at the core of this book are fundamental to China's discussions of what the country has achieved over the past three decades of reform and opening and where policy makers believe society and the economy need to go in the future. Economic growth has been at the center of China's development agenda since 1949 (Brandt and Rawski 2008), although the approach to economic growth shifted radically. The reforms unleashed by Deng Xiaoping, starting in 1979 and then accelerating in 1992 are widely credited with economic growth averaging almost 10 percent a year for the entire period since 1980.[1] Moreover, the Chinese government has particularly prided itself on raising hundreds of millions from abject poverty during this period, an achievement that has been widely recognized by the international development community (Ravallion and Chen 2005).

Throughout the 1980s and the 1990s, there was a broad consensus that an economic policy focused primarily on economic growth met China's most urgent needs (Naughton 2008). One of these was clearly poverty alleviation, and the assumption was that a bigger pie would ensure more for those at all levels of society. But it was hardly the only goal. The Chinese government has always had a major political agenda, both in terms of stability at home and security internationally, and delivering economic growth has been seen as central to both. Domestically, prosperity has tended to keep the public satisfied and maintain cohesion within the Chinese Communist Party (CCP), while from an international security point of view, it has given China both a stronger military and more negotiating leverage in a variety of fora.

But as China has become wealthier, perceptions of its development needs among the general public, within the leadership, and within the broader governmental bureaucracy have shifted, become broader, and more nuanced. At its current stage of development, the need to address the other development issues raised in this book—structural change and environmental degradation—are both widely recognized. Both issues are prominent in the 12th Five Year Plan, China's governing national policy document outlining the major directions in economic planning over the period, 2011 through the end of 2015. These new concerns have not replaced the previous focus on economic growth and social stability, but have been added to the development agenda. Poverty alleviation still continues to be a goal, and indeed international interlocutors are likely to hear from their Chinese partners that China is still a poor country with urgent poverty alleviation needs. However, poverty alleviation has to a significant extent been reframed as requiring income redistribution and social service provision in addition to growth (Wong 2009). These goals are centered by a focus on the "quality" of economic growth that also includes environmental protection.

This chapter focuses on how environmental protection has developed into a meaningful part of this overall program of development. Environmental protection has moved from being a goal that observers both inside and outside China perceived as mere window-dressing to a fundamental national goal that local governments take seriously and where there are measurable national results.

THE COSTS OF POLLUTION

China has suffered the environmental consequences of rapid development with poor environmental regulation for decades.[2] Environmental quality was poor even before China began its period of rapid growth and industrial expansion with its reform and opening policies in 1979. By the time China began to grow rapidly, attitudes stemming both from its communist central planning past and its developing country status led to considerable disregard for environmental issues for a number of years.

The first major study to document the impact of pollution on the Chinese populace was the World Bank's *Clear Water, Blue Skies* report in 1997, which estimated environmental damage to cost China 8 percent of GDP, while estimating 178,000 premature deaths annually in major cities from outdoor air pollution and 110,000 in rural areas from indoor air pollution. More recent estimates of health impacts have been higher, while the GDP percentages have tended to be lower. These indicate considerable improvements in data scope and quality, although data issues remain. The widely cited[3] World Health Organization's 2009 China Country Profile of the Environmental Burden of Disease estimated 299,400 deaths per year from outdoor air pollution and 548,900 from indoor air pollution out of a total of 2.4 million environmental health deaths annually.[4] The most widely known and still the most controversial effort to quantify the impact of environmental damage was the World Bank's 2007 study "Cost of Pollution in China; Economic Estimates of Physical Damages," a document that was released in a conference edition, but never in final form. The study offers wide ranges for its estimates of premature deaths, with, for example, the mean estimates of deaths from outdoor air pollution ranging from 110,000 to 394,000 per year, depending on the methodology used. The more often cited GDP cost estimates that have appeared to be at the center of the controversy are also given with a broad range of 2.7 percent to 5.8 percent of GDP, with the press at the time widely citing figures in the 3 percent range. The GDP costs considered not just health impacts, but also other pollution-related damage, including crop and natural resource losses and infrastructural damage.

The World Bank's health estimates were based on a dose-response approach that is supported by the work of the US-based Health Effects Institute (HEI), whose 2004 study, updated in 2010, *Outdoor Air Pollution and Health in the Developing Countries of Asia: A Comprehensive Review* (HEI 2010) evaluates the existing studies on health impacts in China, along with other countries in developing Asia. The HEI survey of existing data shows that the health impacts from air pollution in Asia are broadly similar to those in the United States and Europe. A critical insight of the HEI survey is that the health effects are dose-related, and thus incremental reductions in the level of air pollution have demonstrable results in improving human health. While these studies all cite health figures going back half a decade or more—generally from before China's major effort to improve environmental quality—we can use this dose-related insight to infer that the improvements that have occurred since 2006 are positive for human health in China.

While the damage of pollution extends well beyond health, the converse is also true: much of what affects overall environmental health is not related to modern air or water pollutants. All of the studies above note that Chinese environmental health is in fact improving, and much of this is due to the control of more traditional sources of environmental disease, primarily poor water and sanitation. Indeed, in recent years, both the World Bank and the WHO have focused on China's non-communicable disease (NCD) burden, as China has already made considerable progress in controlling many of the infectious diseases that disproportionately affect the world's poor. While pollution is one cause of NCDs, the World Bank's 2011 report, "Toward a Healthy and Harmonious Life in China: Stemming the Rising Tide of Non-Communicable Diseases," briefly mentions pollution as a cause of NCDs and recommends enforcing pollution law and regulations, but these are not the priority interventions. The larger causes of NCDs in China are primarily behavioral—with tobacco, salt, and alcohol intake topping the list.

Indeed, it is worth keeping in mind Kirk Smith's admonishment in his discussion of environmental health in China that environmental quality and environmental health are not always closely linked, "just because something is outrageous does not mean it is particularly unhealthy" (Smith 2008). Smith's point is that environmental health impacts relate closely to dose and exposure. Thus, for example, occupational exposure is often more deadly in both developed and developing countries, and yet more focus is generally placed on ambient exposure of the general population. Smith has also been a leader in pointing out the impact of indoor air pollution, and it would be fair to surmise that estimates of the health impact of indoor pollution have risen steadily in China not because there are more farmers with old-fashioned cook stoves (commercial fuel has grown rapidly over this period), but because the issue is better understood. But we can also look at his analysis to realize that health impacts, while widely cited in most of the literature, are just one of many reasons the public wants to see pollution issues addressed.

Indeed, public concern in China can hardly be related to any knowledge of health impacts, which are not well covered in the Chinese press. As the title of the World Bank's original study "Clear Water, Blue Skies" makes clear, environmental quality is valued for itself as well as for its additional benefits. Public discussion of pollution in China is not generally tied to these specific health or economic outcomes—improvements are measured on their own terms. While this can be interpreted as a weakness of analysis, it may also reflect a conviction that environmental improvements are obviously good and do not need further justification.

CHANGING ATTITUDES

Attitudes toward environmental protection have changed dramatically in the past decade, and results are starting to be demonstrable on the ground. Energy efficiency and environmental protection have moved from the periphery to recognition as central issues in Chinese government policy, highlighted in Five Year Plans and major policy speeches. Provinces are under pressure both from the central government and the general public to produce results, and in the past six years they have done so. The 11th Five Year Plan (2006–2010) was the first five-year plan in which a pollution reduction target (sulfur dioxide, SO_2) was met, and in fact exceeded. Moreover, China also came close to meeting its goal to reduce energy intensity (energy used per unit of GDP generated) by 20 percent.[5] This was particularly striking when contrasted with the first half of the decade (the 10th Five Year Plan period), when most indicators deteriorated considerably, including energy intensity which had been improving steadily in the 1980s and the 1990s.

When we look at the major indicators the Chinese government focused on, in particular energy intensity and SO_2 emissions, 2006 appears as a clear inflexion point. Energy intensity had been gradually improving for decades, but actually rose in the early 2000s. With the inception of the 12th Five Year Plan, energy intensity began to improve, and despite considerable challenges over the five-year period, particularly the global economic crisis and China's massive stimulus spending, overall energy intensity was almost 20 percent lower at the end of 2010 than it had been at the beginning of 2006. Moreover, SO_2 emissions, where the goal was a 10 percent reduction, had actually fallen more than 14 percent during the same period.

Clearly a change occurred, but how did it happen? The challenges posed by pollution and high-energy intensity were well known for decades. But a confluence of political, economic, and institutional developments has changed the priority for action and the government's capacity to act.

ENERGY SECURITY

Energy security has been one of China's major historic concerns, going back at least as far as the Sino-Soviet split in the late 1950s/early 1960s, when China was left without a stable supply of imported oil (Calder 2005). While China had been self-sufficient in coal for centuries, it relied heavily on imported oil for the first decade of the new People's Republic. This changed when the Soviet advisors pulled out and China's import source disappeared. The fortuitous discovery of one of the world's largest oil fields at Daqing in Heilongjiang in the early 1960s, just after the Sino-Soviet split, rescued China from an energy crisis. It also paved the way for decades of energy independence, and established itself as one of modern China's great narratives of self-reliance (Andrews-Speed and Dannreuther 2011).

Later oil finds were not nearly as large as Daqing. As the economy grew and Daqing's own reserves were being depleted, it became clear by the early 1990s that China was soon to become a net oil importer. In fact, China became a net importer in 1993, even though publicly delays and corrections in data meant that policy makers were not fully aware of the watershed for a year or two. Analysts had expected this change in trading position to be a major concern for the Chinese government, but in the event the change was barely remarked upon and caused little change in Chinese government policy.

China became a net importer of oil during a period of stable global prices, and energy security slipped to the back burner. This began to change in the 2000s, as energy prices became unstable, political instability in source countries became more apparent, and potential conflict with other consumer countries also became a greater concern. A confluence of events in 2005 brought this message home. The first was the run-up in world oil prices and Chinese imports in 2004. Chinese imports rose particularly rapidly during that year, and while they later slowed down, significant international media attention in 2005 focused on Chinese imports as a cause of higher oil prices. Moreover, there were two votes in the US House of Representatives in 2005—one on the import of nuclear equipment and the other on a proposed purchase of a US oil company (UNOCAL by CNOOC) that made Chinese policy makers nervous. While neither vote was binding, both suggested that there was some opposition to China's efforts to secure its energy supplies internationally.

At the same time, China became increasingly concerned about security of supply, even from domestic sources. Heavy dependency on coal from a single region left China very vulnerable to natural disasters, such as the blizzards of 2008 (French 2008). The net result of these energy security issues was to bring back energy efficiency programs that had lain dormant since the late 1990s. Controlling the rapid rise in China's energy demand was clearly beneficial all around—it reduced the need to turn to international markets, it reduced the pressure on China's own supply lines, and it saved money. Similarly developing nonfossil energy sources reduced competition for foreign energy supplies and diversified supply within China, reducing pressure on the coal transport system (Naughton 2005).

New Wealth and a Broader Notion of Development

The early 2000s were in many ways a watershed period for China's worldview and economic development. China joined the WTO in 2001. Negotiating entry and preparing the economy for this transformation had preoccupied much of Chinese economic and trade policy as well as international diplomacy throughout the 1990s. Now China could reap the benefits (Dollar and Kraay 2003). And these benefits turned out to be considerable. Growth averaged 10.5 percent in the decade 2001–2010 (World Bank), and while the full ten-year average had been the same in the 1990s, in fact, over the course of the 1990s growth had slowed, while in the 2000s it accelerated for much of the decade. The net result of this cumulative rapid growth, extending back to when China initiated reforms in 1979, was that China was vastly richer than it had been just two decades earlier, and by 2005, it was much wealthier than it had been even in the late 1990s. An economy growing at 10 percent a year doubles its size every seven years: thus when China looked at its next five-year plan in 2005, it was more than twice as wealthy as when it had founded its first environmental enforcement agency, the State Environmental Protection Administration (SEPA) in 1998.

Hand in hand with greater wealth, China had gained considerably in institutional capacity. In the lead-up to the accession to the WTO, there was considerable debate about how accession would affect the Chinese economy, with large claims of benefits as well as concerns about the short-term costs of restructuring. While there were a number of estimates of these costs at the time, since then most commentators have been content to point to China's healthy growth rates of GDP and trade as signs of the success of accession. It is, however, not clear whether China's growth after 2000 was due directly to increased trade generated by accession to the WTO, by the institutional developments that were required to meet WTO entry requirements, or by the institutional reform that was simply part of China's domestic reform agenda. Lee Branstetter and Nicholas Lardy (2006) see all three elements as essential and intertwined. They make the case that China's growth in the 2000s was due both to WTO accession and to reforms in the late 1990s, and that WTO accession was a deliberate part of the reform program of the late 1990s. The Chinese central government, along with the State-Owned Enterprises (SOEs), was completely overhauled in the late 1990s. As Branstetter and Lardy argue, reformers led by Premier Zhu Rongji believed that his restructuring was essential to modernizing the Chinese economy. The drive was thus domestic, but WTO accession was a useful tool for getting more reluctant reformers on board.

Reform changed not just the economy, but the government structure as well. The central government and the SOEs laid off tens of millions of workers in the late 1990s. While the majority of these employees came from the much larger SOEs, the result for government and SOEs were much leaner and tighter administrations. In most (but not all) cases,[6] the result was much more effective bureaucracies. While WTO accession has become a shorthand way to describe a number of very different processes—opening to trade, harmonization with international standards and practices, government reform, SOE reform, domestic regulatory reform—there is considerable debate about which contributed in what proportion to the growth rate. From the point of view of their influence on energy and environment policy, it is the sum total of these changes that matters.

This reformist period led to a positive feedback loop of greater institutional confidence and a broader definition of development. As the government and the public felt richer and better able to address additional challenges, the understanding of development expanded. And institutional reforms, whether driven by WTO accession or domestic imperatives, made it possible for the government to address these new development issues, because there was greater confidence in the ability of the government to implement policy and adapt institutions.

This confidence was strengthened and its relevance to social issues made more explicit in the wake of the 2003 SARS crisis. It seems almost forgotten now that President Hu Jintao and Premier Wen Jiabao came to power in the middle of the global panic over SARS, and that there were real fears that SARS could become a global pandemic and a long-term threat to Chinese public welfare and the Chinese economy. The epidemic was already raging in Southern China, Hong Kong, and much of Southeast Asia; the virus had yet to be identified; and on the day President Hu was sworn in, Canada reported its first eight cases. Just a month later, the city of Beijing virtually shut its doors to focus on SARS eradication.[7] Remarkably, by July 5, 2003, the WHO had removed all travel warnings from SARS-affected areas, and the disease apparently had been removed from the human population. The effort to achieve this result was extraordinary, involving government and public mobilization, a rapid ramp up in public health capacity, and extensive international cooperation (Chan et al. 2010). This brief epidemic cost China 0.5 percent of GDP, but it cost harder hit Hong Kong a full 4 percent (Bekedam 2003). Had the epidemic not been contained so rapidly, the risk in lost lives and livelihoods would have been even greater. The epidemic thus brought home to the Chinese leadership that social issues could rapidly and adversely affect development, and that China had the institutional capacity to address these issues. The public health infrastructure moved forward rapidly in the wake of SARS, taking on other challenges, including HIV/AIDS and avian influenza.

But neither the lessons nor the conclusions were restricted to public health. As they faced down SARS, Hu and Wen were also confronted by a public firestorm over the death of a college graduate named Sun Zhigang, who was detained and beaten in a migrant detention facility in Guangdong Province the day after Wen was sworn in. While the migrant detention facilities and their abuses had long been criticized by legal reformers and migrant advocates, middle-class urbanites were galvanized by a story about a middle-class professional in the way they had not been by the plight of ordinary workers. Strikingly, the State Council under Premier Wen Jiabao moved quickly to reform the entire system, not just try to address a smaller subset of cases. The story first surfaced April 25, and by June the central government had eliminated mandatory detention for residency reasons (Shirk 2010).

Through the 1990s the government consensus had been that economic growth was not only the primary goal, but also the only domestic social or economic policy goal.[8] The argument was that there simply were not enough resources for a broader focus. The new government in 2003 dramatically altered the range of possibilities, rapidly initiating new policies in areas ranging from health to public safety, and implementing them at the provincial and local level. This change reflected a growing sense of government capacity and institutional capability, greater wealth and thus economic resources to spend on new priorities, and the interests of the public. Both SARS and the Sun Zhigang case directly affected the middle class and spoke to their anxieties. Having reached a certain level of prosperity, the urban public was much more aware of risks of losing it all—whether by entering a hospital and walking out with a poorly controlled disease or being picked up on the street in a case of mistaken identity. The middle class was expressing its desire for a higher, safer quality of life, and in the early 2000s the government showed much more awareness of these concerns and responsiveness to them.

A Clean Environment as a Development Goal

As the notion of development broadened to include both public health and quality of life, it would seem likely that environmental issues would become part of the package. But in 2003 and 2004, environmental issues and poor enforcement still seemed like back-burner issues. But by 2005, a number of factors increased governmental attention to the stressed state of China's environment. The first was, as discussed above, renewed interest in energy policy. The best approaches to energy security—energy efficiency and diversification of supply—have obvious environmental co-benefits that advocates could highlight.

But the transforming event (Liu 2006) was the November 13, 2005, Songhua River spill—a major environmental incident that received sustained national coverage, first on the web and then in the media. While there were attempts at cover-ups, and ultimately coverage was limited, the public was exposed to a full two months of coverage in the national media, particularly on television (Tilt and Xiao 2010). This was the first such environmental disaster with national coverage, and its impact on the Chinese public was similar to the Exxon Valdez oil spill in the United States in 1987—a notable jump in environmental awareness and demands for greater action. The actual incident involved a fire at a petrochemical plant owned and operated by PetroChina, the world's sixth largest company,[9] and a major economic and political power in China. The fire caused the release of several chemicals, including benzene and nitrobenzene, into the Songhua River near Jilin, upstream of the major city of Harbin, and contaminated river water that flowed into the Heilongjiang or Amur River, causing concern on both sides of the Sino-Russian border (UNEP 2005).

The government's immediate response included two forms of damage control. The first was to address the pollutants in the river. The second was on the public relations front, and specifically to address the public's concern that someone be held responsible. The official fingered was China's top environmental enforcement official, then SEPA administrator Xie Zhenhua, who resigned. While much domestic and international media attention focused on the failure of Xie's agency to enforce environmental regulations at the PetroChina plant, it seems unlikely that anyone in the government leadership actually thought that Xie's subministerial body had the power to enforce regulations at one of the world's largest companies, whose leadership far outranked him in the CCP hierarchy. More likely, Xie took a fall for the team. Indeed he appears to have been rewarded for doing so: he came back to government the following year with full ministerial rank, responsible for climate change in the National Development and Reform Commission.[10]

Ultimately, the response to the spill helped SEPA build momentum for much greater change—setting and achieving clear goals in the Five Year Plan process and gaining greater enforcement authority. The two critical breakthroughs in environmental enforcement in the last decade have been the goal setting process in the 11th Five Year Plan (2006–2010) and the elevation of SEPA to ministerial level—the Ministry of Environmental Protection (MEP)—in 2007. Environmental goals had been part of previous Five Year Plans, but the targets set had never been met. SEPA took a new tack in the 11th Five Year Plan. Instead of setting a large number of goals and then failing to meet them, they chose just two goals—one air pollutant and one water pollution measurement—and focused all efforts on these. This was a novel approach—most developed countries use a combination of human health and ecosystem health factors to set standards, and the recommendations from the WHO, for example, are entirely based on human health. The 11th Five Year Plan targets were much more pragmatic. No one would suggest that reducing SO_2 and chemical oxygen demand (COD) by 10 percent was sufficient, but achieving it was difficult in five years, and for the first time, the goals were actually met.[11]

The next watershed event in China's growing environmental awareness and institutional confidence was the 2008 Beijing Olympics. In bidding for the Games in 2001, Beijing promised an ambitious program to clean the air, and despite international skepticism leading up to the Games it largely delivered. After a very difficult first two days of the Olympics, with extreme heat, humidity, and air pollution, the regional governments came up with a mix of control measures that ensured remarkably good air quality for the rest of the Olympiad period, which included the Olympics and the Paralympics (Wang et al. 2009).[12] The cleaner air was a result of long-term efforts—air quality slowly improved over the several years leading up to the Games—and a set of specific measures to guarantee well above-average performance during the Games. The most well-known measure was the imposition of odd and even driving days, but at least equally important were the reduction in power plant operations by 30 percent and the imposition of restrictions not just on the city of Beijing, but on the other provinces within the Beijing airshed.[13]

Critics at the time doubted the impact of short-term measures given that they by definition would not continue beyond the Olympics themselves. However, the positive impact of those measures added to subsequent pressure to continue to address air pollution issues. The public, and indeed government officials themselves became aware of what an improvement in air quality meant to quality of life. The most immediate public pressure was to continue to restrict driving, since the majority of Beijing's residents are not well-heeled drivers, but public transport and bicycle riders of more modest means who appreciate less crowded streets. The Beijing government initially planned to discontinue driving restrictions after the Games, but public outcry pushed them to modify the plan. The restriction was loosened from odd-even to a one-day-a-week restriction,[14] and the government began actively seeking additional vehicle restriction measures. Since then, Beijing has instituted substantially higher parking fees, kept public transportation prices low and, most recently, has begun to restrict vehicle license plates (Pugliese 2011).

The advances made during the 11th Five Year Plan period—reductions in SO_2 and COD as well as the overall improvement in air quality demonstrated during the Beijing Olympics—combined with the MEP's new bureaucratic heft as a full ministry enabled it to propose more ambitious goals in the 12th Five Year Plan. In addition to continuing to reduce both SO_2 and COD, the new plan added targets for an additional air pollutant, nitrogen oxides (NOx) and an additional water pollutant (ammonia nitrogen) (Seligsohn and Hsu 2011). At the same time, MEP was establishing a new regulatory mechanism for Regional Air Quality (RAQ) control (PRC 2010). Air pollution experts, including those within the SEPA and then MEP bureaucracy, knew full well that serious air pollution control efforts would require a focus on entire regions and not just on major cities. But that level of political coordination is difficult in a country in which most mandates are delegated to the provinces. The Beijing Olympics demonstrated the importance and effectiveness of regional control efforts, and enabled MEP to make the case to the State Council.

RAQ control is more complex than the types of emission standards MEP has enforced to date. Environmental regulations involve a complex mix of regulatory standards tied to outcomes—total emission loads allowed for various periods—hourly, daily, or yearly—with specific standards for sources—technology and emission requirements for automobiles, industrial users, and electric power plants, for example.[15] Given that both the meteorology and the number and type of sources vary by region, to achieve any specific environmental outcome in densely populated, heavily industrial or meteorologically challenging areas requires adjustments to the types of restrictions on sources.

In addition to regulatory limits and standards, there have also been the Five Year Plan goals, which are focused on making progress to achieve certain percentage reductions rather than on specific environmentally determined outcomes. Given the size of the challenge, the Five Year Plans are a realistic way to move forward, but public frustration has grown, as pollution continues to be a major health and quality of life issue.

RAQ management is a major step forward in tying environmental enforcement to environmental outcomes, but it is not easy to implement. MEP needs to add a number of pollutants to its control strategy to address some of the largest health risks, to monitor and measure these effectively, and then to adjust controls to deal with variable conditions on the ground.

As MEP was in the midst of the spadework for implementing the RAQ regulations, public outcry again propelled their efforts forward. In the autumn of 2011, the Chinese blogosphere lit up with criticism of Beijing air quality, and shortly thereafter the domestic press joined the chorus. The trigger for the discussion was in part the poor air quality in the autumn. It may also have been articles in the international press commenting on the poor air quality measured at a monitor set up at the US Embassy that is transmitted via twitter. They were translated and shared on the Chinese Internet. The public outcry very much focused on Beijing. Thanks to a combination of the types of pollution sources in the area and Beijing's difficult meteorology, its air quality is markedly poorer than in other wealthy areas such as Shanghai and Guangdong.

While Beijing city's initial response was quite defensive, MEP was, in fact, well positioned to be responsive. Its annual meeting on RAQ management in November 2011 focused specifically on adding control of the additional pollutants that were needed to address the air quality problems. The focus at the time was on getting initial regulations in place within a year, and national level controls on PM 2.5 by 2016.[16] Over the next several months, implementation sped up, and there are indications that nationwide PM 2.5 monitoring is moving forward.[17] Beijing also announced much more ambitious targets than the national plan, promising to reduce air pollution by 15 percent by 2015 and 30 percent by 2020 (Reuters 2012).

Public concern about water quality has also grown, although public attention has been more sporadic. Air pollution is a near constant concern for urban residents, whereas much water pollution is invisible to the vocal urban public until a crisis occurs. The Songhua River was not the only such crisis in recent years. Two major algal blooms have attracted national attention—in Tai Lake north of Shanghai in 2007 (Goldkorn 2007) and at the Olympic sailing course in Qingdao in 2008 (Yardley 2008). Algal blooms are symptomatic of eutrophication, and there continue to be such blooms, including in both these locations with somewhat less national attention. As a result of the concern over eutrophication ammonia, nitrogen was added as a target in the 12th Five Year Plan. This is a critical step forward, but the challenges overall are even greater than in addressing air pollution.

CLIMATE CHANGE AS A DRIVER

Concern about energy security, economic health, and a better quality of life by reducing local air pollution have clearly driven much of China's actions, but climate change itself is clearly part of China's concerns. The complexity is that the climate change discussion began not so much as a discussion of the impacts of climate change on China's economy and development, but as a discussion of the costs of mitigation on China's future development.[18] Thus, if we look back to the 1990s, the climate negotiations were seen mainly in terms of how to reduce the cost of engaging with the process. To not engage seemed risky, given that China's major trading partners were all engaged, but the process itself seemed to offer few benefits, especially given the time horizon of needs in a poor developed country. With poverty reduction as an immediate concern and the ambition to become a stronger nation, the Chinese government appeared less concerned about problems that at that time were predicted to be decades or even centuries in the future.

With climate change itself appearing much more remote then than it does now, technology transfer became an important issue. If solving the problem was not a sufficient carrot, perhaps offering a development benefit that should also help solve the problem might be useful. The challenge is that technology transfer has since been a major sticking point with China, as well as other developing countries arguing that they have not seen major transfers of technology. This is in part a definitional issue, since developing countries would like to see governments transfer technology, which has not happened under the United Nations Framework Convention on Climate Change (UNFCCC) or the Kyoto Protocol. At the same time, the Clean Development Mechanism (CDM), a program specifically designed to spur new technologies, has been well received and widely used in China. While not all projects have had cutting-edge technology, CDM financing has been critical to such new industries as wind power and important in spurring businesses that may not be cutting edge, but were new to China, such as waste to energy.[19] In creating new energy industries and a whole commercial network to support the CDM market, the CDM created new groups of domestic stakeholders for a climate regime.

The publication of the Intergovernmental Panel on Climate Change's (IPCC) Fourth Assessment in February 2007 (IPCC 2007) marked another turning point in China's climate change awareness. While climate skepticism of the sort found in the United States has had a much smaller influence in China, prior to the Fourth Assessment there were doubts in the policy community that climate change would be all bad for China. If one goes back to the Third Assessment (IPCC 2001), there was very little in the way of quality modeling to make predictions at mid-latitudes. Some research had even suggested that CO_2 might "fertilize" crops, increasing agricultural output. The research that fed into the Fourth Assessment suggested that any such effect would be outweighed considerably by changes in weather systems. Overall, China could expect more droughts in the North and floods in the South, both diminishing agricultural yields, as well as leading to other hardships and losses.

Not only did the Fourth Assessment speak more directly to how China would fare, but for the first time, significant numbers of Chinese researchers were involved in the effort as well. At least 10 percent of the coauthors were Chinese, including Qin Dahe, who headed the Chinese Meteorological Administration and was cochair of the Science Working Group within the IPCC. Even before the report was published, these researchers were presenting their findings to Chinese policy makers. As a result, there was a substantial shift in perspective within China on the extent of the risk of climate change itself, rather than the cost of mitigation. This focus has actually been heightened by the growing discussion of climate security as an international issue. In particular, the United States Defense Department's October 2003 report, "An Abrupt Climate Change Scenario and Its Implications for United States National Security" (Schwartz and Randall 2003), was highly influential in bringing home to the Chinese foreign policy establishment the security implications of climate change.[20]

The complexity for international observers, and especially for negotiating partners, is that the recognition of a national interest in climate mitigation is not one and the same as a commitment to any particular level of domestic mitigation. In fact, it raises the level of frustration within China at the failure of developed countries to act more rapidly after the signing of the 1992 Framework Convention (United Nations 1992), whose text specifically tasks developed countries with "taking the lead" at a time when Chinese emissions were a tiny fraction of what they are today.

Because of the global nature of climate change mitigation and its impacts, there is still a sense of a prisoner's dilemma in who should move first. In fact, the Chinese have moved farther toward seeing mitigation as in their own interest than have the United States.[21] The Chinese also see the range of technologies they have been able to develop and deploy, in particular wind, solar, and nuclear power, as giving them a comparative advantage in the future. Chinese policy makers recognize the positive energy security, economic, and local environmental benefits of most climate mitigation actions—at least up to a point. The question really becomes how to justify actions that are more expensive than those other benefits might call for.

ADDING IT UP: A NEW VIEW OF DEVELOPMENT

China remains a developing country with a per capita GDP still less than $5,000.[22] Thus, development remains the critical domestic policy goal. However, the definition of what development means has changed fundamentally in the past decade. A decade ago, the only real measure was GDP. Today, public health, attractive cities, technological development, long-term sustainability have all become critically important. While China's per capita GDP is modest in global terms, it is dramatically higher than a decade or two ago. The result has been a rapid growth both in public expectations and in policy makers' and leaders' confidence in the ability of government to meet those expectations. Institutions are more sophisticated, and there is a great deal more confidence in these institutions.

At the same time, environmental issues have become recognized as important for energy and national security. Thus, in addition to the solid developmental reasons for supporting better environmental performance, China's leaders now recognize the importance of energy and climate security in existential terms.

Neither of these conclusions suggests that China is willing to go it alone on climate mitigation. Negotiations involve a complex set of considerations of what other countries can offer, and the Chinese are increasingly concerned about how much is offered from the non-EU developed world. It does suggest that China has its own national interest in these issues, and that it will continue to implement energy and environmental policies that align with what it defines as a national interest in sustainability.

Finally, the link to health outcomes continues to be tenuous. While there is good science suggesting that any reduction in pollution levels will achieve some positive health outcomes and thus all reductions should be welcomed, the goals set in the Five Year Plans are not tied to any specific intended health outcomes. Targets are set either in terms of absolute emissions numbers or as percentage reductions, and these are not tied to variations in how these numbers might affect vulnerable populations—variation in proximity, meteorology, geography, etc.

Thus, while the environment has clearly become a part of China's development agenda, there is still considerable scope for augmenting this focus and developing policies addressing specific goals, whether they be human health, ecosystem health, or other quality of life measures.

NOTES

1. Growth rates either from China's own National Bureau of Statistics or the World Bank record these levels.
2. See the World Bank (1997) for an early comprehensive evaluation of China's environmental challenges. Also see SEPA's and now MEP's annual "The State of the Environment" reports for an annual appraisal of China's challenges for the last 13 years.
3. See for example Zhang et al. (2010).

4. The country profile for China does not provide a definition for all the environmental factors included in the total number, but the WHO's accounting of environmental health is quite broad and includes occupational health, housing quality, transport-related accidents, and natural disasters. See Kay et al. (2000).

5. Indicators reported in 12th Five Year Plan.

6. There were some clear exemptions, such as the elimination of the energy efficiency bureaucracy, and over the course of the last decade some bureaucracies have been rebuilt.

7. A full chronology of the SARS epidemic is available at www.who.int/csr/ don/2003_07_04/en/, Hu's and Wen's dates for assuming office are at www.indexmundi.com/china/government_profile.html. The full National People's Congress was March 5–18, 2003.

8. Obviously there were political and foreign policy goals, as well, but development policy was focused on very direct economic issues. For a discussion of priorities under Jiang Zemin and Zhu Rongji, see Dittmer (2003).

9. PetroChina is ranked below Shell, Exxon, BP, and Sinopec (China's other large integrated oil company) in Fortune's Global 500.

10. Xie himself has been internationally recognized as an environmentalist, receiving the United Nation's Sasakawa Environment Prize in 2003.

11. 12th Economic and Social Development Plan of the People's Republic of China, March 2011. See Litao Wang et al. (2010) for a discussion of implementation in the 10th and 11th Five Year Plans and modeled results.

12. Yuxuan Wang et al. (2009) show reductions in ozone levels. Witte et al. (2009) show significant decreases in nitrogen oxides and carbon monoxide. Wentao Wang et al. (2009) document reductions in particulates during the Games, and a continued reduction afterwards.

13. Ibid.

14. Xin (2009) explains the post-Olympics policy, which continues in place.

15. They can also include cap and trade programs, such as the sulfur trading program in the United States, but it is important to remember that the sulfur trading program for acid rain is built on top of local emissions controls to deal with local human and environmental health standards. In China to date, there have been only limited attempts at trading.

16. PM 2.5 are particle matters in the air with a diameter of no more than 2.5 micrometers.

17. The *China Daily* headline of February 21, 2012, read "PM 2.5 to be Monitored Nationwide," www.chinadaily.com.cn/usa/china/2012–02/21/ content_14660835.htm; however the article gave no date. Importantly it discussed how Chinese Center for Disease Control and Prevention plans to link the data to health data, a major gap in how data is used in China.

18. Interviews with key government advisors, including Professors He Jiankun and Zou Ji, 2008. The priority on development costs is also highlighted by Lewis (2007).

19. Lewis (2010) describes the importance of CDM in promoting renewable energy in China, but also documents that the largest number of projects are in hydropower. While these projects may be additional, the technology certainly is not new to China.

20. I am grateful to Professor Zhang Haibin of Peking University for this chronology. He discussed the Department of Defense (DOD) report in an August 2011 talk at the United Nations office in Beijing.

21. US opinion is of course quite varied and the Obama administration advocates a much stronger climate mitigation policy than the United States currently has. However, as a nation, the United States does not have a national climate law.
22. World Bank 2010 data: China's per capita GDP in current US dollars is $4,428.

References

Andrews-Speed, Philip and Roland Dannreuther. 2011. *China Oil and Global Politics*. London and New York: Routledge.

Bekedam, Henk. 2003. Speech at the International Forum on SARS Prevention and Control. Beijing, December 15–16. www.wpro.who.int/china/media_centre/speeches/speech_20031215.htm.

Branstetter, Lee G. and Nicholas Lardy. 2006. "China's Embrace of Globalization." Department of Social and Decision Sciences, Carnegie Mellon University. Paper 49. http://repository.cmu.edu/sds/49.

Brandt, Loren and Thomas G. Rawski. 2008. "China's Great Economic Transformation." In *China's Great Economic Transformation*. Brandt and Rawski (eds.). Cambridge: Cambridge University Press.

Calder, Kent E. 2005. China's Energy Diplomacy and Its Geopolitical Implications. Edwin O. Reischauer Center for East Asian Studies, Johns Hopkins SAIS.

Chan Lai-Ha, Lucy Chen, and Jin Xu. 2010. China's Engagement with Global Health Diplomacy: Was SARS a Watershed? *PLoS Medicine* 7(4): e1000266.

Dittmer, Lowell. 2003. "Leadership Change and Chinese Political Development." *The China Quarterly* 176: 903–925.

Dollar, David and Aart Kraay. 2003. "Institutions, Trade, and Growth." *Journal of Monetary Economics* 50(1):133–162.

French, Howard W. 2008. "Severe Snowstorms Batter China." *New York Times*, January 28. www.nytimes.com/2008/01/28/world/asia/28iht-china.1.9543336.html.

Goldkorn, Jeremy. 2007. "Taihu Lake Pollution: Net Frenzy and Government Response." Danwei, June 1. www.danwei.org/bbs/taihu_lake_pollution_the_inter.php.

Health Effects Institute (HEI). 2010. Outdoor Air Pollution and Health in the Developing Countries of Asia: A Comprehensive Review. Special Report 18. Boston, MA.

Intergovernmental Panel on Climate Change (IPCC). 2001. *Climate Change 2001—IPCC Third Assessment Report*. Geneva, Switzerland: IPPC.

———. 2007. *Climate Change 2007: Synthesis Report*. R. K. Pachauri and A. Reisinger (eds.). Geneva, Switzerland: IPPC.

Kay, David, Annette Pruess, and Carlos Corvalan. 2000. *Methodology for Assessment of Environmental Burden of Disease*. Geneva: World Health Organization.

Lewis, Joanna I. 2007. "China's Strategic Priorities in International Climate Change Negotiations." *The Washington Quarterly* 31(1):155–174.

———. 2010. "The Evolving Role of Carbon Finance in Promoting Renewable Energy Development in China." *Energy Policy* 38(6):2875–2886.

Liu, Tianfu. 2006. "Pollution of the Songhua River: A Catalyst for Environmental Reform." *China Law and Practice* 20(2):66.

Naughton, Barry. 2005. The New Common Economic Program: China's Eleventh Five Year Plan and What It Means. *China Leadership Monitor, No. 16*. Hoover Institution Stanford University.

———. 2008. "A Political Economy of China's Economic Transition." In *China's Great Economic Transformation*. Loren Brandt and Thomas G. Rawski (eds.). Cambridge: Cambridge University Press.

People's Republic of China (PRC). 2010. Notice of the General Office of the State Council about Forwarding Guiding Opinions on Pushing Forward the Joint Prevention and Control of Atmospheric Pollution to Improve the Regional Air Quality Developed by the Ministry of Environment Protection and Relevant Departments. No. 33 of the General Office of the State Council. Original at http://zfs.mep.gov.cn/fg/gwyw/201005/t20100514_189497.htm; translation at www.chinafaqs.org/files/chinainfo/ChinaFAQs_Joint_Prevention_and_Control_of_Atmospheric_Pollution_by_State_Council_translated.pdf.

Pugliese, Tony. 2011. "CHINA: Beijing Drastically Limits New Vehicle Registrations in 2011." *Just-Auto*, January 4. www.just-auto.com/news/beijing-drastically-limits-new-vehicle-registrations-in-2011_id108230.aspx.

Ravallion, Martin and Shaohua Chen. 2005. Fighting Poverty: Findings and Lessons from China's Success. *The World Bank*, http://go.worldbank.org/QXOQI9MP30.

Reuters. 2012. "Beijing to Cut Air Pollution by 15 Percent by 2015." February 9. www.reuters.com/article/2012/02/09/us-china-beijing-pollution-idUSTRE8180C520120209.

Schwartz, Peter and Doug Randall. 2003. "An Abrupt Climate Change Scenario and Its Implications for United States National Security." Washington, DC: US Department of Defense.

Seligsohn, Deborah and Angel Hsu. 2011. "How Does China's 12th Five-Year Plan Address Energy and the Environment?" ChinaFAQs, March 7. www.chinafaqs.org/blog-posts/how-does-chinas-12th-five-year-plan-address-energy-and-environment.

Shirk, Susan L. (ed.). 2010. *Changing Media, Changing China*. New York: Oxford University Press.

Smith, Kirk R. 2008. "Comparative Environmental Health Assessments." *Annals of the New York Academy of Sciences* 1140:31–39.

Tilt, Bryan and Qing Xiao. 2010. "Media Coverage of Environmental Pollution in the People's Republic of China: Responsibility, Cover-Up and State Control." *Media Culture & Society* 32(2):225–245.

United Nations. 1992. United Nations Framework Convention On Climate Change.

United Nations Environment Programme (UNEP). 2005. *The Songhua River Spill China, December 2005, Field Mission Report*. New York: United Nations.

Wang, Litao, Carey Jang, Yang Zhang, Kai Wang, Qiang Zhang, David Streets, Joshua Fu, Yu Lei, Jeremy Schreifels, Kebin He, Jiming Hao, Yun-Fat Lam, Jerry Lin, Nicholas Meskhidze, Scott Voorhees, Dale Evarts, and Sharon Phillips. 2010. "Assessment of Air Quality Benefits from National Air Pollution Control Policies in China." *Atmospheric Environment* 44(28):3442–3448.

Wang, Wentao, Toby Primbs, Shu Tao, and Staci L. Massey Simonich. 2009. "Atmospheric Particulate Matter Pollution during the 2008 Beijing Olympics." *Environmental Science & Technology* 43(14):5314–5320.

Wang, Yuxuan, Jiming Hao, Michael B. McElroy, J. William Munger, Hong Ma, Dan Chen, and Chris P. Nielsen. 2009. "Ozone Air Quality during the 2008 Beijing Olympics: Effectiveness of Emission Restrictions." *Atmospheric Chemistry and Physics* 9:5237–5251.

Witte, J. C., M. R. Schoeberl, A. R. Douglass, J. F. Gleason, N. A. Krotkov, J. C. Gille, K. E. Pickering, and N. Livesey. 2009. "Satellite Observations of Changes in Air Quality during the 2008 Beijing Olympics and Paralympics." *Geophysical Research Letters* 36:L17803.

Wong, Christine. 2009. "The New Social and Economic Order in Twenty-First Century China: Can the Government Bring a Kinder, Gentler Mode of Development?" In *Global Giant, Is China Changing the Rules of the Game?* Eva Paus, Penelope B. Prime, and Jon Western (eds.). New York and London: Palgrave Macmillan.

World Bank. 1997. *Clear Water, Blue Skies: China's Environment in the Next Century. China 2020 Series.* Washington, DC: World Bank.

Xin, Dingding. 2009. "Beijing Car Restrictions to Continue." *China Daily*, April 6. www.chinadaily.com.cn/bizchina/2009–04/06/content_7651378.htm.

Yardley, Jim. 2008. "To Save Olympic Sailing Races, China Fights Algae." *New York Times*, July 1. www.nytimes.com/2008/07/01/world/asia/01algae.html.

Zhang, Junfeng, Denise L. Mauzerall, Tong Zhu, Song Liang, Majid Ezzati, and Justin V. Remais. 2010. "Environmental Health in China: Progress towards Clean Air and Safe Water." *The Lancet* 375(9720):1110–1119.

INDEX

Location of Figures and Tables is indicated by italics.

Printed in the United States of America